ARMS AND INFLUENCE

ARMS AND INFLUENCE

U.S. Technology Innovation and the Evolution of International Security Norms

Jeffrey S. Lantis

Stanford Security Studies
An Imprint of Stanford University Press
Stanford, California

Stanford University Press
Stanford, California

Printed in the United States of America on acid-free, archival-quality paper

Library of Congress Cataloging-in-Publication Data

Names: Lantis, Jeffrey S., author.
Title: Arms and influence : U.S. technology innovation and the evolution of
    international security norms / Jeffrey S. Lantis.
Description: Stanford, California : Stanford Security Studies, an imprint of Stanford
    University Press, 2016. | Includes bibliographical references and index.
Identifiers: LCCN 2015047055| ISBN 9780804793230 (cloth : alk. paper) |
    ISBN 9780804799775 (pbk. : alk. paper)
Subjects: LCSH: National security—Technological innovations—United States. |
    Military weapons—Technological innovations—United States. | United States—
    Military policy. | United States—Foreign relations. | Technology and international
    relations. | International law.
Classification: LCC UA23 .L27 2016 | DDC 355/.070973—dc23
LC record available at http://lccn.loc.gov/2015047055

ISBN 9780804799843 (electronic)

Typeset in 10/14 Minion with Scala Sans display.

Contents

Acronyms

ABM	anti-ballistic missile
ACDA	Arms Control and Disarmament Agency
ADA	Atomic Development Agency
AEC	Atomic Energy Commission
AMIS	A Mission in Sudan (sponsored by the African Union)
ASAT	anti-satellite
ASEA-Atom	Allmänna Svenska Elektriska Aktiebolaget-Atom
AUMF	Authorization for the Use of Military Force
BAMS	Broad Area Maritime Surveillance
CD	Conference on Disarmament
CIA	Central Intelligence Agency
COPUOS	Committee on the Peaceful Uses of Outer Space
DARPA	Defense Advanced Research Projects Agency
EMIS	electromagnetic isotope separation
ENDC	Eighteen-Nation Committee on Disarmament
ENR	enrichment and reprocessing
EU	European Union
EURODIF	European Gaseous Diffusion Uranium Enrichment Consortium
FATA	Federally Administered Tribal Areas
GBI	ground-based interceptors

GGE	Group of Governmental Experts
GMD	Ground-Based Midcourse
GNEP	Global Nuclear Energy Partnership
GPS	Global Positioning System
GSO	geostationary orbit
HRW	Human Rights Watch
HSI	hyperspectral imagery
IAEA	International Atomic Energy Agency
ICBM	intercontinental ballistic missile
ICISS	International Commission on Intervention and Sovereignty
IDF	Israeli Defense Force
IFOR	Implementation Force
IGO	international governmental organization
INFCIRC	Information Circulars
INTELSAT	International Telecommunications Satellite Organization
ISIS	Islamic State of Iraq and Syria
ITT	International Telephone & Telegraph
JEM	Justice and Equality Movement
JNA	Yugoslav National Army
J-UCAS	Joint-Unmanned Combat Air System
KLA	Kosovo Liberation Army
LEO	low earth orbit
MDA	Missile Defense Agency
MEO	medium earth orbit
MHV	Miniature Homing Vehicle
MIRACL	Mid-Infrared Advanced Chemical Laser
MLF	multilateral nuclear force
MSI	multispectral imagery
NASA	National Aeronautics and Space Administration
NATO	North Atlantic Treaty Organization
NCA	nuclear cooperation agreement
NGO	nongovernmental organization
NMD	national missile defense
NNPA	Nuclear Nonproliferation Act
NPT	Treaty on the Non-Proliferation of Nuclear Weapons
NRO	National Reconnaissance Office
NSG	Nuclear Suppliers Group

NSP	National Space Policy
NWS	nuclear weapon state
OST	Outer Space Treaty
PAROS	Prevention of an Arms Race in Outer Space
PPWT	Prevention of the Placement of Weapons in Outer Space
PSI	Proliferation Security Initiative
PTBT	Partial Test-Ban Treaty
PUREX	plutonium-uranium extraction
RAF	British Royal Air Force
R2P	responsibility to protect
SAINT	Satellite Interceptor
SCOT	social construction of technology
SDI	Strategic Defense Initiative
SLA	Sudan Liberation Army
SSN	Space Surveillance Network
SSP	Satellite Sentinel Project
SYNCOM	Synchronous Communication Satellite
UAE	United Arab Emirates
UAV	unmanned aerial vehicle
UCLASS	Unmanned Carrier-Launched Airborne Surveillance and Strike
UN	United Nations
UNAMID	AU-UN Mission in Darfur
UNCLOS	United Nations Convention on the Law of the Seas
UNMIS	United Nations Mission in Sudan
UNOSAT	United Nations Operational Satellite Programme
USSR	Union of Soviet Socialist Republics
VADER	Vehicle and Dismount Exploitation Radar
VOA	voluntary offer agreements
WMD	weapon of mass destruction

Acknowledgments

THIS BOOK EXPLORES HOW CUTTING-EDGE TECHNO-
logical innovations have helped alter the international political
landscape. It is the product of more than five years of research. I am indebted
to a number of institutions and individuals for their support. My work as a
Fulbright Senior Scholar in Australia in 2007 was the genesis of an exploration of norm change as an elite-driven process. I held joint appointments in
the Department of International Relations in the Research School of Pacific
and Asian Studies at the Australian National University and the School of
Social Sciences and International Studies at the University of New South
Wales. I credit valuable discussions with Chris Reus-Smit, then chair of the
department at ANU, and colleagues at both institutions for helping me to
define elements of the model.

I have conducted field research, including elite interviews, archival
research, and participant observation for this project during research leaves
from the College of Wooster in 2010 and 2014. I am grateful to the college as
well as the Henry Luce III Fund for Distinguished Scholarship for research
grants. In 2010, I served as a visiting scholar at the Institute for Security
and Conflict Studies at the Elliott School of International Affairs, George
Washington University. I am indebted to Charlie Glaser, director of the program, and Douglas Shaw, associate dean, for their encouragement and support, as well as the opportunity to interact with many fine colleagues at the
Elliott School and in the Department of Political Science. In 2010 and 2014,

I conducted interviews and archival research in Washington at the National Archives, and the National Security Archives at George Washington University. I also served as an accredited observer at the 2009 United Nations Preparatory Committee (PrepCom) Conference for the 2010 Review Conference of the Parties to the Treaty on the Non-Proliferation of Nuclear Weapons (NPT) at the UN headquarters, New York. Finally, in 2014, I advanced case study research by conducting archival work at the George H. W. Bush Presidential Library in College Station, Texas.

This project has been strengthened by many conversations with colleagues in recent years, including Martha Finnemore and Llewelyn Hughes in the Department of Political Science at George Washington University and Mireya Solis at the Brookings Institution. I benefitted from the guidance of William Burr at the National Security Archives and Paul Kerr and Jeremiah Gertler at the Congressional Research Service. Cameron Hudson, director of the Center for the Prevention of Genocide at the United States Holocaust Memorial Museum, also provided valuable insights. Others with whom I discussed ideas in conferences, workshops, and meetings include Avner Cohen, Maria Rublee, Scott Sagan, Jeffrey Knopf, Shirley Scott, Carmen Wunderlich, Nina Tannenwald, William Walker, Alan Bloomfield, Lyndon Burford, Frank Harvey, Lisbeth Zimmermann, Deepti Choubey, Matthew Kroenig, Victoria Samson, Andrew Oros, Michael Krepon, Scott Pace, Brian Weeden, Andrew Semmel, Miles Pomper, Sandy Spector, Chen Kane, Sharon Squassoni, Corey Hinderstein, Dean Rust, Matthew Fuhrmann, Juliet Kaarbo, Jacques E. C. Hymans, Matthew Krain, Imad El-Anis, Theo Farrell, Jonathan Pearl, and Seva Gunitskiy. In addition, my field research experiences afforded opportunities to speak with other experts and policy-makers. While most spoke on background, I have nevertheless endeavored to bring this information and perspective to the case studies.

My editor, Geoffrey Burn, at Stanford University Press has been supportive of the project from the start, and I am grateful for his assistance through years of manuscript development. This project simply would not have been as strong without him. I also appreciate support from Alan Harvey, James Holt, and other members of the fine editorial staff at the press. Helpful comments from anonymous reviewers also were critical in guiding me toward refined arguments in the book. Needless to say, any errors in the manuscript remain my own.

Finally, I am grateful for research assistance on this project from Rachel Wilson, Isabelle Howes, Lauren Gillis, and Stephanie Sparrow. These talented Wooster students helped me to gather data on technological innovations and norm change and edit versions of the manuscript. Their genuine interest in and curiosity about the project helped propel my work forward. I also express my deep appreciation to my family for their encouragement, love, and support.

Laws and institutions must go hand in hand with the progress of the human mind. As that becomes more developed, more enlightened, as new discoveries are made, new truths disclosed, and manners and opinions change with the change of circumstances, institutions must advance also, and keep pace with the times.

> —*Thomas Jefferson, Letter from Thomas Jefferson to Samuel Kercheval, July 12, 1816*

The pure or fundamental science of today inexorably becomes the applied science and technology of tomorrow, with unforeseeable consequences, either immediate or remote, flowing from its exploitation.

> —*Lord Solly Zuckerman,* Scientists and War

ARMS AND INFLUENCE

1   Introduction

America's capabilities are unique. And the power of the new technologies means that there are fewer and fewer technical constraints on what we can do. That places a special obligation on us to ask tough questions about what we should do.
      —Barack Obama[1]

Politics will, to the end of history, be an area where conscience and power meet, where the ethical and coercive factors of human life will interpenetrate and work out their tentative and uneasy compromises.
      —Reinhold Niebuhr[2]

IN AUGUST 1945, PRESIDENT HARRY TRUMAN announced the United States had developed a revolutionary new weapon, the atomic bomb, through a secret research program known as the Manhattan Project. He said the bomb had been dropped on Hiroshima, effectively destroying "its usefulness to the enemy." Truman hailed the Manhattan Project as "the greatest scientific gamble in history" and expressed optimism that atomic energy could become "a forceful influence toward the maintenance of world peace."[3] However, the heavy responsibilities associated with the ultimate weapon soon generated significant controversy in the halls of power. Some cabinet members and scientists proposed forsaking the bomb and transferring all nuclear technologies to an international regulatory authority, while others argued the United States should seize the advantages provided by the weapons before others acquired them.[4] Two decades later, President Lyndon Johnson pressed for the establishment of a discriminatory international nonproliferation norm and instituted export controls to limit the spread of these technologies. The 1970 Treaty on the Non-Proliferation of Nuclear Weapons (NPT) clearly delineated nuclear haves and have-nots, a distinction that continues to resonate in international politics today.

In the early twenty-first century, technology innovations continued to generate significant leverage in policy-making, but they did not always guarantee success in achievement of preferred normative structures. For example, advances in satellite reconnaissance, communications, and computing technologies provided unprecedented levels of information to U.S. policy-makers about incidents of mass political violence and genocide occurring in other countries. In 2011, President Obama declared preventing ethnic cleansing and genocide "a core national security interest and a core moral responsibility of the United States."[5] To optimists, this suggested an endorsement of the emerging "responsibility to protect" (or R2P) international norm over concerns regarding sovereignty and nonintervention. However, critics charged that even though policy-makers had abundant evidence of human rights abuses in Darfur, the Central African Republic, and Syria, they failed to act to stop mass killings. As a former National Security Council staff director lamented, "at best, we have a rhetorical commitment" to R2P. But, he cautioned, one should not yet assume that "because we know more, we're doing more."[6]

This book explores the complex relationship between technology, policy-making, and international norms. While not designed to establish predictive theory, it sets out to identify stages and processes associated with norm change as well as open theoretical avenues for further exploration. Challenges to traditional norms catalyzed by technology innovations, such as the use of unmanned aerial vehicles (UAVs, or drones) for missile strikes on suspected terrorists that undermines the long-standing norm against assassination of foreign adversaries, have, in turn, prompted a broader effort to redefine international standards on self-defense, sovereignty, and preemptive strikes. These changes fuel significant contestation of international norms. As other governments develop their own drone fleets, Western leaders have scrambled to establish boundaries for a modified norm for targeted killings. In these and other instances, innovations appear to have become potential game changers in global politics.

These developments also suggest contradictions in the dominant historical narrative of U.S. engagement in global politics as a norm leader. The United States has played a critical role in shaping many international security norms—from standards on human rights grounded in the United Nations

Universal Declaration on Human Rights (1948) to UN Security Council Resolution 1540, designed to prevent the proliferation of weapons of mass destruction to terrorist groups. First-generation (or what Andrew Cortell and James
Davis term "first wave") constructivist international relations theory describes
these developments as products of predictable life cycles; ideas for standards
of behavior cascade through political systems and take on constitutive and
regulatory qualities.[7] However, this book examines the potential fragility of
international norms through circumstances of attempted norm change by
great powers. It sets out to document how determined leaders may develop
strategies intended to change or manipulate normative security architectures
for their own utilitarian purposes, and in the process fuel contestation that
may or may not lead to successful outcomes.

Specifically, this study explores the fascinating dialectical relationship that
emerges between the international normative order and endogenous technology advances. It highlights the ways tensions caused by hegemons have altered
the political landscape by catalyzing norm-change processes. This approach
stands in contrast to models that make general reference to "external shocks"
as catalysts for change, and instead acknowledges the balance of internal and
external factors that shape approaches to norms. In fact, technology innovations precede major shocks in many cases, but their implementation and
advancement raise complex questions in the policy process. Technology may
highlight dissonant strands of norms (e.g., nuclear technology sharing versus
preventing weapons proliferation) or dissonance between norms (e.g., absolute sovereignty versus prevention of ethnic cleansing and genocide). New
technologies often heighten awareness of problems or a lack of political consensus, increasing the chances that norms will be subject to contestation. In
essence, "techno-normative dilemmas" fostered by technology innovations
may force a sense of cognitive dissonance on elites, motivating them to solve
the problem at hand.[8] Drawing on insights from social psychology perspectives on idea formation and development, this study attends to the power of
persuasion in domestic and foreign policy development.

In an era of drone strikes in Yemen, advancements in uranium enrichment, and the potential weaponization of space, research on the interaction
between technology, norms, and state behavior has never been more important. While popular accounts of challenges to the global order focus on the
behaviors of rogue states or dramatic events, this book shows how some of
the most profound norm changes may be a function of quiet yet persistent

campaigns by great powers to adapt international standards to emerging realities. This study takes some of the most controversial new developments in military technologies and embeds them in international relations theory; theoretical arguments are analyzed in relation to evolving social practice.

Key research questions in this project include: If norms are truly regulative and constitutive, as most first-generation constructivists maintain, why would states ever consider violating traditional norm frames? Under what circumstances are these considerations most likely? How do great powers reconcile emerging opportunities and challenges related to national interests with international norm strictures? What are the processes by which great powers promote norm change? Have major technological innovations shifted prevailing normative understandings in all cases? Why, or why not? What institutional features make norm change more or less likely? And finally, what are the implications of a model of norm change for policy-makers and theories of international cooperation?[9]

Theoretical Foundations

Constructivism

Constructivism, which reflects a broad sociological turn in international relations theory, offers valuable foundations for the study of international cooperation and conflict. Contrary to realists, constructivists define international norms as "shared understandings that constitute actors' identities and interests," effectively binding the latitude of state policy.[10] They are customary rules that govern behavior in societies, and scholars believe they help shape state behavior. Constructivists Martha Finnemore and Kathryn Sikkink's norm life-cycle model is a seminal first-generation constructivist approach to the study of international cooperation. Finnemore and Sikkink describe three stages of norm life: emergence, broad acceptance (also referred to as a "norm cascade"), and internalization.[11] Finnemore and Sikkink also recognize countries like the United States as critical players in norm development—countries "without which the achievement of the substantive norm goal is compromised."[12] By the late twentieth century, many states appeared to have become embedded in complex normative networks that influenced their foreign policy paths.

First-generation constructivist scholarship adds an ideational dimension to the modern study of international relations, but it presents an incomplete accounting of a range of possible state behaviors. First-generation models focus primarily on norm development and "life." They rarely allow for state challenges to international standards, especially efforts by traditional norm stewards to change the meaning of a norm or rules within multilateral frameworks.[13] These models also tend to disregard negative cases, or instances in which norms may be challenged, rejected, or modified. Works that do recognize the potential for change focus on broad causes, including external shocks, the actions of rogue states, or "world historical events such as wars or major depressions."[14] Constructivism also has not resolved the agent-structure question sufficiently. How exactly are international norms maintained, and by whom? If international norms are manifest in cognitive, evaluative, and expressive dimensions, it is conceivable that actors who support those values might be identified and their impact on state compliance and multilateral negotiations explored.

This study expands the norm life-cycle model to account for episodes where hegemons or great-power leaders play roles as architects of norm change or evolution. It presents a thoughtful look at norm stewardship by modifying the traditional norm life-cycle model to incorporate stages in which leaders may seek to reinterpret the meaning of norms to accommodate exceptions to international standards related to security. This is consistent with calls from international relations scholars for more dynamic models. For example, Robert Axelrod recommends theoretical treatments of "how norms arise, how norms are maintained, and how one norm displaces another."[15] Sikkink suggests the value of an "agentic constructivism" frame that "focuses on the role of human agency in the origins of new norms and practices, and is thus better positioned to explain change."[16] Such models may help restore some balance to theoretical treatments of the agent-structure relationship and provide more comprehensive explanations of international politics.

Technology and Norm Change

Technology advancements are particularly salient among the factors that may foster leaders' perceptions of gaps between general rules and state interests.[17] Innovations may encourage leaders of powerful states to revisit critical normative structures of the past and adapt them to new material and ideational boundaries. While there is ample evidence that countries support some norms some of the time, this book shows that technological competitiveness may foster a much greater role for agency in norm discourse than allowed for by traditional constructivism. These connections may be critical, but they have received surprisingly limited treatment in international relations theory. As noted above, default explanations of change in international relations tend to focus on system dynamics and balances of power, not endogenous pathways of development.

Studies of the sociology and history of technology and international law inform this model of norm change. Counter to the "technological imperative" hypothesis that technology is an exogenous factor that dictates state behavior—most closely associated with realist arguments from Barry Buzan, Michael Howard, Robert Heilbroner, and Daniel Deudney—contemporary works recognize a dialectical relationship between political decisions and technological opportunities.[18] Beginning with pathbreaking scholarship by Merritt Roe Smith and Leo Marx (1994), social construction of technology (SCOT) theorists frame innovations as the impetus for social trends and transformations.[19] Advancements in this literature highlight how this relationship is mutually constitutive in that social forces shape the evolution of technologies. SCOT theory tends to focus on how different groups compete to control and interpret the implications of technology designs rather than the expectation of a preordained path from innovation to application. Instead, Wiebe Bijker and Trevor Pinch focus on a process of mutually constitutive stabilization by which one social group or set of innovations prevails over the others. Innovation is thus a complex process of construction where technology and society negotiate the meaning of new technological artifacts through thoughts, frames, practices, and actions.[20]

Though this literature devotes less attention to the impact of technology on political systems, SCOT theory is consistent with constructivist international relations theory in its emphasis on subjective interpretations of the meaning of scientific advancements and knowledge. For example, Wayne Sandholtz and Kendall Stiles contend that great-power development of steel-hulled ships had very different meanings for different groups.[21] A social construction model of technology recognizes a synergistic relationship between technological advances and political processes.[22] As another study explains, SCOT theory emphasizes "the 'interpretive flexibility' of an artifact. Different social groups associate different meanings with artifacts leading to interpretive flexibility appearing over the artifact. The same artifact can mean different things to different social groups of users."[23]

Historical sociology explains the role of technology in a broader social context, exploring how interests are shaped and, critically, the key players involved in the policy process. Geoffrey Herrera's *Technology and International Transformation* (2006) begins to try to bridge technological change and international politics. The book summarizes key insights from the last two decades of work in the history of technology. It challenges traditional balance of power approaches and instead advances constructivist interpretations of international relations. Herrera's overall argument is that certain technologies—especially large technical systems—may have direct consequences for the international system. Counter to what realists assert, technological innovations may spur on system transformation, but "institutions, social practices and politics surrounding it" are critical to an endogenous process of change, "giving it political (and military) meaning."[24] As Herrera argues, this exploration is valuable because technology is a critical element of global politics (he calls it a "medium of interaction for international actors")—yet there is little established theoretical understanding of mutually constitutive "complex sociotechnical systems that are political to their core."[25] This relationship is clearly intersubjective. The most comprehensive models of these connections must eschew pure technological determinism (the idea that technology will have a certain, singular political effect) as well as the social constructionists' preoccupation with the political effects of brand new technologies.[26] In sum, the SCOT literature suggests there are important possible connections between technological advances and changes in social and political structures.

The United States, Technology, and Contestation of International Norms

The United States has been a major player in the development of traditional international security norms and an architect and enforcer of multilateral arrangements for managing global challenges—an agent of hegemonic norm change. At the same time, the United States was the world's primary developer, innovator, and exporter of high-technology products throughout the second half of the twentieth century and a leader in basic science and industrial applications.[27]

Some U.S. technological advances have occurred as a direct product of wartime efforts, and thus achievements in science often contributed to both national security and economic prosperity. U.S. spending on research and development in the post–World War II period remained high, fueling even greater innovation and productivity growth. Research in the United States paved the way for advancements in production of fissile material for nuclear weapons. The country led the world in high-technology goods such as aircraft, semiconductors, computers, drugs, plastics, and engines and turbines.[28] Even when rivals like the Soviet Union made advances in space technology and expanded their industrial capacity, U.S. high-technology production continued to dominate global markets. This trend only began to fade in many categories in the 1980s when imports surged and other competitors, such as Germany and Japan, gained larger market shares, but even then U.S. players tried to maintain a competitive edge in high technology.

The relationship between technology innovations and American military strategy has been explored in some past works. For example, in his 1973 book *The American Way of War*, Russell Weigley described the U.S. approach to military strategy as one that emphasized "total war" as an extension of technological advancements. U.S. economic development (including significant innovation) was inextricably linked with its ambitious foreign policy agenda over time. Ultimately, Weigley argues, the United States way of war became one that emphasizes annihilation: the "destruction of the enemy's armed force and with it the complete overthrow of the enemy."[29] A classic example of technological advantage and military strategy came during the Persian Gulf War when U.S. armored divisions used Global Positioning System data for the first time to outmaneuver Iraqi Republican Guard forces in the open desert. These and other achievements bolstered the mind-set that the United States could spend less on the military overall and focus resources on decisive technology with an information network-centric focus.[30] "Spurred by dramatic advances in information technology," Max Boot writes, the U.S. military has adopted a new style of warfare focused on "a quick victory with minimal casualties on both sides. Its hallmarks are speed, maneuver, flexibility, and surprise."[31]

Contrary to realist studies of the impact of technological change on military strategy, though, technology here is cast as an important ideational variable that changes the nature of the political debate and sometimes produces uncertain outcomes. This study focuses instead on the ideational implications of techno-normative dilemmas—the way state leaders may pursue persuasion in the domestic political arena and social influence in multilateral institutions to change international perspectives on acceptable or legitimate behaviors. For example, the development of armed drones in the 2000s gave the United States unprecedented power to assassinate foreign adversaries by remote control. While drones have been hailed as a technological wonder that expanded the global reach of the United States, this book focuses on how military innovations shifted domestic political discourses and the framing of multilateral normative standards regarding their use. Indeed, the George W. Bush administration's 2003 *National Strategy for Combating Terrorism* described how the United States must win "the war of ideas" in order to defeat terrorism. It states, "with our friends and allies, *we aim to establish a new international norm* regarding terrorism requiring non-support, non-tolerance, and active opposition to terrorists."[32]

Technology innovations also may have negative implications for international security norms, spurring contestation and attempts to change the security architecture. For example, when great powers recognized that "peaceful" nuclear energy technologies like uranium enrichment and reprocessing could be diverted by would-be nuclear proliferants, they acted to change the international normative structure. U.S. leaders pressured their counterparts to endorse a discriminatory nuclear nonproliferation regime in the NPT that expressly sanctioned just five countries as nuclear weapons states. In the 2000s as it became clear that even the more discriminatory regime had not prevented nuclear weapons proliferation, the George W. Bush administration tried to reengineer the nuclear order through a series of more restrictive export controls. A senior government official said the result has been a continual struggle "to try to fix the problem" of inconsistency in national and international policies regarding uranium enrichment and reprocessing.[33] These developments are so vast, and the dynamics so new, that it is important to examine the potential implications for the global normative order.

Plan of the Book

This book explores the synergistic relationship between technology innovations and international norms—and the power of political discourse to shape normative change through contestation. Because norms need stewards, government leaders regularly engage in assessments of their commitments to norms. Specifically, the study proposes a model of a top-down pathway of norm change that infuses greater agency into constructivist perspectives on change. There are few in-depth examinations, to date, of the process by which elites may address multilateral commitments and normative standards and seek constructive substitution to achieve instrumental objectives.[34] Domestic political deliberations in democratic states can shape state behavior in multilateral forums related to norms, including the pursuit of norm change. Problems with compliance may occur regularly, and policy changes relative to a norm are often incremental. The goal of this study is to take some of the most controversial new developments in military technologies and embed them in international relations theory to develop a more reflexive understanding of norm stewardship as a dialectical political process.

The book contains eight chapters. Chapter 2 develops the theoretical foundation for the project. It surveys both early constructivist scholarship on the life cycle of norms and newer work on agentic constructivism, international law, and the social construction of technology that recognizes the potential for norm evolution. The chapter presents a new, three-stage model of norm change and a research design outlining the method of structured, focused comparison of cases that is employed in the project. Chapters 3 through 7 of the book survey case studies of technological innovation and attempts at normative change. They explore some of the most controversial developments in military technologies in recent memory and embed the examination fully in international relations theory. Chapter 3 examines one of the earliest modern examples of norm change: the invention of the atomic bomb and the subsequent development of a discriminatory nuclear nonproliferation norm. Chapter 4 explores contemporary debates about nuclear technology sharing, and the tightening of the international nonproliferation norm in the wake of the discovery of clandestine nuclear weapons programs. Chapter 5 examines the role of satellites in the evolution of the new "responsibility to protect" norm to prevent crimes against humanity. Chapter 6 explores the implications of unmanned aerial vehicles for international security. It examines the development of drones and the innovation of arming drones for the purpose striking designated targets on the ground. This advance has profound implications for the existing norm against assassination of foreign adversaries. Chapter 7 addresses the challenges of technology innovations for outer space, including anti-satellite technology innovations and their potential for changing the way the United States views protection of the global commons. Finally, Chapter 8 summarizes the findings of the study and explores implications for both international relations theory and technology studies.

2 Theorizing Norm Change

Just as the international order is made by national ideas, so it is
unmade. . . . In some instances states turn toward . . . the dominant rules,
institutions, and norms that characterize the international system. In other
situations, nations understand their interests as best served by separating
themselves from that society, or even by dramatically revising it. This
variation begs for analysis.
—*Jeffrey W. Legro*[1]

They always say time changes things, but you actually have to change them
yourself.
—*Andy Warhol*[2]

THIS CHAPTER ESTABLISHES THEORETICAL FOUNDA-
tions for a new model of norm change. It surveys scholarly
advances in first- and second-generation constructivism and related insights
from sociology and international law that support a dynamic model of norm
development.[3] The model features three stages of elite-driven change: technology innovations and the recognition of "techno-normative dilemmas," redefinition of commitments in the domestic political arena, and contestation and
constructive norm substitution in multilateral settings. This chapter also out-
lines the research design and methodology for the study, including the potential for different levels of success for strategies of norm change.

Constructivism and the Norm Life Cycle

Constructivism describes ideational foundations of state behaviors and international cooperation. As noted in Chapter 1, it highlights the role of ideas in

shaping foreign policy behavior, where state identities and interests can be seen as "socially constructed by knowledgeable practice."[4] To first-generation scholars, "constructivism is about human consciousness and its role in international life."[5] Given its fresh focus on ideational factors that shape human interactions and the breadth of this approach in the first decade after the Cold War, constructivism quickly emerged as a leading contender to rationalism in international relations theory. Constructivists devote special attention to norms as "intersubjective beliefs about the social and natural world that define actors, their situations, and the possibilities of action."[6] Social norms help govern behavior in societies and may have additional social functions such as motivation. These "shared expectations about appropriate behavior held by a community" are more than merely functional, exogenous constraints on state behavior; they help constitute identities, beliefs, and expectations.[7]

Constructivists also theorize the norm-development process, how norms are conceived over time and constitute and affect state behavior (e.g., through shaming or public pressure).[8] Studies typically examine grassroots activism by agents such as nongovernmental organizations (NGOs) to build societal pressure for norms through the raising of moral consciousness. In this sense, norm development reflects a moral cosmopolitanism—a drive for universal ideals in rooting out dangers such as genocide and other human rights abuses, or land mines and cluster munitions. Once established, norms are characterized as both regulative and constitutive in that they shape national interests and identity. Norms are expected to elicit conformity. Norms that intersect with international legal structures, optimists contend, foster significant pressure for state compliance.[9] Harold Koh's theory of obedience suggests states may be so highly penetrated by international law that they fully internalize a norm and it becomes a part of their own value system. From this perspective, compliance is thus a function of the internalization of both norms and laws through transnational legal processes.[10]

The Norm Life-Cycle Model

As noted in Chapter 1, Martha Finnemore and Kathryn Sikkink's norm life-cycle model features three stages of norm life: emergence, broad acceptance (also referred to as a "norm cascade"), and internalization.[11] It characterizes norms as developing up through "social processes and logics of action" that affect actors' behaviors.[12] The first stage represents early development of the norm, often from domestic origins and discourse. "Norms do not appear out of thin air," Finnemore and Sikkink contend, rather they "are actively built by agents having strong notions about appropriate or desirable behavior in their community." Those primary agents are norm entrepreneurs, typically non-governmental organizations or groups who then attempt to persuade a critical mass of states of the rightness of the new principles. Entrepreneurs strive to create new cognitive frames that will resonate broadly and to promote new ways of considering issues. Norms can thus be understood as identity pre-scriptions for behavior.[13]

This model also identifies a tipping point, or threshold, in norm life when "a critical mass of relevant state actors adopts the norm."[14] This sets up both the second and third stages of development. The transition to the second stage involves both persuasion and imitation. Norm entrepreneurs attempt to socialize other states "to become norm followers." Norm cascades occur "through a combination of pressure for conformity, desire to enhance international legitimation, and the desire of state leaders to enhance their self-esteem."[15] Here, norms begin to "stick" in the international community through a process of cross-national moral consciousness-raising and insti-tutionalization and habitualization.[16] Actors engage in processes of strategic social construction that include ideas and morality in shaping state behavior. Norms are reproduced through policy and discourse, and many actors are socialized to accept them as standards for appropriate behavior.

The third stage in the norm life-cycle model is internalization. Through political discourse, norms cascade and gain acceptance in the international security community. In this context, "norms acquire a taken-for-granted quality and are no longer a matter of broad public debate."[17] This stage is often equated with acceptance, compliance, and routinization of a norm by a critical mass of states. Norm internalization typically involves a transition for actors from following a "logic of consequence" (as described by rational-ism) to a new collective understanding based on the "logic of appropriateness" (sociological institutionalism).[18] Shared meanings and practices begin to help organize state interaction as accepted social constructs. Agency appears to fade as norms define a new, communitarian perspective reflected in recurrent social behaviors. According to this logic, institutional cooperation and iden-tities are mutually constitutive, providing legitimacy and reinforcement for positive practices; defection would be unexpected.

The norm life-cycle model has had a powerful influence on scholarly understanding of norm development. Many first-generation works addressed the dynamics and implications of stages of progression. For example, Thomas Risse, Stephen Ropp, and Kathryn Sikkink developed a spiral model of the socialization process of human rights norms that included five stages. The model was designed to highlight both the progressive influence of transnational advocacy movements to shape international norms and the normalization of state policy through internalization.[19] Scholars also have extended and questioned the model in creative ways in recent years, such as Christine Ingebritsen's work on how Scandinavian states have become norm entrepreneurs in promoting global humanitarian causes and conflict resolution and an investigation by Mona Lee Krook and Jacqui True of gender inequity in world politics.[20]

Limitations

While first-generation constructivist scholarship has broadened our understanding of global politics, its assumptions have not been internalized by all who study norms. Critics charge that first-generation models focus primarily on norm development and life, but do not well capture change or the possibility of contestation of international standards. Studies of norm entrepreneurs, such as nongovernmental organizations, in action tend to miss the potential for states seen as norm stewards to later seek to change the meaning of a norm or rules within multilateral frameworks. Matthew Hoffmann suggests the traditional literature has been guilty of "freezing" norms conceptually. Norm content (and state compliance patterns) would be expected to remain relatively static. This challenge is especially ironic given that the original life-cycle model portrayed norm adoption and implementation as a dynamic process.[21]

The few first-generation works that acknowledge the potential for change tend to discuss possible causes in the broadest of terms, such as world historical events or wars or major depressions.[22] Wayne Sandholtz interprets norm change as an ongoing transformative process, where outcomes of interpretational disputes "inevitably modify the rules, giving them new content, making them stronger (or weaker), clearer (or less), more specific (or less), more subject to exceptions (or less)."[23] Jeffrey Legro argues the scholarship on ideational transformations tends to rely too much on the idea of external shocks or psychosalient events as catalyst for change, while missing endogenous processes that may have a greater impact on policy development and normative direction.[24]

An emerging, second-generation of critical constructivist approaches has begun to examine the importance of opposition in existing norms discourses.

Scholars characterize norms as products of strategic social construction and pay more systematic attention to the role of agency in norm diffusion processes. They also recognize the potential for what Harald Müller and Carmen Wunderlich call "norm dynamics," including norm decay and unintended consequences of normative evolution.[25] This newer work has opened debates regarding norm diffusion, internalization, and compliance. Norms are characterized as contested, ambiguous, and sometimes indeterminate in their impact on global politics. Related works explore the potential for norm decay, regress, and even setback. Conventional constructivism favors regulative and constitutive effects, but critical constructivists argue that the very legitimacy of norms hinges on contestation and dialogue over their viability.

Constructivism also has not resolved the agent-structure question sufficiently. First-generation studies of norms clearly focus on development, diffusion, and the constraints imposed by norms on state behaviors. The scholarship tends to explore positive cases of norm development, implementation, and success instead of negative cases, or instances in which norms may be challenged, rejected, or modified by leaders or governments. The logic of norm internalization infers that state interests will simply shift to comply with the norm. This leaves open critical questions of agency, though, including: How exactly are international norms maintained, and by whom? What are the processes by which agents engage in contestation and replacement of norms?[26]

Norm Change

Many constructivists adopt broad, static, even existential views of the power of norms. Conversely, this study asserts norms may change at the hands of vested great powers and the process of attempted norm change by democratic regimes is often observable. Powerful countries play the role of norm stewards, the keepers of normative principles. But stewardship may take many forms. It demands that actors regularly engage in assessments of their commitments to norms and domestic political deliberations in democratic states that can shape state behavior in multilateral forums related to norms. Such dialogues are necessary to maintain the effectiveness and legitimacy of normative commitments. However, in the process of reflecting on traditional norm frames, leaders may sometimes determine there is a need to persuade others of disjunctures between emerging realities and established rules. This typically involves persuading key political actors, both domestic and international, to acknowledge the need for change. As Legro asserts, "just as the international order is made by national ideas, so it is unmade." States may engage norms and institutions that characterize the international system. But "in other situations, nations understand their interests as best served by separating themselves from that society, or even by dramatically revising it. This variation begs for analysis."[27] This is especially the case for leaders of democratic states that serve as norm stewards, where discourse is a natural extension of social reflection and practice.[28]

Thus, it is important to try to understand the political process of deliberations, both internally and externally, in relation to norm development. Agents who were instrumental in helping to build norms also may impact norm compliance and foster norm challenges. James March and Johan Olsen argue that a shift toward rule-guided behavior (logic of appropriateness) evolves as a conscious process of choosing the appropriate normative or rules structure.[29] While actors will endorse collective norms and understandings that constitute identities and regulate behavior, the establishment of a norm involves developing consensus about the right thing to do.[30] This study accepts the premise of ongoing dialogue and anticipates that dialectical processes occur at both the domestic (through redefinition) and international level (through constructive norm substitution). It places greater weight on agency than structure, and explores the dynamic tensions in normative systems that impact rules development.[31]

Elite Agency

While the goal of the study is not to advance a mono-causal theory, it highlights the role of elites among relevant domestic political actors involved in security policy-making.[32] For the purposes of this study, elites are identified as top government officials with the authority to allocate government resources, and they are expected to play critical roles as norm stewards in the development and maintenance of international regimes. Specifically, this study focuses on the roles of U.S. presidents and high-ranking administration officials who may interpret and contest norm meanings in relation to national interests.[33] Presidential positions on issues like nuclear proliferation or human rights help set the tone for cooperation with international regimes. This occurs as a function of ongoing arguments about the interpretation of the rules.[34] In the process, leaders can become policy entrepreneurs by exercising influence to direct and induce others to adopt a particular line of policy. In sum, leaders may embrace established multilateral regulations on an issue, or develop their own interpretations of historical narratives and attempt to build coalitions in support of an alternative foreign policy path.[35]

As noted above, studying elite norm stewardship challenges prevailing approaches in constructivism. The norm life-cycle model, for example, emphasizes that norms develop primarily through bottom-up, grassroots processes. Shared assessments regarding new norm frames in a community are constructed through the first two stages of the life cycle: emergence and cascade. This study counters that elites, too, can be critical agents for norm change. Once established, ideas must have carriers, or stewards. While social institutions, including policy norms and principles, appear to gain some causal efficacy by embodying human agency, this study focuses on elites as norm stewards who are uniquely positioned to imagine change. In the process, these entrepreneurs attempt to leverage ideational influence and persuade state actors of the appropriateness of particular norms and ideas. Elites also may be more likely to emerge as norm entrepreneurs in some highly technical policy areas. Governments work closely with corporations on some cutting-edge technological innovations, and thus leaders are often the first players to see the potential of these new systems as well as the need to regulate them through establishment of an international code of conduct.

A norm stewardship model highlights how actors may make strategic use of norms in pursuit of interests. In this context, interactions between agents and institutions help establish and reestablish constructs.[36] They may challenge claims of validity or legitimacy of normative constructs and try to build new understandings of stable orders through contestation. Perhaps norms and ideas are best depicted as tools that enable agents to accomplish various objectives. As noted earlier, a focus on elite latitude challenges first-generation assumptions regarding internalization. Contrary to some constructivist models that assume leaders fully internalize normative principles (and thus that all interests are constituted by existing norms), elites may not take the standard of legitimacy for granted. In this context, legitimacy is more of an external institutional resource and constraint than an internalized barrier to imagined change.[37]

Finally, adopting an elite framing or strategic approach for the study of norm change clearly challenges traditional arguments about internalization and the acceptance of the logic of appropriateness. As Michael Barnett suggests, "the normative structure that constitutes and constrains actors also provides the wellspring for social practices and allows for strategic action" which might be "designed to rewrite the cultural landscape in order to legitimate foreign policy change."[38] Scholar Liesbet Hooghe, in a rare study of socialization focused on individuals within international organizations, finds that supranational norms are often less taken for granted (and players' strategic calculations less focused on "ought-ness") than is assumed by traditional constructivism.[39] The argument that leaders consciously select among competing normative interpretations suggests a lower level of norm internalization among elites than is often assumed.

Elites can and do attempt to change the structural landscape as a function of their perception of strategic advantages or even their own principled beliefs. Such an approach is well supported in the emerging critical constructivist literature, where scholars like Amitav Acharya and others investigate such themes as localization and adaptation of universal norms to regional contexts.[40] Ultimately, as critical constructivists Antje Wiener and Uwe Puetter argue, "What actors make of norms matters . . . [for] moving the social practice of governance beyond the boundaries of modern states."[41] In related work, Wiener also argues contestation is a positive phenomenon, as it is the condition for a deliberation over meanings of norms, which is necessary to produce norm legitimacy.[42] Theoretical approaches to this phenomenon can be strengthened to determine how and when elites follow traditional normative narratives rather than pursue or support norm change.

"Techno-Normative Dilemmas" and Dissonance

As noted in Chapter 1, this study asserts that one of the most important and understudied catalysts for norm change may be great-power technological innovation. Major technological advances with political and military applications can highlight dissonant strands of norms (e.g., nuclear technology sharing versus weapons proliferation, or contradictions between sovereignty and humanitarian intervention) and foster reconsideration of state commitments. These developments may heighten awareness of problems or a lack of consensus and increase the chances norms will be subject to contestation. In such circumstances, elites have the opportunity to break with traditional bounds of normative principles. Studies from political psychology show that individuals facing cognitive dissonance often seek to minimize the condition by changing their behaviors or justifications to "solve the problem at hand."[43]

Traditional works on technology and international politics tend to treat technology as exogenous to the political system and theoretically insignificant. In contrast, this study frames technology as endogenous to political systems and explores processes of norm change. Norm change may begin when leaders learn of significant technological innovations that cause them to reevaluate the effectiveness and appropriateness of the boundaries of international norms. Techno-normative dilemmas may prompt decisions to engage in contestation by challenging the validity of central principles and pursuing redefinition and constructive norm substitution through discursive rhetoric, policy actions, and persuasion. Here, technology is a *political subject* worthy of detailed scrutiny, and explanations of state behavior must be multilayered, encompassing technical, political, cultural, and economic dimensions, as well as multiple players. Understanding the place of new technologies from a sociological perspective means recognizing the role of cultural and psychological factors that both impact, and are impacted by, technological advances (see Figure 2.1).

This approach also draws on reflexive sociology and sociological models of institutional change. Reflexive sociology highlights the importance of dynamism in interpretation of the agent-structure relationship and warns that international relations theory tends to over-socialize actors based on structuralist perspectives. In this spirit, this study highlights situations in which established norms are contested by great powers, sometimes leading to norm change. The route for this contestation is typically policy innovation and discursive interventions to promote reconstruction of the principles entailed in a standing norm. Discursive interventions as social practices entail and reconstruct the meaning of norms. Thus, this study adopts a neo-Giddensian understanding of the dual quality of norms as structuring and constructed— "the structural properties of social systems are both the medium and the outcome of practices that constitute those systems."[44] In this context, "rules and practices only exist in conjunction with one another." Giddens described technological development and political discourse as involving recurrent social practices, suggesting that technological innovation could allow a process by which states "recursively instantiate and thus reconstitute the rules and resources that structure their social action."[45]

Leaders who interpret traditional norms as constraints have three basic options. First, they may reject a standing norm and openly declare their

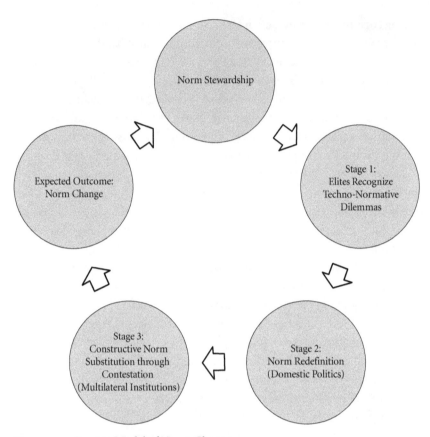

Figure 2.1   Process Model of Norm Change

intention to pursue new behavior. This might take the form of a sudden change in negotiating stances in international institutions or even formal abrogation of a treaty.[46] Second, states may simply comply with traditional norm prohibitions. Third, and much more likely, leaders of great powers may identify dissonance between traditional normative constraints and new opportunities and pursue a path of redefinition and constructive norm substitution through contestation. Persuasion and social influence are at the heart of this process, a struggle to redefine norm frames and gain support for substituted alternatives. Ideas spread through a process directed at "changing attitudes about cause and effect in the absence of overt coercion."[47]

Norm Redefinition

Norm stewardship requires regular interventions to steer the ship of state carefully between normative pressures and state self-interest. Leaders participate in dialogues related to normative limits and prescriptions on a regular basis—and these dialogues are necessary to maintain the effectiveness and legitimacy of normative commitments. Thus, in a weakly socialized setting, a dialectical process may be at work in the life and evolution of norms: elites typically pay respect to prevailing norms, but they may sometimes determine standards are obsolete or ineffective relative to strategic goals. They can then pursue the path of redefinition through discursive rhetoric, institutional actions, and persuasion, which can have the effect of challenging inhibitions. Modeling norm stewardship as a two-way street also helps explain the potential for hypocrisy, manipulation of rhetoric, and contestation over interpretation of rules by state leaders.[48]

Great-power leaders who identify normative dissonance fostered by technological innovation may pursue a path of redefinition and constructive norm substitution through contestation. Redefinition refers to a process of domestic recalculation of a state's commitment to a traditional norm or its interpretation of the meaning of the norm and implications for policy behavior. This process may be most transparent in democratic states, where accountability and power sharing necessitate the constructive exchange of ideas among leaders. Redefinition typically occurs in domestic political arenas through rhetorical means, and may be especially visible when leaders of governments that serve as traditional enforcers of a norm raise questions of normative utility or legitimacy. Actors critically evaluate normative guidelines through a "logic of truth-seeking or arguing," which includes recognition of both theoretical and practical discourses.[49]

Frame theory suggests elites have a unique opportunity to characterize phenomena through focused discourse. Norm redefinition through framing effectively casts doubt on old orders by challenging their legitimacy. William Gamson and Andre Modigliani define a frame as a "central organizing idea or story line [in a communication]. . . . It suggests what the controversy is about, the essence of the issue."[50] Frames can be central to political discourse—they "help receivers of information define problems, diagnose causes, make moral judgments, and suggest remedies."[51] Actors may strategically deploy frames to help contextualize events or mobilize actions.[52] And redefinition can be confrontational. In some circumstances, "elites wage a war of frames because they know that if *their* frame becomes the dominant way of thinking about a particular problem, then the battle for public opinion has been won."[53]

Support for a model of differential levels of norm internalization also can be found in sociological studies of internalization, second-generation (or "second wave") constructivism, and debates over the law. Recognizing the potential for variable levels of internalization, sociologists turned to questions of conditions of probability defining conforming behavior.[54] Legal theory also has long fostered debates over degrees of interpretation of founding documents. Scholars contend that the courts are populated by justices who adopt varying perspectives toward the U.S. Constitution, ranging from originalists, who refer back to the framers' views as the full extent of the law, to interpretationists, best characterized as constructivists who view the Constitution as having a dynamic meaning (the so-called living Constitution). Unsurprisingly, differences between these camps become magnified over interpretation of general, vague, or contradictory legal standards from the past. Debates over interpretation and depth of legal standards have continued in international law.[55] Cass Sunstein argues norms are much more often external than intrinsic constraints.[56] And in an exploration of the "microprocesses of acculturation," Ryan Goodman and Derek Jinks contend internalization might be better understood as providing a measure of "cognitive comfort" for leaders derived from the social-psychological benefits of group conformity.[57]

The Process of Redefinition

Both day-to-day governance and norm stewardship require elite management and regular interventions through policy-making to steer the ship of state. In general, first-generation constructivists expect continuity and see norm conformity as the default option. To play out the analogy, this study accepts the premise that leaders will typically guide the state within marked channels—including those that conform to domestic political, strategic, and normative parameters. Traditional channels become established over time, and navigating along the prescribed course provides both political balance and legitimacy in state behavior.

However, leaders also may contemplate diverging from the traditional course for two primary reasons: principled beliefs or instrumental gains. Both are considered equally powerful motivations for norm redefinition for the purposes of this study. Redefinition occurs primarily through rhetorical means and exchange in the domestic political arena. This refers to a process of leaders' recalculation of state commitments to a traditional interpretation of the meaning of the norm and its implications for state behavior and subsequent efforts at persuasion in the domestic policy arena. Elites may experience dissonance when they believe the primary principles for which their country stands are being challenged or violated by developments in the international community. Navigating the ship of state can, of course, be seen as a continual process of leaders' evaluation of the ideational environment around them and of adjustment. Elite calculations of instrumental gains are another source of norm change. Indeed, technological innovations may offer profound opportunities for instrumental gains. Innovations may highlight dilemmas or tradeoffs between perceived "national interests" and norm parameters. Because elites occupy a unique vantage point to determine short- and long-term strategic interests, they might become aware of circumstances that could impact their interests vis-à-vis international norms and national security and try to steer governance in line with opportunities versus constraints.[58]

In the redefinition stage, leaders reevaluate the effectiveness and appropriateness of international norms relative to their own assessment of interests and national security. They may question the validity of central principles and pursue the path of redefinition through discursive rhetoric, policy actions, and persuasion. This also may be seen as a strategic framing process where stewards establish understandings of the world and work to communicate their vision of legitimate action within normative parameters. By redefining normative commitments based on an assessment of strategic developments and determining a preferred alternative policy course, leaders use frames to challenge old normative commitments and champion new ones. The goal is to establish a new frame of reference for an established norm that is supported by the domestic polity and commutes legitimacy to the enterprise.

Specifically, this study posits that redefinition in domestic political settings involves elite-driven processes of political engagement and persuasion. In the United States, the executive branch often initiates contact with the legislature with persuasive messages designed to "change actor preferences and to challenge current or create new collective meaning." Persuasion provides the "mechanism for constructing and reconstructing social facts."[59] Of course, such messages are "not transmitted in an ideational vacuum," but rather in a contested terrain in which elites have a special responsibility to help frame the new narrative.[60] The goal of this discourse is to formulate successful frames that will resonate with the largest possible audiences.[61] Marc Lynch suggests a carefully crafted interpretive frame, therefore, can help establish a social resource that is apart from material power resources. While norm entrepreneurs "overtly exploit material levers all the time," Rodger Payne argues that inducing change also plays on the "instrumentality and social functions of alternative frames."[62] Frames become the foundation for construction of broadly resonant norms and thereby serve to legitimate normative orders. Consistent with the social psychology literature, redefinition involves primarily using persuasion to achieve transformation of state interests and pursuit of new objectives in foreign policy.

Constructive Norm Substitution through Contestation

The third stage of the norm-change process typically involves constructive norm substitution through contestation, as orchestrated by determined national leaders in multilateral settings. This entails debate and engagement with other member states in multilateral venues to promote new frames for cooperation. The success or failure of norm substitution can be seen in the outcome of rule changes.

Assertions that norms can undergo contestation in multilateral institutions derive primarily from the newest generation of agentic constructivism. Scholars suggest that norm development may be seen as a "product of the constant interplay between rules and behavior [that] follows a cyclical, or dialectical pattern," suggesting the potential to theorize contestation dynamics.[63] Hoffmann asserts, "Social norms are contested at every turn. . . . Contestation is inherent in the process through which actors subjectively interpret intersubjective notions of appropriateness, act on that understanding," and in turn, alter them. He concludes that mutual contestation may allow more analytic scrutiny as a mechanism for institutional change.[64] Second-generation agentic constructivists recognize the potential for leaders to have significant latitude in shaping policy conformity to international agreements or standards. They assert studying the role of human agency in the development of norms and procedures makes agentic constructivism "better positioned to explain change" than social constructivism.[65] In this context, disputes and contestation flow from debates over the meaning of norms.

International diplomacy is a critical tool for constructive norm substitution through contestation. Consensus-building is an important element in the struggle to define prevailing norms, as ideas spread through processes of persuasion and social influence. Agents may engage in negotiation, arm-twisting, and rhetorical pressure of their peers in multilateral settings. Leaders will attempt to frame their cause in ways that resonate with others, with special attention to issues of power and legitimacy. Noting that international relations theory is typically limited in explaining socialization in noncoercive settings such as multilateral institutions, Alastair Iain Johnston suggests a model of "degrees of internalization." He argues that "not all actors are exposed to exactly the same configuration of social pressures, nor do they enter into a social interaction with exactly the same prior identifications. . . . This leaves a vast amount of pro-social behavior produced by neither process."[66] Even if hegemons cannot effectively persuade their counterparts of the need for cooperation—thereby changing their cognitive perspectives and assessments of causality—they can still wield social influence. This study focuses on ways that norms may change as a function of concentrated elite action in a sequential, dialectical process. Central to problem solving is argumentation and exploration of validity claims and identities.

Scholars suggest that not only is contestation a reality for most international agreements, it is also necessary to establish and maintain legitimacy.[67] Legitimacy is constructed through "communicative action during which different socio-culturally determined preferences are adapted and changed based on the willingness to be persuaded by the better argument. Norm validation then is the result of deliberation in transnational or supranational negotiations."[68] This perspective on norms as dynamic is only developed in limited form in existing studies, however. For example, Wiener argues, "As an intersubjective process, discursive interaction draws on resources which have been created prior to the negotiating and/or bargaining situation. Communicative action thus not only contributes to the social construction of norms, but also reconstructs socio-cultural patterns of the life-world."[69] This is critical because "normative structure is constituted by discursive interventions that secure the (re)construction of the values, norms, and rules entailed in it."[70] This approach fosters a more reflexive understanding of the conflictive interaction that shapes the meaning of norms (at least for critical players) at a given point in time.

The Process of Constructive Norm Substitution
Constructive norm substitution involves attempts by states to persuade their peers in multilateral venues that a new normative frame is legitimate. As

noted in Chapter 1, leaders seldom seek to destroy existing norms, given the potential to damage the reputation of state policies and the need for a semblance of regulatory order. Rather, studies in international relations theory and law suggest great powers tend to prefer to remake norms rather than violate them.[71] The social costs and potential repercussions of simply breaking with traditional norms may be perceived as too high; thus, leaders may try to bend norms to their advantage through new interpretations. In a multilateral contestation, just as in domestic settings, competing normative commitments are present in the system, and actors may dispute key values. Norms may be mutually constitutive, but ideational foundations for strategic action also "can be designed to rewrite the cultural landscape in order to legitimate foreign policy change."[72]

Leaders engage in persuasion and social influence in the process of constructive norm substitution. They do so through discourse and negotiations in multilateral venues to gain broader political support for a new norm frame. The process is constructive because it is assumed that leaders seldom desire the elimination of entire norms (perhaps given their marginal constitutive and regulatory effects), but rather to bend the will of the international community toward a new frame of reference or definition of acceptable behavior. New normative frames rarely discard old institutional frameworks or patterns of behavior but instead modify them. It is also constructive (rather than destructive) in that it entails persuasion as a primary mechanism for norm substitution. This occurs through a process of negotiation, arm-twisting, and rhetorical pressure with a program to "frame their cause in ways that resonate" at all levels.[73] Again, this model suggests a dialectical process at work—what Mlada Bukovansky calls "the complex interplay between elite discourses about political legitimacy and strategic struggles for power within and among states."[74]

The process begins when norm stewards foster debate and negotiate new guidelines or standards for international normative principles and agreements. Great-power representatives may make direct or indirect statements in multilateral institutions that the international community should revisit existing standards in light of new challenges or opportunities. This would then generate a policy discourse and debate in the international institution, as leaders consider a range of possible new or modified solutions to the issue at hand. Once again, it is expected that during this process different leaders would exhibit different degrees of commitments to international multilateral regime principles. Some may be highly committed to multilateralism and willing to subsume state interests under multilateral regimes, while others may be predisposed to view these commitments as less pressing and thus may be more willing to take risks grounded in national self-interest. Like redefinition, constructive norm substitution can be seen as a war of frames, which implies that different actors may approach questions of normative principles differently.

In addition, recent social psychology literature suggest that building legitimacy and state bandwagoning behavior need not match the standards of "internalization" ascribed by first-generation constructivism. A process of "social influence" represents a synthesis of considerations of material and social interests, including the valuation of social conformity, rather than internalization in the spirit of first-generation constructivism. As Maria Rost Rublee contends, "It does not have to be all-or-nothing: either states transform their attitudes and behavior (validating constructivism) or they don't (validating realism). Constructivism allows us to explore ways in which the social milieu created by regimes can influence state behavior without 'converting' them."[75] Thus, even if leaders do not fully persuade their counterparts of a genuine transformation of preferences, they may achieve a measure of social conformity (behavior resulting from the desire to maximize social benefits and/or minimize social costs without a change in underlying preferences) that serves to modify the norm frame. In her book, *A Theory of Contestation* (2014), Wiener argues that as a social activity "that involves discursive and critical engagement with norms of governance, whether voiced or voiceless, contestation is constitutive for social change for it always involves a critical redress of the rules of the game."[76] Taken to its logical conclusion, then, this argument suggests there can be a "reverse-tipping point" for normative development.

Expected Outcomes

Norm change is defined for this study as the substantive alteration of acceptable (read: "right") or unacceptable ("wrong") behavior as articulated by a critical mass of players. But how do we know norm change when we see it? And when do actions by great powers to seek "exceptions" to international normative standards become more the "rule"? As noted above, norms are generally understood as fundamental values, organizing principles, or standardized procedures that exist in varying degrees of abstraction and specification in multiple forums (such as treaties, agreements, official policies and laws, and so on). This study focuses on normative standards that are fairly well organized and specified in terms of multilateral institutions, treaties, and agreements, but yet undergo challenges and debate in multilateral institutions.

In addition, the larger process benefits from priming the pump of contestation. Scholars agree that this dynamic is latent in all multilateral institutions, where competing narratives reside regarding problems, processes, and solutions. Indeed, these differences help fuel regular discussions regarding current and future rules structures. Wiener contends contestation is a "necessary condition" to establish and maintain legitimacy for normative agreements.[77] But agents with intentions to change the framing of a traditional norm may also use contestation to their advantage. In such situations, there is a need for great powers to persuade others of the legitimacy of their position. Players work to frame themes and debates so that they can convince others of their preferred "solution" to a challenge. The goal is to shift legitimacy from the old order, or Norm 1.0, to the new order, Norm 2.0. This is achieved when a new version of the norm gains legitimacy or validation "as the result of deliberation in transnational or supranational negotiations."[78] As noted above, this approach is informed by the social psychology literature, which tells us that gaining legitimacy and drawing state bandwagoning behavior need not match the standards of "internalization" ascribed by first-generation constructivism. While leaders may seek consensus in the domestic political arena to achieve a transformation of state interests (persuasion), they may focus instead on exertion of social influence in multilateral institutions.

As noted above, there are two primary measures of norm change for this study. First, legitimacy may be a key to establishing a threshold to assess the robustness of old or new norm frames. Under legitimate, alternative normative structures, "actors accept and support the rules as desirable, proper, or appropriate within some socially constructed system of norms, values, believes, and definitions."[79] Thus, a norm change represents a shift in standards of acceptability. This suggests a process by which new norms may either gain or lose salience, but this study expects to find evidence that through the multistage process states begin to endorse new, alternative orders as legitimate.[80] New approaches are thus authorized by the imprimatur of the institution. Policies such as trade with a nation that was previously sanctioned or behaviors of states or alliances that were previously opposed by the sheer force of will of international institutions demonstrate that a normative frame has evolved. This outcome may be measured by examining public records of multilateral institutions, outcome documents, resolutions, or other institutional endorsements or policy statements.[81]

A second measure for evaluating norm change is bandwagoning behavior. Contestation by major players may be the catalyst for a shift in communal attitudes toward norms that could lead to change. That is, change may signal a new response to an international challenge that leads a critical mass of actors to follow suit. As multiple states endorse the alternative and perhaps implement policy changes, the normative frame is reset. Bandwagoning behavior may be seen in discourse and policy actions toward prevailing norms. For example, the viability of a norm may be understood as a reflection of state commitment. If a fundamental policy change taken by a great power leads other countries to support a different interpretation of the normative order, then a breach may have occurred reflecting norm redefinition and substitution. State leaders may no longer believe that others will abide by the rules and pursue policies that benefit perceived national interests. Thus, bandwagoning behavior is a sign that a new norm (or version of a norm) has acquired salience and/or legitimacy manifest in policy changes.[82]

For the purposes of this study, "successful" norm change will be coded as evidenced by both legitimacy in the form of multilateral institutional changes in rules and standards and significant policy changes in bandwagoning behavior by great powers. That is, for an attempted norm change to be coded as successful, one would expect to see that international organizations endorse the new or evolved principles through resolutions and outcome documents and that great powers alter their policies and behaviors in support of the new norm frame. "Contested" norm change can be identified when either multilateral institutions have issued new standards or great powers are changing their behaviors, but one of the critical elements of legitimacy or bandwagoning behavior is limited or absent. As noted in the critical constructivist literature, contestation may have the effect of strengthening a norm, and so this category of assessment recognizes pending or possible norm change. A third outcome, "failed" norm change, may occur when states pursue a new course that is rejected by international institutions and not emulated by other great powers. Informed by constructivist ideas on foreign policy as discourse and ideational models of change, this study explores a more reflexive theoretical model of life, contest, and decline of prevailing norm frames.

Research Design

Method

This study sets out to explore the utility of this model of normative change by conducting a structured, focused comparison of case studies. Specifically, it compares cases where technological innovation produced significant normative change to those where innovations did not shift prevailing normative understandings, with the goal of identifying important processes and institutional features of the cases that make agency possible. It also identifies some conditions that appear to mitigate technological innovation and normative change. Ultimately, this analysis is designed to get to the heart of the relationship between technology advances and normative changes, address questions of causality (necessity versus sufficiency), and clarify order and timing of decision-making processes in the case studies. The theoretical contribution is based on an analysis of emerging and evolving social practice.

This plausibility probe of the model employs the comparative case method, supported by elite interviews, archival research, analysis of declassified government documents, and participant observation. It applies a set of theoretically relevant, standard questions to examine some of the most controversial military technological innovations and their implications for political processes.[83] The study will examine three stages of case development. First, each case explores the historical foundations of traditional norm architectures and technology developments that prompt the emergence of "techno-normative" dilemmas. The next stage is redefinition, where elites reconsider the state's commitment to the traditional norm in light of innovation and initiate a policy process for change. In the United States, this stage involves presidential drives to shift or shape foreign policy and their interactions with other domestic actors, especially Congress, in these processes. Third, leaders champion alternatives to traditional normative interpretations at the international level through a process of constructive norm substitution via contestation in institutions. The goal is to bring about desired norm changes that generate both legitimacy and bandwagoning behavior from the international community. Process tracing offers an appropriate method to examine the phenomena of norm redefinition and substitution in the constructivist tradition—and may be especially valuable in relation to the evolution of frames of legitimate state behavior within a normative framework.

Case Studies
The book explores the model of norm change in five original case studies. The case studies were selected, in part, as representations of contemporary debates in international politics, or defining moments when problems force political actors to debate foreign policy behavior. They also were selected based on the expectation of variance in outcomes; that is, they demonstrate the evolution of normative standards in a way that differs from traditional models of norm development (or the norm life cycle). It is clear from preliminary investigation that the outcomes of these attempts at normative change vary (see Table 2.1). Finally, these cases explore important research puzzles, including why traditional stewards would promote a redefinition of normative standards and how countries avoid (or ignore) significant international pressure to conform in multilateral settings.

The goal of this study is to demonstrate that endogenous technology innovations are the start of a complex political process, and to explore the dynamics of stages of norm change. It is not enough simply to show that outcomes are consistent with technological change, of course. Rather, my goal is to develop a stronger model of causality through a structured, focused comparison of the case studies and outcomes. This study will analyze the power of technology innovation as an endogenous cause of change by comparing cases where technological innovation produced normative change to cases where it appears not to have shifted prevailing normative understandings. This should help to identify important institutional features of the cases that have made agency possible. It will help get to the heart of the relationship between technology advances and normative changes, address questions of causality (necessity versus sufficiency), and clarify the order and timing of decision-making processes in the case studies.

Technological innovations and policy development in the United States relative to international normative standards are the focus of this study for several reasons. First and foremost, the United States is a democracy with a self-proclaimed commitment to restraint in the use of force externally and the power of public opinion in its internal governing process. The U.S. government has embraced its role as a norm leader, and government officials have spoken out for decades about regime standards. In the nuclear realm, for example, the United States was one of the originators of the Nuclear Suppliers Group (NSG), as well as a strong proponent of limits on missile technology and the production of fissile materials. The United States also has played an important

Table 2.1   Case Studies of Norm Change

Traditional norm	Technology innovation	Potential norm change
Prohibition against weapons of mass destruction	Atomic fission, the atom bomb	Development of discriminatory nonproliferation norm (NPT)
Peaceful uses of nuclear energy	Uranium enrichment and reprocessing technologies	Convention banning sensitive technology transfers
Sovereignty and nonintervention	Satellite imagery, government and NGO monitoring	Humanitarian intervention and the responsibility to protect
Norm against assassination of foreign adversaries	Unmanned aerial vehicles and drone strikes	Revising the doctrine of self-defense through preemption and counterterrorism
Prohibition on militarization of outer space	Lasers and kinetic-kill vehicles	Development of discriminatory norm against space-based missile defenses and anti-satellite technologies

role in articulating the value of sovereignty and asserting its sovereign right to carry out actions in the international arena. Theory suggests that key norm stewards would be heavily vested in existing standards. For these reasons, U.S. actions to promote changes in prevailing norms might seem least likely cases. Second, traditional studies of U.S. foreign policy have tended to focus on systemic factors, such as balances of power and correlations between the power dynamics and decisions on technology such as nuclear supply. Third, this study shows that norms are living and dynamic entities in global politics that have undergone fundamental changes over time. Some of these changes have drawn international attention, while others have been incremental in nature, but all have contributed to the evolution of a surprisingly dynamic normative structure. Finally, cases were chosen as representative of contemporary debates in international politics.

Data for these original case studies have been collected through elite interviews, archival research, and participant observation over a six-year period. Dozens of interviews were conducted with current and former policy-makers from the White House, the Department of State, and the Department of Defense, in addition to experts on all subject areas in the project. The National Security Archive, housed at George Washington University, as well as reviews of original documents at the George H. W. Bush Presidential Library, provided detailed background information for the case studies. This study also draws on participant observation from the Third Preparatory Committee meetings for the 2010 NPT Review Conference at the UN headquarters in New York.

In summary, this book represents an original study of norm evolution plus in-depth explorations of decision-making related to norm change. By analyzing classic and contemporary cases of norm change, it illuminates the role of leaders in the complex game of crafting multilateral solutions to global problems. Preliminary analyses of the cases suggest the United States has had mixed levels of success in attempts to evolve norms. In the process, the study raises a number of interesting theoretical and empirical insights worthy of further exploration.

3   The Atom Bomb: Constructing a Nuclear Order

When you see something that is technically sweet, you go ahead and do it, and you argue about what to do about it only after you have had your technical success. That is the way it was with the atomic bomb.
        —J. Robert Oppenheimer[1]

Each nuclear-weapon State Party to the Treaty undertakes not to transfer to any recipient whatsoever nuclear weapons or other nuclear explosive devices or control over such weapons or explosive devices directly, or indirectly; and not in any way to assist, encourage, or induce any non-nuclear weapon State to manufacture or otherwise acquire nuclear weapons or other nuclear explosive devices, or control over such weapons or explosive devices.
        —Treaty on the Non-Proliferation of Nuclear Weapons[2]

THE UNITED STATES BECAME THE WORLD'S FIRST atomic power and the only nation in history to use atomic weapons in war in 1945. The two U.S. bombs dropped on the Japanese cities of Hiroshima and Nagasaki killed over 130,000 people instantly; 200,000 more would die of the effects of radiation. They were the largest explosions ever produced at the time.[3] While U.S. president Harry Truman proclaimed the atom bomb "the greatest marvel . . . the greatest achievement of organized science in history,"[4] he privately professed unease about it. Reflecting the spirit of past efforts by the international community to regulate weapons of war, Truman initially backed plans for the creation of a multilateral commission to control, and perhaps even eliminate, nuclear weapons. Cabinet members also debated ways the atom could be harnessed for peace.

U.S. policies evolved significantly in the face of changing circumstances over the next two decades, though. The nuclear nonproliferation norm that eventually emerged from a process of contestation was multifaceted and discriminatory. The 1970 Treaty on the Non-Proliferation of Nuclear Weapons (NPT) granted "the inalienable right of all the Parties to the Treaty to develop research, production and use of nuclear energy for peaceful purposes without discrimination," in exchange for a pledge not to pursue nuclear weapons. Countries ratified the treaty with the assurance of equal access to technologies to establish their own energy programs, and atomic energy became associated with economic development and hope. Yet, Articles I and II defined a set of "nuclear weapons states"—those that had acquired weapons by that time, including the United States, China, Russia, the United Kingdom, and France—and "non-nuclear weapon states" (all others). The NPT helped regulate the spread of nuclear weapons and promote peaceful nuclear energy cooperation, but it also modified traditional principles of universalism in arms control to create a discriminatory regime.

This case study adopts the three-stage model of norm change to explore the construction of the modern nuclear nonproliferation norm, with an emphasis on its subjective and dynamic character. It tells the story of innovation, the redefinition of atomic weapons by U.S. leaders as a viable instrument of warfare, and the establishment of a discriminatory normative architecture. This case appears to demonstrate a successful effort to transform international norm frames from one following universal restrictions to a discriminatory architecture featuring commitments to disarmament, nuclear nonproliferation, and peaceful nuclear energy development.

The Traditional Arms Control Norm: Universalism before World War II

The international community often seems to respond to dramatic advances in military technology with a mixture of awe and horror. Machine guns, armored vehicles, and chemical weapons all had devastating effects when they were used on battlefields in the nineteenth and early twentieth centuries. The advent of steel-hulled warships and aircraft that could accurately bomb targets on the ground represented micro revolutions in military affairs of their own. Many new weapons offered overwhelming advantage to one side at tremendous cost to those who lost the battle or war. In a number of these circumstances, the international political community seemed to respond reflexively by trying to ban, or at least significantly limit, the use of these types of weapons.

Universal prohibitionary regimes for weapons had their early origins in the laws of armed conflict. President Abraham Lincoln commissioned a study in 1863 to codify military standards and practices for the Union during the Civil War (which became known as the Lieber Code). Over time, this persuasive set of standards became a more universal guide to wartime practices. Among the elements of the code were calls for humane treatment of prisoners of war and protection of civilian populations in occupied areas. Other ideas in the code now seem prescient, including prohibitions against the use of poisons in warfare (calling this "entirely outside the pale of civilized nations and peoples") and the use of torture to extract confessions. At a convention in St. Petersburg, Russia, in 1868, to discuss the rules of war, diplomats produced a declaration prohibiting the use of small explosive projectiles, or dum-dum bullets, which had ghastly effects on the battlefield. This was considered the first formal disarmament agreement, and it was supported by most European powers at the time.[5]

Diplomats negotiated new conventions at the turn of the century that further defined practices for the treatment of noncombatants and prisoners of war, among other principles. A key focus of the first and second Hague International Peace Conferences (1899 and 1907) was to establish laws of war and treaties restricting the use of particular weapons and military practices.[6] Diplomats negotiated conventions including prohibitions against aerial bombardment (or the launching of explosives from balloons), the use of submarine mines, and bans on poison gas. The Hague Conventions also established codes of conduct for war at land and at sea, declarations on standards of opening and closing hostilities, and statements on the rights of neutral powers and the freedom of maritime commerce. The Permanent Court of Arbitration was founded to promote nonviolent conflict resolution between states, a precursor to international tribunals established from World War II to the present.[7]

A series of Geneva Conventions also helped codify the laws of war. The first Geneva Convention (1864) called for the protection of medical facilities, their personnel, and any civilians aiding the wounded in wartime. The second convention, in 1882, extended the protection of the first convention to combatants at sea (wounded or shipwrecked sailors). The third and fourth conventions, completed in 1929 and 1949, respectively, reaffirmed standards for the treatment of prisoners of war and protections for civilians during wartime. The Geneva Protocols also called for employment of proportionality in the use of force and prohibited the use of asphyxiating and poisonous gases and bacteriological weapons in international conflicts—though this rule would not apply to defensive, internal, or civil wars. Taken together, these regulations even suggested the emergence of a norm against offensive war. By the twentieth century, Michael Walzer opined, war became "a rule-governed activity, a world of permissions and prohibitions—a moral world, therefore, in the midst of hell."[8]

Technology advances related to the battlefield in the nineteenth and early twentieth centuries appeared to spur on the evolution of international legal standards regulating behavior in wartime. The threat of Clausewitz's "total war" loomed large by the twentieth century, but new weapons with devastating effects were ruled out of bounds in an evolving moral code of war.[9] This was well illustrated by international cooperation after World War I. The devastation of the Great War marked a turning point in the establishment of new standards for wartime behavior. Some past Hague Convention standards on the use of asphyxiating gases and the prohibition of aerial bombardment were flagrantly violated during the war. Diplomats began working almost immediately through conferences and the newly established League of Nations to address ways to tighten and extend international prohibitions on armaments. For example, the Washington Naval Conferences (1921–1922) addressed issues of disarmament and arms control with vigor, as diplomats worked to halt a new naval arms race between the world's leading powers. The United States, the United Kingdom, France, Italy, and Japan agreed to limit the number and tonnage of capital ships, and even to scrap vessels that exceeded the limits. In 1928, the Kellogg-Briand Pact was the first major treaty designed to outlaw war. The language of the pact was expressly written to prohibit offensive wars, or wars of aggression, rather than wars of self-defense; the pact also called upon signatories to settle their disputes by peaceful means. Within several years, nearly seventy countries, including all the major powers, had ratified the pact.[10]

Technological Innovation: The Atomic Bomb

The Manhattan Project that produced the atom bomb was a massive scientific undertaking. President Franklin Roosevelt ordered the establishment of the secret atomic weapon research program during World War II, under the leadership Army Brigadier General Leslie Groves and theoretical physicist J. Robert Oppenheimer. The foundations of the project lay in advanced scientific discoveries in European laboratories in the 1930s and early 1940s. Oppenheimer tapped the best and brightest North American scientists, plus a number of wartime émigrés from Europe, including Leo Szilard and Enrico Fermi, for participation in the Manhattan Project. The project eventually employed thousands of scientists and engineers at research and production sites.

The goal of the enterprise was straightforward: "to produce a practical military weapon in the form of a bomb in which the energy is released by a fast neutron chain reaction in one or more of the materials known to show nuclear fission."[11] The incredible (yet fearsome) technological achievements that followed came from one of the most elaborate scientific research programs in history—a virtually unparalleled feat of physics, mathematics, and engineering. Scientists worked on every possible aspect of the challenge, including conversion of natural uranium, uranium enrichment for use as fissile material in a bomb, bomb design and manufacture, delivery systems, and even management of nuclear waste. These became critical elements of the modern nuclear fuel cycle and weapons production process.

Three technological innovations at the heart of the atomic bomb program were fission, uranium enrichment, and bomb design. Each reflected new technologies that would provide the United States with unprecedented power, but each was highly complex. Even when the basic physics, mathematics, and chemistry behind an atomic bomb had been worked out, many doubted that the rapid technical advances needed could be made in so short a time. Scientists thus approached the challenge with what historian Richard Rhodes called a special mixture of science and faith.[12]

The birthplace of atomic fission (or splitting the atom) was not the United States, but rather scientific laboratories in Europe. In 1932, British physicist James Chadwick, who had begun experiments with radioactivity and atomic disintegration (and for which he later won the Nobel Prize in Physics), discovered the existence of the neutron, a subatomic particle without an electric charge. German laboratories under the direction of theoretical physicist Werner Heisenberg also made significant advances in atomic research. Hungarian-born scientist Leo Szilard, who had studied under Albert Einstein and Max Planck in Berlin in the 1920s, emigrated to London in the 1930s, and played a critical role in understanding and translating the implications of these advances in atomic research for Western audiences.[13] Within months of news of the discovery of neutrons, Szilard had developed an idea of a controlled release of atomic power through a neutron chain reaction and advanced the concept of "critical mass."[14]

Soon, several European laboratories were experimenting with bombardment of elements with neutrons and the discovery of new radioactive isotopes. Enrico Fermi's laboratory in Rome published a study in 1934 of experiments with neutron bombardment of uranium and their confusing scientific results. As the heaviest naturally occurring element on Earth, uranium carries a number of protons that reacted in ways that fascinated scientists (indeed, this became known as the "uranium problem"). The splitting of the nucleus of the uranium atom yields mass, but also releases a significant amount of its binding energy. Neutrons released by one atom would then impact nearby atoms, producing a chain reaction explosion. In 1938, German scientists Otto Hahn, Fritz Strassmann, and Lise Meitner reported conclusive evidence of atomic fission in a published study; they also coined the term atomic "fission."[15]

On January 26, 1939, Danish physicist Niels Bohr made an historic announcement of the discovery of fission at an annual theoretical physics conference in Washington, DC. The news seemed to set off a different sort of scientific and political chain reaction. Within weeks, both Szilard and American scientist Oppenheimer recognized independently that splitting the atom would produce excess neutrons that must be shed, creating an atomic chain reaction. They also quickly realized this might make it possible to amplify the splittings in a runaway chain reaction in the form of a bomb.[16] A fast flurry of scientific research continued in European and U.S. research laboratories on radioactivity and the different properties of the element uranium. Szilard, who had moved to Columbia University by that time, was co-inventor of the first nuclear reactor. In the summer of 1939, Szilard also appealed to his former mentor, Albert Einstein, to pen a letter directly to President Franklin Roosevelt that called for government action.

Einstein's letter served to notify President Roosevelt and the highest levels of the government of important scientific research with military potential. It also included a warning that scientific research was underway in Berlin as well, and that Nazi Germany could be making rapid progress toward its own atomic bomb. Roosevelt took notice and ordered the establishment of a research committee including military and civilian representatives.[17] Government-funded research also advanced at several universities, including

Columbia, the University of Chicago, and the University of California at Berkeley. By 1941, sufficient progress had been made to order a larger program by the Army Corps of Engineers to establish a secret, nationwide research program known by its code name, the Manhattan Project.[18]

Its beginning highlighted what would become the second major technological challenge to overcome in the endeavor: how to attain enough fissile material in enriched form to create a chain reaction explosion. Scientists determined that two elements with high atomic numbers offered the best prospects for fission: uranium and plutonium. Uranium ore would be processed to produce uranium oxide, containing the isotopes U-238 and U-235. Understanding the different properties of the two isotopes was critical to understanding the feasibility of the bomb, not to mention the potential for generating nuclear power.

At the start of the program, uranium-235, a highly fissionable isotope, was such a rare element that it could only be found in high concentrations in two mines in the world outside of Axis control: the Eldorado mine in Canada and the Shinkolobwe mine in the Belgian Congo. The uranium ore was recovered and shipped to the United States to be processed in Manhattan Project facilities. Early uranium conversion involved experimental mixes of chemical processes, electrolysis, and high temperatures. U-238 is a much more ubiquitous part of the ore, and so the isotopes had to be separated and amounts of U-235 concentrated for use in nuclear power reactors or nuclear bombs. Scientists developed several methods for uranium enrichment—technically, isotope separation to enrich the amount of U-235 required for the core of an atomic bomb.[19] Researchers also focused on the potential for plutonium to serve as the core of a weapon. Plutonium, a man-made element that could be created by bombarding uranium with neutrons, was produced in secret reactors located in Hanford, Washington.

Enrichment was to prove an incredibly complex and energy-intensive experimental process. Scientists in the Manhattan Project developed two parallel research and development lines. Groves built an entire city and laboratory complex for the purpose out of the scrubland west of Knoxville, Tennessee, which became known as Oak Ridge. Scientists established separate facilities for electromagnetic isotope separation (EMIS) and gaseous diffusion, employing the gas uranium hexafluoride (UF6). EMIS was a simplified process employing "calutron" devices, but it was found to be highly energy-intensive and inefficient; the United States eventually abandoned this method.

Gaseous diffusion designs became more efficient over time, and this method won out and became the preferred U.S. approach to enrichment. Subsequent scientific advances in enrichment using uranium hexafluoride gas (UF6), especially centrifuges, have significantly advanced the process. At the same time, these systems have greatly increased the risk that clandestine nuclear programs could successfully enrich fissile material for a bomb (see Chapter 4).

Weapons design was a third critical innovation. The scientists' goal was to build devices that would set off a chain reaction of uranium-235 or plutonium to produce a powerful explosion. Researchers experimented with two primary designs of the atomic bomb. First, a "gun-type" weapon design that would generate an explosion from a carefully timed collision of two subcritical amounts of U-235 together for a powerful weapon. The gun-type weapon design featured a plan to propel one mass of uranium or plutonium into another at high velocity. While the basic design of the weapon was simpler, experiments found that the use of plutonium in such a weapon would be far less efficient than separate masses of uranium. The design also suffered from potential problems, though, including that it was susceptible to accidental detonation through ground contact, electrical shorts, or exposure to fire.[20]

Next, an implosion device was designed that would require extremely precise triggering to crush the uranium into a critical mass at the core. This alternative design addressed concerns about the efficiency of a plutonium-core weapon. The weapon would produce a spherical explosive wave to compress a critical mass of plutonium at exactly the right instant. Nicknamed "the Introvert," this design would trap neurons to enhance its explosive power. A critical player in this design was chemist George Kistiakowsky, another émigré from Europe. Kistiakowsky and his team designed and tested a combination of different explosive shapes and sizes, including molding explosive charges into three-dimensional lenses that would focus the shockwave inward.[21] In the end, this proved a more sophisticated, stable weapon design, and scientists gravitated toward it as the preferred schema for atomic bombs. The implosion device was the first weapon tested, on July 16, 1945, in the desert near Los Alamos, New Mexico.

The scientific process of atomic bomb development was one of the most deeply held secrets in the history of statecraft during the presidency of Franklin Roosevelt. After Roosevelt's death, Harry Truman was sworn into office and briefed on the "atomic fission bomb" project by Secretary of War Stimson and General Groves.[22] The president worked with groups of scientific and political advisors on the questions of how, and whether or not, to use these weapons, and by spring of 1945 had resolved that the weapon should be dropped without warning on military targets in Japan. Three weeks after the successful test, Truman ordered the use of two bombs over Hiroshima, on August 6, 1945, and Nagasaki, on August 9, 1945. Two days later, the Japanese government sued for peace.

Stage I: New Technology Meets Traditional Norms

News that the United States had unleashed weapons of unprecedented power on Japan at the end of World War II was greeted with a mixture of awe, relief, and uncertainty. Different actors soon developed subjective interpretations of the meaning and significance of the atomic bomb for U.S. foreign policy and international politics. Reflecting the normative arc of the early twentieth century in relation to powerful weapons, President Truman's first impulse after the war seemed to be to establish an international authority to secure control of nuclear technology. However, by the 1950s and 1960s the United States came to favor an exclusive, discriminatory nonproliferation norm. Key factors in this evolution included the views of the Eisenhower, Kennedy, and Johnson administrations, as well as disagreements among leading political and scientific advisors and interagency struggles. Externally, the development of the atomic bomb by the Soviet Union in 1949 and spiraling Cold War tensions also had a significant impact on U.S. policies.

A Pregnant Pause: Monopoly or Prohibitionary Norm?

With the development and use of the weapon in Japan, the United States had secured a powerful technological advantage over all other nations. Beyond the successful use of the weapon to leverage an end to the war, though, policymakers, scientists, and concerned citizens knew that something had profoundly changed. Many began to weigh the implications of this technological achievement, producing a period of reflection—a pregnant pause—that stretched from Pennsylvania Avenue to Main Street. The president himself reflected on the double-edged nature of the atomic bomb, writing in his diary at the Potsdam conference on July 25, 1945: "We have discovered the most terrible bomb in the history of the world. It may be the fire destruction prophesied in the Euphrates Valley era, after Noah and his fabulous ark."[23] Physicist Niels Bohr lobbied colleagues at atomic labs in Los Alamos and Chicago in favor of openness and universality regarding technology sharing.[24] Editorials also appeared in major newspapers after the war calling on restraint. The *Los Angeles Times* said, "Not only must this uranium be controlled, but just in case a substitute is found, any suspect nations will have to be kept under surveillance to prevent the building of atom bomb plants."[25] Renowned journalist Edward R. Murrow opined, "Seldom if ever has a war ended with such a sense of uncertainty and fear, with such a realization that the future is obscure and that survival is not assured."[26]

This was, of course, the first time any nation had deliberated on the implications of nuclear weapons and nuclear power. Truman's cabinet was divided on the question after the war. The president himself had mixed feelings, though he did move to assert civilian control over the atomic energy complex. Secretary of State James Byrnes believed the United States atomic monopoly offered incredible diplomatic and security advantages that would last for a decade or more. Byrnes was skeptical of the motives of the Soviet Union and believed nuclear weapons should be wielded as any instrument of statecraft. Meanwhile, Secretary of War Henry Stimson warned the technological secrets of the atomic bomb project would eventually leak out to other countries' research programs. Stimson saw the Soviet preoccupation with power as the primary reason it would be driven to create its own bombs at all costs, and he urged the president to negotiate with Stalin to find a reasonable settlement. The only solution, Stimson argued, was to right the nuclear imbalance through unilateral disarmament and international control.[27]

The Truman administration faced a dilemma: how to use the atomic bomb as a diplomatic tool to advance U.S. interests and promote peaceful cooperation for scientific research yet keep others from developing the weapon. Differences inside the cabinet resulted in some initial diplomatic fumbling in multilateral settings. For example, during the first postwar meeting of Allied foreign ministers in London in October 1945, Byrnes stood firm on the U.S. nuclear monopoly but ran up against significant Soviet challenges. Soviet foreign minister Molotov publicly chided Byrnes for the U.S. position of "no negotiation" regarding the atomic bomb as well as its intransigence on other postwar settlement matters, and the conference collapsed in acrimony. In response, Byrnes recognized the United States might have to reconsider its monopoly position in light of international diplomatic pressures. He ordered his deputy, Undersecretary of State Dean Acheson, to draw up a plan for a system of international control of atomic weapons that could be discussed at the next meeting of foreign ministers.

Early nuclear activists and concerned citizens also pressured the government to consider international control and development of a prohibitionary norm. Prominent voices included Hamilton Holt, Andrew Carnegie, and Oppenheimer. Holt, the president of Rollins College, was a champion of world government and helped found the nongovernmental organizations the American Society of International Law and the American Peace Society. At a conference on world government at Rollins, delegates called for the United States and the world to ban nuclear weapons and establish an international legal framework to eliminate them from the earth.[28] Oppenheimer, too, had grown troubled by the destructiveness of the atomic bomb in the days that followed its first test and uses, and he was determined to try to influence the Truman administration to ban the bomb. In personal appeals to officials in Washington he suggested that the bomb should be made illegal, "just like poison gases after the last war," but he received a largely tepid response.[29]

The Baruch Plan

Truman appeared to be leaning toward maintaining the U.S. monopoly of weapons, but he allowed continued deliberations on the question. He appointed Acheson, along with David Lilienthal, of the Tennessee Valley Authority, to direct a study for the administration that might eventually be submitted to the United Nations. The Acheson-Lilienthal Report was finalized in early 1946. The report recommended the establishment of a prohibitionary regime, to be overseen by an international Atomic Development Agency (ADA) to regulate dangerous nuclear activities.[30] The ADA would be responsible for controlling technology that might be used for nuclear warfare while supporting the development of civilian atomic energy programs. The report recommended that the new agency, perhaps administered by the United Nations, should take guardianship of all atomic research facilities in any country of the world, and that there be no future national or commercial ownership of dangerous nuclear technologies.[31] Finally, the United States would abandon its monopoly—destroying its existing arsenal of bombs and revealing everything to the Soviet Union in exchange for a mutual agreement for prohibition. In sum, the report was a far-reaching proposal to create an international prohibitionary norm. As historian Tom Zoellner observed, "That such a dovish proposal could have ever come from the White House of Harry Truman, even when he believed the Russians were incapable of building the bomb, is testament to the millennial panic and social readjustment that had swept through the country after Hiroshima," as well as the influence of opinion-makers in the newspapers.[32]

However, the U.S. position evolved when, at Byrnes' suggestion, the president appointed Bernard Baruch, a well-known financier and political consultant, to present the Acheson-Lilienthal plan at the United Nations. Baruch immediately revised the plan. His proposed alternative was to advocate a position that if countries violated the agreements of the prohibitionary norm they would relinquish their veto power in the UN Security Council.[33] On June 14, 1946, the U.S. envoy made his pitch to the United Nations:

> We are here to make a choice between the quick and the dead. That is our business. Behind the black portent of the new atomic age lies a hope which, seized upon with faith, can work our salvation. If we fail, then we have damned every man to be the slave of fear. Let us not deceive ourselves: we must elect world peace or world destruction. . . . Nuclear weapons give an unqualified advantage to the aggressor . . . [and] there can be no adequate military defense.[34]

The new atomic energy authority should be granted complete control over the weapons and technology, Baruch proposed, and it should be supported by an international inspections regime to verify compliance. As expert Henry Sokolski later opined, the plan seemed to have a straightforward goal "to prohibit nations from owning *anything* that might help them make a bomb and to ensure that the penalties for violating the prohibitions were 'swift and condign.'"[35] All potentially dangerous nuclear activities were to be owned and controlled by the International Atomic Energy Authority alone.[36] And critical to the plan was Baruch's argument that violators of the agreement would be severely punished and lose their veto power to forestall sanctions.

Unsurprisingly, Soviet diplomats strongly opposed the plan. Some historians have since suggested that by the spring of 1946 Truman already was beginning to adopt the view that the Soviet Union was an adversary that could not be trusted. They suggest that the appointment of Baruch—a strong-willed leader not well known for taking orders—was actually a set-up for the plan to fail. Privately, one expert suggested, "The White House already knew that the plan would be dead on arrival. The USSR objected to the idea of giving up its uranium deposits and enrichment facilities, both of which it was frantically developing in secret. The United States also continued to manufacture weapons even while the plan was under debate, giving the Soviet UN delegate Andrei Gromyko license to accuse his negotiating partners of hypocrisy."[37]

Soviet diplomats countered that the United States should take the lead by destroying all of its nuclear weapons, and then the international community might be able to negotiate a new framework for management of the technology. The Soviet Union rejected the Baruch Plan in December 1946.

Stage II: Redefinition for the Cold War: A Discriminatory Framework

The collapse of the Baruch Plan in the United Nations represented an important turning point in U.S. diplomacy regarding nuclear weapons. Many inside the Truman administration came to believe the United States could, and should, redefine its position on nuclear weapons and strengthen its nuclear arsenal in the face of future challenges. General Groves privately concluded, "If there are to be atomic weapons in the world, we must have the best, the biggest, and the most."[38] U.S. positions in negotiations with the Soviet Union hardened. On August 29, 1949, the Soviets shocked the world with their first atomic bomb test.

The election of Republican Dwight Eisenhower to the presidency in 1952 helped formalize the redefinition the U.S. position on nuclear weapons. Eisenhower adopted a three-track approach to the nuclear question. First, the United States would continue to build up and modernize its nuclear arsenal, and it would threaten to use nuclear weapons against rivals. Second, it would advance commercial nuclear power development in the United States by ending the federal government's monopoly on materials, technologies, and research and development. Third, the Eisenhower administration would embrace international cooperation on peaceful nuclear energy development— and use its assistance to developing countries as a valuable incentive to draw countries to its side. Critically, most facets of the approach garnered significant support in Congress and among most executive agencies in Washington.

Eisenhower ordered the military to devote billions of dollars to research and development of atomic weapons. Against the advice of the military brass, the president supported the advent of new, more tactical atomic weapons, including warheads that could be launched by battlefield cannon. His National Security Council principals also gave serious consideration to the use of atomic weapons in the Korean War. Eisenhower asserted in his memoirs that he was prepared to use atomic weapons if necessary to get a settlement at the peace talks and that he "would not be limited by any world-wide gentleman's agreement."[39] This strategy of modernization and consideration of the possible use of atomic weapons in the 1950s was supported by the president's top advisors. For example, Secretary of State John Foster Dulles had experienced somewhat of a personal conversion over time, a shift from "viewing the bomb in the immediate post-war period as an immoral device unsuited for Christians to being an equally enthusiastic proponent of it in the 1950s."[40] In January 1954, Dulles gave a high-profile speech to the Council on Foreign Relations in which he articulated the Eisenhower administration's massive retaliation policy. This stance, Dulles said, represented a decision "to depend primarily upon a great capacity to retaliate, instantly, by means and at places of our choosing."[41] Both Dulles and the president repeatedly articulated that they saw atomic weapons as viable weapons of war, part of an arsenal that might be employed in escalating conflicts. They also authorized forward deployment of U.S.-owned weapons and technology sharing with allies, and in 1958 the United States negotiated a first-of-its-kind agreement to exchange classified data on the history and technical functions of the U.S. nuclear program.[42]

Second, the Eisenhower administration encouraged planning by the Atomic Energy Commission (AEC) in the early 1950s to shift the government monopoly on nuclear technologies and materials to commercial enterprises, and the government explored avenues for stimulating industrial development of nuclear power. This resulted in a significant modification of the U.S. Atomic Energy Act (AEA) by a supportive Congress in August 1954. The AEA was designed to promote the development of peaceful atomic energy while at the same time framing a safety and security regime.[43] For the first time, the government established a framework allowing privatization of the nuclear energy industry as well as set out guidelines for civilian development of nuclear energy, safety, monitoring, and disposal of nuclear waste.[44] Thomas Murray, a member of the AEC, fully supported the end of the nationalization of the nuclear industry. He opined, "For years, the splitting atom, packaged in weapons has been our main shield against the Barbarians—now, in addition, it is to become a God-given instrument to do the constructive work of mankind."[45]

Third, Eisenhower also endorsed the advancement of U.S. interests through exports of peaceful nuclear energy plants to promote economic development in the Third World. On December 8, 1953, the president formally presented the Atoms for Peace program at the United Nations, which endorsed the rapid development of commercial nuclear power programs around the world. The Atoms for Peace announcement was a watershed moment; indeed, some likened it to the soaring rhetoric of the announcement of the Marshall Plan in terms of scope and ambition. At the same time, though, this program also served a dual purpose: a global program for nuclear energy technology sharing virtually guaranteed U.S. technical dominance of the competitive energy market.

The president effectively laid out a three-dimensional plan—nuclear arms modernization, commercialization of nuclear power and research and development at home, and peaceful energy assistance to developing countries—for a new normative posture that could sell at home and abroad. On Capitol Hill, a number of congressional leaders signaled their support for the plan. Nuclear arms modernization coupled with new opportunities for U.S. corporations in the energy sector were an easy sell to most constituents. Nuclear cooperation agreements under the auspices of Atoms for Peace began in 1955. While the early nuclear export market consisted primarily of U.S. companies (with government consent and backing) selling nuclear technologies to client states, other countries gradually developed commercial nuclear programs and technology sharing agreements.

However, the sharing of technologies was to have a significant proliferation impact. Experts came to recognize the growing problem of proliferation of nuclear technologies in the 1960s and called on the White House to pursue multilateral negotiations to address the challenges. The State Department warned that with the trade in sensitive technologies and very limited oversight, other countries could legally reach full "nuclear pregnancy." They called for a rigorous new system of safeguards authority and supported the creation of the International Atomic Energy Agency (IAEA) in 1957. Subsequent discussions focused on the extent of IAEA authority to conduct inspections in aspiring nuclear countries as well as nuclear weapons states. Recently declassified documents show that the Arms Control and Disarmament Agency supported progress toward a new international agreement as necessary to "develop . . . political inhibitions against the development of further national nuclear capabilities" because "a world in which there are ten and then possibly twenty states having national nuclear capabilities . . . would be a world of the greatest danger and insecurity."[46] In 1965, the president's Committee on Nuclear Proliferation argued that "preventing the further spread of nuclear weapons is clearly in the national interest despite the difficult decisions that will be required." Calling the matter one of great urgency, the committee advised the president that the world was "fast approaching a point of no return in prospects of controlling the spread of nuclear weapons" and that "success in preventing the future spread of nuclear weapons requires a concerted and intensified effort." One of its primary policy recommendations was that measures "to prevent particular countries from acquiring nuclear weapons are unlikely to succeed unless they are taken in support of a broad international prohibition applicable to many countries."[47]

Stage III: Constructive Norm Substitution

The 1960s brought a new set of challenges and opportunities for the emerging international nuclear nonproliferation regime. Prominent U.S. leaders intended to create a regime that would bolster international security, yet preserve and legitimize their own instruments of power. Gone was the idea of prohibition. Instead, by the 1960s the United States and close allies saw themselves as guardians of critical technologies and began to construct a new norm architecture to legitimize this arrangement. They recognized the double-edged nature of the technology: the science of the atom offered the prospect of tremendous opportunities for energy production and economic growth; at the same time, determined regimes could divert some of these technologies to develop clandestine nuclear weapons programs. To many, guardianship or stewardship implied a need to maintain dominance and control of nuclear technologies.

More experts were calling out the dangers of unfettered sharing of nuclear technology and materials through the Atoms for Peace program. Noted strategists Albert and Roberta Wohlstetter warned of the military potential of civil nuclear energy technologies, suggesting that drawing a dividing line between atomic weapons research and nuclear energy was "a distinction without much difference."[48] British journalist and nuclear security specialist Leonard Beaton called Atoms for Peace "one of the most inexplicable political fantasies in history." He went on: "Only a social psychologist could hope to explain why the possessors of the most terrible weapons in history should have sought to spread the necessary industry to produce them in the belief that this could make the world safer."[49] Looking back at the implications of the technology sharing deal decades later, experts Thomas Reed and Danny Stillman charged that Atoms for Peace "tore a gaping hole in the dikes holding back the spread of nuclear weapons."[50] It was certainly the case that scientists from around the world learned the secrets of nuclear technology through Western educational programs. As sensitive materials and technologies were shared with developing countries, more governments *could* pursue development of nuclear energy and nuclear weapons.

The Treaty on the Non-Proliferation of Nuclear Weapons (NPT)
Presidents John F. Kennedy and Lyndon Johnson saw a new nonproliferation regime as one response to a multidimensional problem. Not only were Western officials concerned about a U.S.-Soviet arms race, they also feared the number of countries possessing nuclear weapons might soon grow exponentially as a result of sharing materials and technology. They recognized this would require confidence-building measures between the superpowers and nuclear aspirants. They embarked upon negotiations for new norm construction in the 1960s with a broad, stated goal of promoting multilateral principles of restraint. Meanwhile, the unstated, surgical goal of the White House remained to try to lock down Western control of an increasingly dangerous technology.

Tensions between the superpowers had contributed to a spiraling arms race. By 1960, the United States had accumulated more than 15,000 nuclear warheads; the Soviet Union around 10,000. But because the precise number of warheads on both sides was unknown to the other, the reality of circumstances at the time was fueled by misperceptions. Advances in delivery systems and weapons modernization further complicated the situation. After all, it was the Soviets who first developed intercontinental ballistic missile (ICBM) technology, symbolized by the launch of the *Sputnik* satellite in 1957. This technology gave them the capability to deliver warheads to targets in the United States in a matter of minutes. By the late 1950s, some officials were concerned that the West was falling significantly behind the Soviets in ICBMs (the so-called missile gap), and both countries rushed to develop new technologies. President Kennedy ordered a shift in nuclear doctrine from massive retaliation to flexible response. Following the Cuban missile crisis, the superpowers negotiated a "hot-line" agreement and the Partial Nuclear Test-Ban Treaty (PTBT).

The Kennedy administration also was alarmed by the threat of horizontal proliferation—the spread of nuclear weapons to many new countries. U.S. allies France and Britain had developed nuclear weapons in the 1950s, and intelligence reports suggested the People's Republic of China might be moving toward a bomb of its own. A secret Department of Defense memorandum predicted that at least eight countries—Canada, China, India, Israel, Italy, Japan, Sweden, and West Germany—could have the ability to produce nuclear weapons within ten years. And President Kennedy publicly warned, "I see the possibility in the 1970s of the president of the United States having to face a world in which 15 or 20 or 25 nations may have [nuclear] weapons. I regard that as the greatest possible danger and hazard."[51] The president ordered the National Security Council, Department of Defense, and State Department to explore creative diplomatic avenues to address the challenge.

Negotiating the NPT: Substituting Norms through Contestation
U.S. representatives approached negotiation of a nonproliferation treaty with the intent to create a discriminatory normative architecture. Their goal was to establish a treaty that would define nuclear weapons states and non-nuclear-weapon states, as well as ensure there were no loopholes that might allow direct or indirect proliferation. In essence, then, the United States and its Western allies undertook an ambitious agenda in multilateral forums to substitute traditional prohibitionary norm frames with a discriminatory regime.

Diplomats from Ireland launched some of the first overtures, but their initial efforts were founded upon prohibitionary norms of the past. They proposed a resolution to "establish an *ad hoc* committee to study the dangers inherent in the further dissemination of nuclear weapons and recommend to the General Assembly for its fourteenth session appropriate measures for averting these dangers"[52] A ten-nation UN Disarmament Committee was established by an agreement of the major powers in 1959. That year also saw the signing of the Antarctic Treaty, prohibiting military activities in that polar region. In December 1960, Ireland sponsored UN General Assembly Resolution 1576, calling upon both nuclear- and non-nuclear weapon states to refrain from acts that would lead to further proliferation. This was seen as a temporary measure that might set the foundations for a broader agreement. But committee deliberations had the almost immediate effect of highlighting differences between traditional prohibitionary norm frames and discriminatory alternatives. The first proposals to emerge in the Disarmament Committee were true to the spirit of the enterprise: diplomats proposed blanket disarmament plans that called for the superpowers to stop producing and destroy existing arsenals of nuclear weapons. For both the United States and the Soviet Union, however, such proposals were dead on arrival. The negotiations on possible outcomes did stir up many of the issues that would eventually become critically important in nuclear nonproliferation negotiations, including nuclear deterrence, safety, verification, and compliance.

By 1961, the United States and its Western allies inserted an alternative plan—a discriminatory regime—into the discourse. U.S. diplomats began championing a UN resolution geared primarily to the "prevention of wider dissemination of nuclear weapons," instead of a plan to eliminate the stockpiles of weapons held by the superpowers. Any such deal would need to include plans for verification, the United States asserted, which might help ensure that nuclear weapons technologies did not spread to would-be nuclear nations. An international agreement with verification measures would help ensure the protection of technologies. The Kennedy administration supported this new discriminatory normative architecture, and the "Irish Resolution" of 1961, as it came to be known, gradually gained support in the UN General Assembly. The basic elements of the plan called for:

- A treaty that would try to balance mutual responsibilities and obligations of the nuclear and non-nuclear powers;
- The treaty should be considered a step toward the achievement of nuclear disarmament;
- The treaty should establish workable provisions to ensure its effectiveness;
- The treaty should not adversely affect the right of any group of states to conclude regional treaties in order to ensure the total absence of nuclear weapons in their respective territories.

The Kennedy administration viewed this outline for a discriminatory treaty much more favorably than past proposals. It would still address the general goals of arms control but would allow the United States to retain its significant weapons advantage (compared to most of the world). In 1962, the administration also supported the establishment of a new, Eighteen-Nation Committee on Disarmament (ENDC), which worked alongside the UN's First Committee to debate disarmament resolutions and initiatives. General Assembly resolutions were passed on disarmament that promoted urgent negotiation of nonproliferation measures—"to take all necessary steps conducive to the earliest conclusion of a treaty on the nonproliferation of nuclear weapons"— including a call for the convening of a conference on nonproliferation no later than July 1968. At the same time, the Soviet Union challenged U.S. plans for establishment of a NATO multilateral nuclear force (MLF) and questioned whether "peaceful nuclear explosions" should be prohibited in any treaty.[53]

President Kennedy used the momentum of the Irish Resolution to successfully substitute a normative architecture of discriminatory control in place of a prohibitionary norm, and he also launched a concerted drive to achieve meaningful agreements with the Soviet Union and other major powers. In 1963, the United States, the United Kingdom, and the Soviet Union completed the first major nuclear arms control agreement: the Partial Nuclear Test-Ban Treaty (PTBT). This agreement banned the testing of atomic weapons in the atmosphere, under water, and in outer space. Henceforth, the superpowers agreed to permit only the testing of weapons in underground, controlled chambers. The deal was first signed by the original parties, but then broadened to multilateral forums for support. By 2010, the PTBT had been signed, ratified, or acceded to by 125 countries.

In the twentieth session of the UN General Assembly in 1965, the United States supported a resolution on nonproliferation that called for formal negotiation of a treaty following the lines of the 1961 Irish plan. U.S. diplomats supported a detailed agreement both to close any loopholes that might permit nuclear or non-nuclear powers to proliferate and to balance the responsibilities of nuclear and non-nuclear-weapon states. The plan would include a call for general and complete nuclear disarmament. At the same time, steps to bolster atomic energy control were underway. In 1961, the International Atomic Energy Agency (IAEA) established its first safeguards system, which specified protocols for reporting and inspection of civilian and military nuclear facilities. The goal of the new safeguards was to ensure greater certainty, even transparency, regarding nuclear activities. The safeguard protocols were upgraded in the mid-1960s with the support of the United Nations.

However, while the president stated his support for a comprehensive, universal safeguards program, administration officials quietly rebuffed a push by non-aligned countries in 1965 and 1966 for greater obligations on the part of nuclear weapon states. Johnson declared, "We do not believe that the safeguards we propose will interfere with the peaceful activities of any country. And I want to make it clear to the world that we in the United States are not asking any country to accept safeguards that we are unwilling to accept ourselves," but the reality of U.S. behavior overshadowed its rhetoric. Johnson promised that the United States would cooperate with safeguards, so long as they did not undermine national security.[54] But behind these claims, officials held the line that the original Irish proposal of 1961 set a sufficient foundation for a treaty and that the specific obligations of nuclear weapons states in a formal treaty should be circumscribed. After the NPT entered into force in 1970 all of the countries which joined the treaty as nuclear weapons states eventually concluded so-called voluntary offer agreements (VOA) with the IAEA permitting basic safeguards. At the same time, however, none of the VOAs provide the IAEA the level of access to nuclear materials and facilities that it enjoys in non-nuclear-weapon states.

Superpower maneuvers slowly helped advance multilateral negotiations on the NPT. In August 1965 the United States submitted a draft treaty to the UN Disarmament Committee that included a call to ban the transfer of nuclear weapons by any nuclear weapon state to any non-nuclear-weapon state. The latter would agree to apply International Atomic Energy Agency or equivalent safeguards to their peaceful nuclear activities. In late September 1965, the Soviet Union submitted a similar draft treaty to the UN General Assembly for consideration. Resolution 2028 launched formal negotiations on the NPT in November 1965. The UN Committee on Disarmament also continued to give priority to the question of nonproliferation. In 1967, Latin American countries introduced and signed the Treaty of Tlatelolco, creating a nuclear-free zone across the region. By late 1967, the United States and the Soviet Union submitted separate but identical texts of a draft treaty on nuclear nonproliferation for extensive debate in the United Nations, and later offered security assurances to non-nuclear-weapon states.

Subsequent negotiations on the NPT focused on development of a network of legal and normative frameworks to regulate the proliferation of WMD. This was to be a grand bargain: this agreement distinguished between states with nuclear weapons and those without. It also created a quid pro quo arrangement (i.e., offering assistance with peaceful nuclear programs in exchange for agreements to negotiate the elimination of nuclear weapons) that make it different from traditional universal arrangements in international treaties.[55] But in others ways, the Johnson administration recognized that it would have to deal with the demands and positions of non-nuclear-weapon states, especially nonaligned developing countries, and in a broader context of U.S.-Soviet relations. For example, strict delineation of nuclear weapons states, as distinct from non-nuclear-weapon states, as framed in Articles I and II, was the subject of protracted negotiations. China's position on the negotiations evolved through the 1960s, most notably with its attainment of status as a nuclear weapons state in 1964. Meanwhile, states like Pakistan, India, and Australia expressed concerns about regional security and remained noncommittal. Diplomats from Italy, Egypt, and other countries expressed frustration at an architecture that would establish a second-class status of non-nuclear states, and Indian prime minister Indira Gandhi told Western leaders that India would not sign on and instead wanted to "keep its options open."

An issue that slowed serious negotiations through 1967 was safeguards and inspections. While nuclear weapons states were focused on establishing a system of verification of treaty compliance by utilizing an IAEA inspections regime, non-nuclear-weapon states were concerned by the lack of application of safeguards on nuclear weapons states. A U.S.-Soviet draft of the treaty that was advanced in the summer of 1967 was tabled partly because it did not include language on safeguards nor a specific article on disarmament. Developing countries like Brazil objected to the proposed treaty framework as an "affront to . . . sovereignty." Subsequent negotiations focused on the details of Article III regarding safeguards and IAEA authority, which the United States called a "key element in the effort to curb nuclear proliferation."[56] Short of this, the State Department warned, aspiring countries could legally reach a full "nuclear pregnancy" under the treaty and then withdraw from it and quickly acquire a weapons capability.[57]

Declassified government documents show that the United States carefully practiced strategies designed to change dynamics. For example, in a memo to President Johnson, William Foster, the director of the Arms Control and Disarmament Agency, argued: "In the course of our intensive consultations during the last few weeks, many of the non-nuclear-weapon countries, including many of our important NATO allies, have expressed concern that the proposed safeguards requirements in our draft non-proliferation treaty might hinder their peaceful nuclear programs and leave them vulnerable to industrial espionage. It might help to overcome these objections if the United States were to invite the International Atomic Energy Agency to apply its safeguards on a broad scale to U.S. peaceful nuclear facilities."[58] Another internal State Department cable shows that the U.S. diplomats worked out a strategy that would attempt to isolate voices of new and aspiring nuclear nations and build the necessary support for a draft that could move forward.[59]

Outcome

U.S. leaders and their allies successfully established a new normative architecture through the Treaty on the Non-Proliferation of Nuclear Weapons. The legitimacy of the new arrangement was fortified with endorsements from the great powers and codification in the treaty and corollary agreements. More than fifty nations—including the United States, the Soviet Union, and the United Kingdom—signed the NPT when it was formally presented at the United Nations on July 1, 1968. However, ratification of the treaty proved more problematic given the turbulent times. The Soviet crackdown in Prague, Czechoslovakia, in 1968, new pressures from non-nuclear-weapon states, and questions about the extent of the inspection authority to be granted the IAEA all seemed to cloud the picture of the treaty. The U.S. Senate voted to ratify the NPT on March 13, 1969, by vote of 83 to 15. Other countries, including advanced industrialized nations of Western Europe, were also slow to ratify the agreement due to concerns about Soviet adventurism.

By 1970 the bandwagoning appeared successful when forty-three signatory states ratified the treaty and it formally went into effect. The treaty established a new nuclear nonproliferation regime oriented around three pillars: (1) nonproliferation: in Articles I and II of the treaty, non-nuclear-weapon states pledge not to acquire weapons, while nuclear weapons states pledge not to share them; (2) peaceful uses of nuclear energy and civilian cooperation under "full-scope safeguards": the treaty provided the "inalienable right of all the Parties to the Treaty to develop research, production, and use of nuclear energy for peaceful purposes without discrimination," but Article III outlined mechanisms for monitoring and control, including the prevention of diversion of nuclear technology for weapons, through safeguards monitored by the IAEA; (3) disarmament: a pledge in Article VI of the treaty for nuclear weapons states to "pursue negotiations in good faith at an early date on effective measures regarding cessation of the nuclear arms race and disarmament." When the NPT was introduced in the UN General Assembly in July 1968, it was supported by three of the five nuclear powers—the United States, the Soviet Union and the United Kingdom—and dozens of non-nuclear states.

The result of this norm substitution was a nonproliferation treaty that was also a technology denial regime. Membership grew significantly over time to encompass nearly all countries in the world. The NPT advanced with the accession of the two remaining nuclear powers, France and China (1992), the former Soviet republics (including Belarus and Kazakhstan as *non*-nuclear-weapon states in 1994 and 1994), and two former rivals and nuclear aspirants, Argentina and Brazil (in 1995 and 1998, respectively). The steady increase in membership over time made the NPT the most widely accepted arms nonproliferation treaty in history. Given the contractual nature of state commitments to the NPT, signatories adopted uniform principles, including a commitment to forsake weapons development in exchange for the perceived greater goods of assistance in economic development and the benefits of nuclear research.[60] Parties to the NPT held Review Conferences every five years. Important progress was made to cement sanctions and safeguards programs to prevent diversion of peaceful technologies or materials to weapons programs. Some issues were referred to the United Nations for further deliberation; others were handled through direct action by nuclear supplier states. Perhaps the most significant step to sustain the NPT came in the Fifth Review Conference in 1995, where parties agreed on the "indefinite extension" of the terms of the agreement into the future.

4 Atoms for Peace? New Nuclear Technology Export Controls

> Nothing in this Treaty shall be interpreted as affecting the inalienable right of all the Parties to the Treaty to develop research, production and use of nuclear energy for peaceful purposes without discrimination.
>   —*Treaty on the Non-Proliferation of Nuclear Weapons*[1]

> The 40 nations of the Nuclear Suppliers Group should refuse to sell enrichment and reprocessing equipment and technologies to any state that does not already possess full-scale functioning enrichment and reprocessing plants. This step will prevent new states from developing the means to produce fissile material for nuclear bombs. Proliferators must not be allowed to cynically manipulate the NPT to acquire the material and infrastructure necessary for manufacturing illegal weapons. For international norms to be effective, they must be enforced.
>   —*George W. Bush*[2]

THE GLOBAL NUCLEAR NONPROLIFERATION ORDER established during the Cold War offered different things to different players. For great and middle powers, the Treaty on the Non-Proliferation of Nuclear Weapons (NPT) represented an international agreement providing a measure of control over nuclear weapons proliferation. For developing countries, the NPT offered hope for assistance with peaceful nuclear energy production to fuel economic growth in exchange for a simple pledge not to develop nuclear weapons. In addition, the five declared nuclear weapon states gained legitimacy and influence as managers of the new, global nuclear order.

However, it became clear in the 1970s that some countries that had received peaceful nuclear energy assistance were diverting the technologies for clandestine nuclear weapons programs. India conducted its first nuclear test explosion in 1974, and several other countries, including some NPT signatories, appeared to be moving quickly toward acquiring nuclear weapons of their own. Countries were diverting sensitive technologies, including centrifuges for gaseous diffusion uranium enrichment and reprocessing, to develop fissile material for bombs. It appeared that would-be nuclear states had found ways to use technology to subvert the nuclear order.

The great powers responded to these challenges with supply cartels and export controls, but tightening the nonproliferation norm over time through redefinition and constructive norm substitution has been fraught with challenges. After all, Article IV of the NPT guaranteed countries the "inalienable right" to develop peaceful nuclear energy programs, and thus potential restrictions on the nuclear trade threatened a core principle of the nuclear order. Debates over new restrictions continued for nearly four decades before the international community agreed to major new export restrictions. In 2011, the Nuclear Suppliers Group (NSG) endorsed a "new normal": a requirement that in order to engage in nuclear commerce, countries must commit to the IAEA's intrusive inspections and reporting requirements known as the Additional Protocol. At the same time, though, some Western leaders have been unable to prevent the spread of enrichment and reprocessing (ENR) technologies and unwilling to impose this requirement in all modern nuclear deals. Thus, while there are some indications of progress toward redefining and substituting a new, more restrictive norm frame, the outcome of the case remains contested.

This chapter adopts the three-stage model of norm change to explore the evolution of the modern nuclear nonproliferation norm. It tells the story of technology innovations with military implications, the redefinition of U.S. export policies, and efforts to establish new multilateral nonproliferation regime standards restricting sensitive nuclear technology exports. Given the limited success of the U.S. drive to establish a cohesive, discriminatory norm frame preventing the spread of enrichment and reprocessing technologies, this case study underscores the contested and politicized nature of the norm-change process.

The Traditional Nonproliferation Norm

As discussed in Chapter 3, the Treaty on the Non-Proliferation of Nuclear Weapons became the cornerstone of the nonproliferation norm during the Cold War. The NPT formalized a regime founded on several pillars. First, states endorsed the principle of nonproliferation. Non-nuclear-weapon states pledged not to acquire weapons, while nuclear weapons states promised not to share them. Second, countries agreed to basic principles of peaceful uses of nuclear energy. The treaty provided the "inalienable right of all the Parties to the Treaty to develop research, production, and use of nuclear energy for peaceful purposes without discrimination." At the same time, Article III outlined mechanisms for monitoring and control, including the prevention of diversion of nuclear technology for weapons through safeguards managed by the International Atomic Energy Agency (IAEA). Third, nuclear weapons states pledged to pursue disarmament negotiations. As membership in the nonproliferation regime grew, signatories adopted uniform principles, including a commitment to forsake weapons development in exchange for the perceived greater goods of assistance in economic development and the benefits of nuclear research. As noted in Chapter 3, parties to the NPT held Review Conferences every five years, and in 1995, member states agreed on the "indefinite extension" of terms of the agreement.

Building on the momentum of the Atoms for Peace program, advanced industrialized states and developing countries began cooperating on atomic energy research. This became a symbol of hope for the future, wrapped in the NPT norm frame. The result was a flourishing civilian nuclear energy network around the world. In 1960, 17 nuclear power reactors were in operation in France, the Soviet Union, the United States, and the United Kingdom; by 1970, 91 plants provided power for fifteen different countries. By the 2000s, more than 400 reactors were operating in thirty countries, and fifty-six countries possessed operational research reactors.[3]

It was in this context that the IAEA emerged to become a critical enforcement mechanism for the new multilateral nonproliferation regime. The agency was established in 1957 out of the early momentum in the United Nations on nonproliferation. Forerunners to the IAEA included the Baruch Plan to internationalize the nuclear fuel cycle, a proposal to establish an International Atomic Development Authority that would oversee the emerging nuclear order, and later, the UN Atomic Energy Commission. The Atoms for Peace program envisioned an agency at the center of the operation that would help redirect nuclear materials and technologies from military to civilian purposes.[4] The statute of the IAEA granted it the authority "to establish and administer safeguards designed to ensure that [nuclear items supplied by or through the agency] are not used in such a way as to further any military purpose; and to apply safeguards, at the request of the parties, to any bilateral or multilateral arrangement, or at the request of a State, to any of that State's activities in the field of atomic energy."[5] The statute also provided a framework for a safeguards system, though some details of implementation were left open to negotiation.

The 1960s saw parallel efforts to promote a nuclear order through the NPT and formalize regulations that would enable peaceful nuclear energy cooperation yet regulate against state diversion of nuclear assistance for bombs. In 1961, the IAEA Board of Governors issued its first Safeguards Document (INFCIRC/26) with guidelines for oversight investigations of reactors as well as for the conduct of inspectors. Over the next decade, these were broadened to include other types of reactors as well as other critical nodes of the nuclear fuel cycle. The IAEA also created standards for nuclear material accounting and inspections for verification of state claims of the holding and use of nuclear materials. This included measures such as the installation of monitoring devices and cameras at nuclear facilities around the world, with the potential to uncover diversions of materials or technologies for secret nuclear weapons programs.[6]

The safeguards system requires agreements between the IAEA and individual countries or groups of countries linked closely to the NPT. The NPT called for all member non-nuclear-weapon states to conclude safeguards agreements with the IAEA that would cover all the nuclear materials in their territory (known as comprehensive, or "full-scope," safeguards).[7] The IAEA Board of Governors can notify the UN Security Council if a country violates IAEA safeguards, and the council can impose economic, political, or military sanctions on the violator. The IAEA also established a limited-scope (or "item-specific") safeguards program placed on individual plants, shipments of nuclear fuel, or supply agreements between importers and exporters of nuclear fuel or technology. These were typically concluded between the IAEA and states not party to the NPT, such as India, Pakistan, and Israel. The IAEA also allows what it terms "voluntary offer agreements" of declarations of nuclear activities or materials without inspections or regulation. Finally, in line with the NPT, all nuclear export arrangements should include a bilateral safeguards agreement between supplier and recipient state, even if the importer is not a member of the NPT.

With mounting evidence that some countries were diverting civilian assistance for nuclear weapons, the IAEA advanced a new safeguards system

(INFCIRC/66) with additional provisions for safeguarded nuclear materials in other stages of the nuclear fuel cycle (such as in conversion and fuel fabrication plants). According to the IAEA, the purpose of the new safeguards system was "to provide credible assurance to the international community that nuclear material and other specified items are not diverted from peaceful nuclear uses . . . [enabling] the Agency to independently verify the declarations made by States about their nuclear material and activities."[8] The inspections regime was widely considered effective at its outset. It offered a template for similar safeguards agreements for multilateral and regional treaties, including the 1967 Treaty for the Prohibition of Nuclear Weapons in Latin America and the Caribbean (Tlatelolco Treaty), the South Pacific Nuclear Free Zone Treaty (Rarotonga Treaty), and the Treaty on the Southeast Asia Nuclear Weapon-Free Zone (Bangkok Treaty).

Technology Innovations: Enrichment and Reprocessing

Nuclear technology innovations that changed the world originated with scientific advances in the 1930s and 1940s. Uranium ore mined in the Belgian Congo was processed for the Manhattan Project to produce uranium oxide. Next, the isotopes had to be separated through a process of enrichment in order to concentrate uranium-235 for use in nuclear bombs (and later, for nuclear power generation).

As noted in Chapter 3, scientists developed two primary systems for uranium enrichment in the Manhattan Project: electromagnetic isotope separation (EMIS) and gaseous diffusion. While electromagnetic isotope separation worked, it proved to be an energy-intensive and inefficient method, and the United States eventually abandoned it after World War II.[9] The first facility for large-scale gaseous diffusion, the secret new K-25 plant at Oak Ridge, Tennessee, was the world's largest building at the time of its construction. Much of the building was a complex network of pipelines and machines through which uranium hexafluoride gas (UF6) was pumped. Porous membranes called "barriers" helped separate isotopes with different velocities. Lighter UF6 gas molecules containing U-235 atoms diffused faster through the barriers than those containing U-238, allowing separation and enrichment of concentrations of U-235. At the end of the process the gas was condensed back into a liquid, then cooled and solidified before being fabricated into fissile material for bombs.[10] As complicated as this design was, scientists learned quickly how to refine it and make it more efficient, and it became the preferred U.S. method for enrichment after World War II. New gaseous diffusion plants were constructed at Oak Ridge and in Kentucky and Ohio in the early 1950s. This was also the primary method adopted by France to power its large-scale civilian nuclear power industry. France set up a consortium in the early 1970s, called EURODIF, with Italy, Spain, Belgium, and Iran to produce uranium fuel for light-water reactors.

The Centrifuge: Democratizing Dual-Use Technology

The development of the centrifuge for enrichment by gaseous diffusion represented a major technological accomplishment. Centrifuges allow more efficient production of enriched uranium for nuclear power generation, but determined actors also may use them to produce fissile material for nuclear weapons. This dual-use technology would come to play an important role in the saga of nuclear proliferation. In the 1930s, a scientific team at the University of Virginia led by physicist Jesse W. Beams first developed a vacuum centrifuge that could separate isotopes in some elements. Laboratory directors at the Manhattan Project considered employing this method for enrichment, but the science was not yet advanced enough; large-scale gaseous diffusion plants offered simpler and more reliable results. Nevertheless, Beams and his colleagues continued to advance designs for a counter-flow gas centrifuge in their laboratory and began promising experiments with uranium.[11]

The principle at the heart of the centrifuge process for uranium enrichment is the application of centrifugal force to separate isotopes. Uranium hexafluoride (UF6) gas is spun inside a centrifuge, a cylindrical container with a rotor that spins rapidly and generates a force thousands of times greater than gravity. Heavier U-238 atoms are drawn toward the outside of the centrifuge while the lighter U-235 gas molecules collect near the center of the cylinder. Modern uranium enrichment plants are constructed with chains of thousands of centrifuges, each one feeding into the next in a cascade effect to produce higher concentrations of U-235 enriched uranium.

The Soviet Union was the first country to design a centrifuge that would become the model for modern systems. Soviet research scientists relied on captive scientists from the Third Reich, especially Austrian Gernot Zippe, to help develop an efficient centrifuge design in the 1940s. When the prisoners of war were later repatriated, they helped transfer information about this design to Western governments, including West Germany, the United States, and the

Netherlands. These nations, along with other advanced industrialized powers like the United Kingdom, France, Australia, Sweden, Italy, and Japan, soon started centrifuge programs for the expressed purpose of achieving energy self-sufficiency. Germany, the Netherlands, and the United Kingdom eventually joined forces in 1971 to establish URENCO, a civilian enrichment program designed to promote commercialized development. It was a dramatic success, and in many ways served as a model for the establishment of a global civil nuclear fuel cycle.[12] Today URENCO supplies enriched uranium for nuclear power plants in more than a dozen countries and controls roughly 30 percent of the global market.

U.S. researchers at the University of Virginia continued to explore centrifuge enrichment in the 1950s, but their programs faced various technical hurdles. Professor Jesse Beams invited collaboration with Zippe and other repatriated German scientists to duplicate the centrifuge project they had worked on in the Soviet Union. They quickly overcame past hurdles in design and development of what became known as "short-tube" centrifuges using improved metal alloys available in the West. They also made advances in a new, classified program on a high-speed long-tube centrifuge program. Critical to its development was the invention of new, stronger steel and equipment that would allow higher rotation speeds and overcome problems with the introduction and extraction of gases. At the same time, companies like General Electric and Westinghouse became active in the game, exploring centrifuge enrichment as an economic means to advance nuclear energy production. By forming cooperatives and producing enriched uranium on a large scale, they hoped to contain the technologies and dominate the global supply chain.[13]

Throughout the development of industrial-level enrichment, government leaders were mindful that centrifuges could be used for clandestine weapons programs. However, several forces worked against a Western monopoly. First, several scientific papers on centrifuge design authored by Zippe were published in open sources in the late 1950s.[14] Their release appeared to stimulate a significant increase in research and development of centrifuge programs around the world. Second, new centrifuge designs were smaller, more efficient, and far less energy-intensive than other methods of enrichment. Centrifuge cascades could be fashioned in an industrial facility and run to produce steady supplies of enriched uranium for nuclear energy plants. Third, developing countries became very interested in centrifuges to offset their concerns about factors like cost and reliability of supply of enriched uranium for power generation from the great powers. In 1973, U.S. officials actually halted sales of enriched uranium to client states because they were concerned sales might outstrip their capacity to supply the U.S. infrastructure. The Arab "oil shock" and tensions in the Middle East at the time, coupled with the U.S. maneuver, fostered doubt about the reliability of the supply of enriched uranium worldwide. For this and other reasons, governments in many countries moved to establish their own programs using public information. Physicist Scott Kemp characterizes what followed as a "cascade of cascades," including the spread of centrifuge technologies to "Israel (circa 1960), France (1960), China (1961), Australia (1965), Sweden (1971), Italy (1972), India (1972), Japan (1973), and Brazil (1979)."[15]

In many ways, the advent of centrifuge enrichment marked a major turning point in nuclear weapons proliferation—a democratization of the means to acquire fissile material for the most destructive, yet most coveted, weapon on Earth.[16] Most governments developed centrifuges for nuclear energy production in the years that followed, but some viewed them as a means to accelerate their secret bomb programs. The governments of Iran, Iraq, and Pakistan took determined steps to develop large-scale centrifuge plants, for example. In a classified report from the 1950s, the U.S. Atomic Energy Commission warned, "It would not be too difficult to build a secret plant to produce highly enriched uranium." Scientists at major corporations agreed. The Union Carbide Nuclear Company sent a report to the AEC echoing the warning that, "in general, it would not be too difficult to build a relatively small clandestine gas centrifuge plant capable of producing sufficient enriched uranium for a small number of nuclear weapons."[17] The report recommended the United States reach out to its European allies regarding control of technology and limitations and "an expanded U.S. development program costing about $6 million over three years should proceed expeditiously and independent of negotiations."[18] Corporate representatives and government officials began to meet regularly for high-level discussions of the "Nth power problem" and sensitive new technologies, including an important gathering with President Eisenhower at the White House in February 1960.

While many focused on the dangers of new state acquisition of sensitive technologies and materials, black-market proliferation rings also contributed to the spread of sensitive technologies. In 1975, Pakistani metallurgist A. Q. Khan made a fateful decision to steal designs and supply network information for centrifuges from the Dutch firm where he worked as a contractor. He returned to Pakistan and became the architect of that country's clandestine bomb program by buying centrifuge components on the open market. In turn, he also directed a vast black-market supply network that sold sensitive technologies and designs to North Korea, Iran, and Libya.[19] His network provided technology for centrifuge enrichment programs in those developing countries, as well as high-quality assistance (including providing engineers as project consultants) for programs in Brazil, Iraq, and South Africa.

Reprocessing

Reprocessing, chemically separating and recovering fissionable uranium plutonium from irradiated (spent) nuclear fuel, is another sensitive technology.[20] Scientists in the Manhattan Project discovered they could also produce fissile material, plutonium, by treating spent fuel from a research reactor with a chemical separation process. The first atomic test explosion was powered by an implosion-design plutonium device. Later, the United States experimented with the process at facilities in Hanford, Washington, in the 1940s and 1950s, refining the PUREX (plutonium-uranium extraction) method of extraction of fissile material using acids and organic solvents to separate plutonium from other materials.[21]

Countries that have commercial-scale reprocessing plants in operation today include France, India, Russia, the United Kingdom, and Japan (which opened a new reprocessing plant in 2013). China is also designing a pilot-scale reprocessing facility at this writing.[22] Other countries, such as North Korea, Syria, and India, have experimented with the technology as well. North Korea launched its clandestine program focusing on reprocessing and plutonium-extraction, but has since replaced it with a centrifuge capability. Scientists in Syria's nascent nuclear program have reportedly experimented with reprocessing and centrifuge systems (though sanctions may have limited their uranium enrichment capabilities).[23] Of these, India advanced the farthest. The Indian nuclear program began in the late 1940s, and India received significant assistance for its civilian nuclear energy program from the United Kingdom, the United States, and Canada in the Atoms for Peace program. India's first power reactors, at Tarapur and Rawatbhata, were supplied by the United States and Canada respectively, and the United States provided India with a design for its first reprocessing plant, in Trombay. Some of these technologies and materials contributed to the production and separation of the plutonium used in India's 1974 nuclear weapon test. This link between spent nuclear fuel and reprocessing to produce fissile materials also occurred at plants in Yongbyon, North Korea, and in the Dimona facility in Israel.[24] Indeed, one dire estimate warned that clandestine programs to reprocess fuel could have rogue states building facilities to separate plutonium from spent fuel in less than one year and extracting plutonium capable of being used in nuclear weapons within days of operation.[25]

Stage I: Technology Meets the Traditional Norm

The Treaty on the Non-Proliferation of Nuclear Weapons was the cornerstone of a new, multidimensional nonproliferation norm, but U.S. support for the treaty seemed to begin to waver almost immediately after signing it. The U.S. government delayed ratification of the treaty in the Senate for nearly two years, in part to protest the 1968 Soviet crackdown in Czechoslovakia.[26] In general, the Nixon White House seemed unconcerned about the nonproliferation pillar of the NPT. While Secretary of State Kissinger believed the United States had a "special responsibility" to prevent nonproliferation, the president was not interested in the treaty regime. At one of the first meetings of Nixon's National Security Council in 1969, the president lamented, "treaties don't necessary get us very much. . . . For example, suppose a country wanted to make their own weapons, then they could obviously abrogate the treaty without sanctions."[27] According to declassified documents, Nixon "believed that the NPT was unenforceable and irrelevant." Exemplifying this attitude were remarks he made to Security Adviser Kissinger in 1972. He "wasn't for" the NPT, the president said, which he saw as an alien intrusion, foisted upon him by the State Department. He characterized the treaty as having "nothing to do with the security of the United States."[28]

The Nixon White House believed the best way to "control" proliferation was to maintain a dominant market share as a reliable nuclear supplier state. So long as countries received uranium fuel and nuclear technology from U.S. suppliers, it could effectively maintain oversight through bilateral agreements coupled with IAEA safeguard inspections. In hindsight, concern about the waning U.S. dominance in nuclear technology market appeared justified: the Soviet Union concluded two important deals to transfer enriched uranium to France and Sweden in 1970, and other countries, including Germany, Canada, France, and Belgium, were building a competitive edge in nuclear exports.

The Soviet Union also made progress in advancing and marketing its breeder reactor technologies.[29] Breeder reactors, which were designed to run on pluto- nium extracted from spent nuclear fuel, offered countries the opportunity to extend the nuclear fuel cycle.

To help boost U.S. influence in the changing global nuclear market, the Nixon administration announced federal government backing of commer- cial programs to pursue new research and development initiatives, includ- ing breeder reactor research. This decision was taken in full awareness that it might send the "wrong" signals to the international community that breeder technology and reprocessing were acceptable elements of the global nuclear fuel cycle.[30] It also demonstrated the seeming complacency with which the administration approached the issue of foreign countries developing latent or real nuclear weapons capabilities. In spite of these new initiatives, though, the U.S. nuclear industry continued to lose market share. Not only had the Soviet Union concluded deals to transfer enriched uranium to France and Sweden, the U.S. Atomic Energy Commission reported at the time, "the Soviets had achieved [an] advantage in breeder technology and were in the process of marketing it."[31] European companies such as Framatone (France), ASEA-Atom (Sweden), and a French-Belgian-Spanish-Italian consortium (EURODIF) began exporting reactor technology, and the German-British- Dutch consortium URENCO expanded its market share in enrichment ser- vices and technology.

Various conditions, including a determined Indian government, the weak stance of the Nixon administration, and a competitive international nuclear market, seemed to contribute to a surprising outcome in India's nuclear test detonation in May 1974. India had successfully diverted technologies and materials that it had received from key supplier states, including a nuclear reactor from Canada and heavy water from the United States and Canada, through the Atoms for Peace initiative for a clandestine bomb program. The test shocked the world—and it generated intense debates in a number of gov- ernments regarding state commitments to a flawed nonproliferation regime. Indeed, the test and political fallout had the potential to shatter the nonpro- liferation regime, especially given that it demonstrated the capabilities of non-member states to develop weapons through clandestine means and diver- sion of materials from peaceful nuclear energy technologies supplied by the West. It also had the potential to change the policy consensus in Washington regarding nonproliferation.

Stage II: Redefinition

Nixon resigned from office two months after India's test. President Gerald Ford and Secretary of State Henry Kissinger played key roles in advancing new ideas regarding export controls. U.S. government departments conducted reviews of policies and patterns related to the spread of nuclear technologies, with concern about potential breakouts by other players. Kissinger described the nonproliferation problem as being "at a crucial stage" at the time, and warned India's test "could lead others to acquire independent nuclear explosives capabilities in a 'chain reaction' effect."[32]

The snap judgment of many U.S. officials in the administration and Congress was that export controls established through the IAEA and embedded in the NPT had proven ineffective. Declassified documents from the summer of 1974 suggest a range of concerns. Fred Ikle, the head of the Arms Control and Disarmament Agency (ACDA), and Winston Lord of the State Department Policy Planning Group argued in a memorandum that in the wake of India's test, Western allies would have to develop new frameworks "for attacking the proliferation problem through global policies aimed at containing technical capabilities, strengthening legal-political barriers, and dealing with the special issue of peaceful nuclear explosions." They outlined new strategies for the United States to "strengthen political, legal, and security-related inhibitions against proliferation" with the goal of denying other countries "the full range of materials, equipment, services, and technology needed to produce nuclear explosives."[33] Critically, they recognized the need for multilateral cooperation: "The United States cannot, solely through its own actions, hope to establish an effective and durable non-proliferation regime. Concerted international policies are needed."[34]

The Ford administration reached out to other supplier states, including the Soviet Union, Canada, France, Japan, the United Kingdom, and West Germany, on the question of controls in 1974. Diplomatic coordination meetings began in London in late 1975. The so-called London Group of nuclear suppliers readily agreed that the Indian explosion had "sharpened" the issues associated with nonproliferation, though there was less clarity in these and other multilateral forums on the proper response. According to recently declassified documents, the primary U.S. objective at the London Group meeting was to obtain a consensus in principle on nuclear policies. Officials directed greater scrutiny to the spread of sensitive technologies, including revisiting key clauses of the NPT.[35] A National Security Council report suggested "the most effective approach to slowing down the spread of nuclear weapons is for the advanced nuclear industrial states to tighten controls on weapons-grade material and related production capabilities." A summary document from the National Security Council Under Secretaries Committee called on the West to "restrict the spread of independent national uranium enrichment and chemical reprocessing facilities."[36] Nevertheless, there remained significant debate over what level or intensity of safeguards would be requested, including on transfers and special controls on sensitive facilities and materials and control of retransfers.[37] These differences continued at the same time the nuclear industry was diversifying, and countries like France and Germany were emerging as significant suppliers.

Later, the Jimmy Carter administration (1977–1981) initiated a strong, executive-driven effort to redefine the U.S. stance toward the nonproliferation norm and exports. In 1978, the administration worked with a bipartisan group of legislators led by Senators Glenn (D-OH) and Charles Percy (R-IL) to develop the Nuclear Nonproliferation Act (NNPA). The NNPA represented a plan to modify the 1954 Atomic Energy Act by instituting new, restrictive nuclear export controls. Key measures of the NNPA included plans to tighten the criteria for nuclear cooperation and reshape the nuclear fuel cycle, provide for better coordination of export approval and control processes among government agencies, and even renegotiate retroactive agreements to improve nonproliferation controls. The centerpiece of the legislation was new restrictions on sensitive nuclear technology exports, especially the requirement for U.S. consent for client states to subject U.S.-origin nuclear fuel to further enrichment or reprocessing. The plan focused on finding legitimacy for the U.S. position in multilateral standards and setting them as preconditions for nuclear assistance. It required that countries belong to the NPT to receive U.S. nuclear exports, a measure not embedded in past export legislation, which ensured that full-scope safeguards would be a prerequisite for supply (a measure not implemented by the NSG until after 1992). The legislation also was intended to draw a clear line between civilian and military uses of nuclear technologies. Supplier states would be encouraged not to transfer sensitive uranium enrichment and spent fuel reprocessing technologies to other countries. Coupled with assurances of a steady, reliable supply of low-enriched uranium and an emphasis on IAEA safeguards, the Carter administration believed the NNPA was "a major step toward fulfillment of an objective which the United States shares with other nations—a halt in the spread of nuclear weapons capability while preserving the peaceful use of nuclear energy."[38]

U.S. policies wavered over the next two decades. In the Reagan administration (1981–1989), the United States reverted to a free-market orientation that allowed countries like Argentina, Brazil, India, and Pakistan—all non-members of the NPT who did not comply with full-scope IAEA safeguards—to receive nuclear assistance through legal transfers from supplier states. The Reagan administration rejected Carter's support for a "multilateral policy of technical denial," and tried unsuccessfully to repeal parts of the NNPA.[39] U.S. officials refused to reengage with the Nuclear Suppliers Group—the body did not meet during the entire decade of the 1980s to revise its trigger list of export control items.[40] The 1990s brought a new set of challenges, including the revelation that Saddam Hussein's regime in Iraq had come very close to the development of its own nuclear bomb through clandestine means. In 1998, Pakistan and India engaged in a series of nuclear tests, declaring their status as nuclear powers at the dawn of a new century.[41] Presidents George H. W. Bush and Bill Clinton adopted a somewhat more conciliatory tone toward multilateral engagement and support for the nonproliferation regime. The Bush administration's nonproliferation focus was clearly on superpower arms control, and the U.S. government was actively engaged in working to dismantle the old Soviet nuclear arsenal and stop the spread of materials and scientific know-how to developing countries. The Clinton administration demonstrated much greater support for multilateral negotiations on nonproliferation, and it targeted countries that were seen as violating the existing regime for sanctions, including North Korea, India, and Pakistan. Symbolic of Clinton's commitment to multilateralism was U.S. support for the declaration to reaffirm and indefinitely extend the Treaty on the Non-Proliferation of Nuclear Weapons at the 1995 Review Conference.

Stage III: Norm Substitution through Contestation

The United States' stance toward the nonproliferation norm began to evolve again following the terror attacks of September 11, 2001, and the discovery of the A. Q. Khan network. The Nuclear Suppliers Group became one of the most important venues for U.S. diplomacy to engage in constructive norm substitution. Formed in 1975, this was a multilateral consortium of supplier states that agreed to coordinate export controls governing transfers of nuclear technology. Capable nuclear suppliers during the Cold War included countries like Argentina, Brazil, China, France, Germany, the USSR/Russia, and the United States. Many were original members of the NSG, but several, including India, Israel, Pakistan, and Serbia, remained apart from the group.[42] All supplier states could conceivably transfer sensitive nuclear materials and technology to other states.

The group of suppliers began negotiations in 1977 and 1978 to coordinate their export controls on transfers of civilian nuclear material and nuclear-related equipment and technology to non-nuclear-weapon states. Their ultimate goal was to prevent nuclear exports for commercial and peaceful purposes from being diverted to make nuclear weapons. Negotiations shifted toward development of a "trigger list" of nuclear technologies that would henceforth be subject to significant controls. Carter administration diplomats lobbied other countries on the importance of controlled technology and materials transfer, using the India case as an example of the perils of dual-use transfers. The group successfully negotiated an official set of NSG Guidelines for Nuclear Transfers (INFCIRC/254) in 1978.[43] New export controls were put into place for nuclear materials, reactors, plants and equipment related to reprocessing, enrichment, and conversion of nuclear materials and for fuel fabrication and heavy water production. Export of these items required that states adhere to comprehensive IAEA safeguards. NSG guidelines were coordinated with the IAEA to apply to nuclear transfers to ensure through regulations and monitoring that they would not be diverted to unsafeguarded nuclear fuel cycle or bomb programs.

While this represented the first major multilateral effort to curtail sensitive nuclear technology transfers and define an important dimension of the nonproliferation norm architecture, NSG standards only confirmed that holders of sensitive nuclear fuel technology would "exercise restraint" in decisions about exports, and suppliers could opt out in select circumstances. Diplomats maintained that this would be the most achievable, best multilateral stance for the times. The NSG recommended that in ENR transfers, suppliers should encourage recipients to accept, as an alternative to national facilities, supplier involvement and/or other appropriate multinational participation in resulting facilities. Leaders of major supplier states seemed to appreciate the duality of the standards and policy latitude and sometimes used this to their advantage. For example, Russia transferred nuclear fuel to India even though many members of the NSG argued this would contravene multilateral commitments and principles. China exported sensitive nuclear materials and technology to Pakistan and Iran in the 1980s, despite U.S. objections.[44]

NSG members returned to the trigger list in the wake of revelations that Saddam Hussein's regime in Iraq had made significant progress toward the development of nuclear weapons through clandestine means. At a 1991 meeting in the Hague, NSG members welcomed six new governments and moved to compile a new control list focused on dual-use technology transfers. The new guidelines encouraged suppliers to look at the comprehensive nonproliferation record of potential clients in reviewing export licenses. Most notably, the NSG took a decision to exceed the original standards of the NPT by requiring that any client state receiving trigger list items be subject to full-scope IAEA safeguards.[45] This would differ from the traditional regulation network in which states had to meet safeguards for all sources or special fissionable material in all peaceful nuclear activities in order to verify their obligations under the NPT that such material was not diverted to nuclear weapons or other nuclear explosive devices (INFCIRC/153). States would periodically provide information to the IAEA about nuclear materials, facilities, inventories, containment, safety standards, and organization and management. Safeguards emphasized accounting for nuclear materials in order to detect if significant quantities of fissile material were being diverted from peaceful uses.

The new program, which became known as the Additional Protocol, would allow a tighter safeguards system. States would be required to make broader declarations of activities and more detailed inventories of materials and activities related to the nuclear cycle. They also would have to be more forthcoming with the agency regarding nuclear research and development programs, and the IAEA would have much greater authority to conduct intrusive, surprise inspections of facilities where suspect activity might be under way. Finally, where the old system of safeguards allowed member states to separate out military and civilian nuclear programs, the Additional Protocol requires full declarations of all nuclear-related activities. The IAEA is granted the authority to access sites and even to conduct environmental sampling around facilities where it suspects clandestine nuclear activity.[46]

Proposed New Restrictions on ENR Technology Sharing
The aftermath of the 2001 terror attacks on the United States led to a new, intensified focus on constructive norm substitution to stop proliferation of weapons of mass destruction. President George W. Bush responded with a

barrage of policies meant to substitute a new normative frame for the existing nonproliferation regime, including tightening restrictions on ENR technology exports to close loopholes for access to latent nuclear weapons capability. The result was a period of dynamism, debate (and even confusion) regarding international nonproliferation norm frames. Some hailed the Bush administration for articulating concrete policy stances; others criticized the president's norm stewardship as sending mixed signals at a dangerous time in international affairs.

In 2004, more than fifty years after the launch of Eisenhower's Atoms for Peace program, President Bush outlined his administration's "changes in thinking and strategy" on nonproliferation in a high-profile speech. For the first time, a U.S. president addressed embedded tensions in the nonproliferation regime head on by linking issues of technology sharing and proliferation threats. Bush charged that enrichment and reprocessing were unnecessary for peaceful nuclear programs given the global market for nuclear fuel. He said the United States and its allies should cooperate on several initiatives to "close the loophole" in the nonproliferation norm that allowed states to legally acquire ENR technology in the existing regime. He argued such transfers should be sharply curtailed. The president called on the Nuclear Suppliers Group to "refuse to sell enrichment and reprocessing equipment and technologies to any state that does not already possess full-scale, functioning enrichment and reprocessing plants." Second, Bush called for client states to "renounce enrichment and reprocessing" in exchange for a U.S. "guarantee of reliable access at reasonable cost to fuel for civilian nuclear reactors." The president concluded forcefully: "Proliferators must not be allowed to cynically manipulate the NPT to acquire the material and infrastructure necessary for manufacturing illegal weapons. For international norms to be effective, they must be enforced."[47]

U.S. officials pushed a stringent set of criteria to limit countries that would be eligible to acquire uranium-enrichment and plutonium-reprocessing technologies, in multiple venues. In contrast to the "restraint" on sensitive technology transfers in past NSG guidelines, the Bush administration demanded clients be states-parties to the NPT and have no outstanding breaches of IAEA safeguards. Any ENR that was shared should protect technological secrets (using a so-called black box approach to impede recipients from replicating the technologies or building their own indigenous facilities). At the same time, the Bush administration also championed other programs designed to curtail the spread of ENR technologies, such as the Global Nuclear Energy Partnership, a plan to promote the virtues of spent nuclear fuel reprocessing in safeguarded facilities and the civil use of plutonium as a nuclear waste management strategy. The Proliferation Security Initiative also was launched to interdict illicit weapons shipments through allied intelligence cooperation and military operations.

Contestation

U.S. and French proposals for new ENR restrictions created a number of controversies in NSG plenary sessions in 2004 and 2005 and other multilateral settings. Countries like Canada and South Africa (both of which have large uranium deposits but no enrichment capabilities) were opposed to these restrictions from the outset, while Brazil and Argentina foresaw the potential for a discriminatory new regime. No consensus on imposition of new ENR restrictions was reached in the NSG. The forum also was deadlocked over requiring the Additional Protocol, a plan for a much more rigorous inspection program for future trade of all nuclear materials.[48] Reasons for stalemate included frustration with the Bush administration's style of negotiating, which many perceived as dogmatic, and the U.S. government's willingness to go outside normal multilateral channels and establish new programs and initiatives (such as Global Nuclear Energy Partnership and the Proliferation Security Initiative) based on its own rules.

Another important reason other countries balked on dramatic ENR restrictions was their concern about reliable access to nuclear fuel. President Bush proposed fuel assurances only to states that renounced enrichment and reprocessing plants. John Bolton, then under secretary of state for arms control and international security, told an NPT Preparatory Committee meeting bluntly, "the Treaty provides no right to such sensitive nuclear technologies."[49] Developing countries were outraged by this perceived contravention of the principles of Article IV and took every opportunity to challenge the emerging restrictive regime standards. At the Seventh NPT Review Conference in 2005, fundamental differences arose over such issues as stronger pledges to pursue disarmament, how to respond to the actions of noncompliant countries such as Iran and North Korea, and the implications of secret supplier networks for states and non-state actors to acquire WMD. Distrust and division among players with vested interests in nonproliferation created a serious impasse, and for the first time ever, an NPT Review Conference collapsed in

acrimony.[50] Many decried the episode as a low point for multilateral cooperation on nonproliferation.

In response to deadlock in multilateral institutions and a failure to achieve
successful norm substitution, Bush shifted the focus to implementing his
agenda through mini-lateral and bilateral agreements. The administration convinced the Group of Eight industrialized powers to agree to a one-
year suspension on ENR technology transfers in 2004. And U.S. diplomats
launched a concerted effort to sign a series of memoranda of understanding
for nuclear cooperation with countries in the Middle East, including Saudi
Arabia, the United Arab Emirates, Jordan, and Bahrain, that carried a critical
clause banning uranium enrichment and reprocessing. This would effectively
rule out the possibility that any nuclear client state could work to establish
its own elements of the fuel cycle and, by default, would help close the ENR
loophole. The United States was able to finalize the first deal of this kind with
the United Arab Emirates in 2009.

A Pyrrhic Victory in the NSG?

In June 2011 the Obama administration appeared to achieve some of its objectives in the long and winding road on multilateral ENR restrictions. After
seven years of stalled negotiations, the 46-member Nuclear Suppliers Group
agreed on tighter restrictions on exports of ENR technology. The new, more
restrictive language stated, "suppliers should authorize transfers, pursuant to
this paragraph, only when the recipient has brought into force a Comprehensive Safeguards Agreement, and an Additional Protocol based on the Model
Additional Protocol or pending this, is implementing appropriate safeguards
agreements in cooperation with the IAEA including a regional accounting
and control arrangement for nuclear materials, as approved by the IAEA
Board of Governors."[51] This defined several, concrete changes. First, the NSG
stipulated that states must be party to and in full compliance with the NPT
to receive sensitive technologies. Second, they must have and comply with a
comprehensive safeguards agreement with the IAEA, and be in good standing with the agency. Third, they must report on national export controls as
called for under UN Security Council Resolution 1540, an initiative designed
to bring greater transparency to the trade regime. Fourth, supplier and client
states must adhere to international nuclear safety norms and adopt the Additional Protocol, an enhanced safeguards agreements with the IAEA. Finally,

the NSG agreed to a side arrangement for Brazil and Argentina for a regional accounting and control of nuclear materials.

President Obama had to overcome differences on a number of issues to achieve this agreement. Russia and China were concerned about limits on burgeoning relationships with client states, and once again, the U.S.-India civil nuclear cooperation agreement faced potential challenges under a more restrictive system for ENR.[52] NSG members Argentina, Brazil, and South Africa sought exemption from the Additional Protocol. And late in the negotiations, Turkey challenged more restrictive language for fear it could inhibit its peaceful nuclear energy programs. Ultimately, U.S. officials maintained, the 2011 agreement affirmed that being "eligible" to receive enrichment and reprocessing exports did not equate to a "right" to receive them. The net result was a new, more standardized, and specific multilateral framework to regulate ENR transfers, something that had not been achieved in forty years of concern about sensitive nuclear technologies.

However, with the multilateral achievement in its pocket, the Obama administration appeared to take a step back from unilateral imposition of renunciations of ENR ambitions by client states. In late 2011 U.S. officials gave their first indication they might no longer require ENR renunciations in future nuclear cooperation agreements (NCAs), though they maintained the issue was still undergoing interagency review. Diplomats had been engaged in nuclear cooperation negotiations at the time with three new states, Jordan, Saudi Arabia, and Vietnam, but discussions had stalled on the question of an ENR ban. Foreign diplomats insisted they would not sign a pledge similar to that in the UAE deal, reserving the right to develop nuclear technologies in the future.[53] Each country rejected the restrictions on principle, as a violation of sovereignty and Article IV rights under the NPT. They also warned they were ready to shift their business to other countries. After years of internal administration debates over ENR restrictions in future NCAs, President Obama dropped the demand in order to allow policy flexibility and bargaining leverage.[54] At the 2011 Carnegie Endowment's International Nuclear Conference, the administration's lead envoy for nuclear cooperation agreements, Richard Stratford, announced that the United States was moving forward on negotiation of up to fourteen new or renewed bilateral deals by 2014.[55] Finally, while the Obama administration loudly announced it would stand by principles of nonproliferation, officials could not fully articulate what they stood *for* in terms of the new normative architecture. When asked whether the

U.S.-India agreement would be the exception or the new rule, a high-ranking official stated that India was an "aberration" and that most of the world saw it that way. Ultimately, the Obama administration argued its new stance was to endorse a "principled approach" to NCA negotiations, "but also pragmatic."[56]

Outcome

This case study shows the partial success of an elite-driven program of change in the nonproliferation norm—from basic IAEA safeguards to the Additional Protocol. It also demonstrates the evolution from more open technology sharing to sharper restrictions and monitoring. President Obama proclaimed his support for the nonproliferation norm through initiatives including a speech on disarmament in Prague in 2009, the Washington Nuclear Security Summit, the 2010 NPT Review Conference, and the appointment of the Blue Ribbon Commission on America's Nuclear Future. Yet, by upholding some of the controversial export policies of the Bush administration—especially the spirit of the 2004 call not to allow the spread of ENR technologies—U.S. foreign policy fostered divisions among supplier states. Taken together, the mix of tactics suggested the absence of legitimacy for an overriding strategic concept regarding nonproliferation during the Obama years. Perhaps also, this was a president who was simply more comfortable with dissonance in policy frames than some of his predecessors.

Short of a legitimate new U.S. foreign policy stance, technology advancements like enrichment and reprocessing continued to foster serious reflection and reassessment of state capabilities, interests, and normative commitments. As Geoffrey Herrera argues, this dynamic was certainly a two-way street. Not only have these technologies impacted policy development, but they also have been impacted by international politics.[57] Three years after completion of the UAE deal, the U.S. government quietly acknowledged that it would no longer require renunciations of ENR technology in future NCAs and would instead diversify its agreements around a common set of principles. A senior government official interviewed in 2014 said that while the United States still prefers ENR renunciations, it would have to be realistic in negotiating renewals and future cooperation agreements. The "gold standard" might seem like a positive solution, he stated, but at the same time the United States and major corporations were "nervous we were shutting ourselves out of the market for no good reason." Would-be client states could easily secure nuclear contracts from other supplier states that would not require ENR pledges. [58]

The Obama administration's new "principled approach" to negotiations by 2014—using all tools available in relation to negotiations of NCAs, including threats that Congress would not approve of deals that allowed client states to pursue enrichment or reprocessing—suggests a less than coherent new normative architecture. There has been little international bandwagoning in support of these changes. Where the United States continued to demand ENR renunciations in ongoing negotiations with Saudi Arabia and Jordan, other supplier states, such as South Korea, Russia, and France, were quite happy to offer bids for nuclear energy plants. Even where the government opted not to require ENR renunciations, as in the recent cases of Vietnam and a renewal of the Taiwan NCA, the United States was still seemingly behind the competitive curve. While the U.S. government stands for a principled approach, a high-ranking official acknowledged in 2014 that after all, "This is a catch-as-catch-can business. We negotiate for what we can get."[59] This characterization suggests a normative architecture that remains very much contested.

5   Satellites and Sovereignty: Humanitarian Intervention and the "Responsibility to Protect"

In just eight years since it was adopted at the United Nations World Summit, R2P has emerged as a widely shared norm in international relations. Every country in the world has recognized its responsibility to protect citizens from genocide, war crimes, crimes against humanity, and ethnic cleansing, and, at least in theory, a responsibility to act . . . [but] R2P remains very much an evolving concept, neither the panacea that some had hoped for nor the hollow promise that others resigned themselves to expect.
> —*Madeleine K. Albright and Richard S. Williamson*[1]

I count tanks in space for George Clooney. . . . No one is doing what we are doing right now. It is a splitting the atom moment for the human rights community. . . . It is no longer just enough to stand at the graveside snapping pictures; that doesn't cut it anymore.
> —*Nathaniel Raymond*[2]

THE NORM OF STATE SOVEREIGNTY AND NONINTERvention has guided the international community for centuries. Grounded in the 1648 Treaty of Westphalia, this system offered relative stability for Europe following the devastating Thirty Years' War. Sovereignty granted leaders absolute authority to control affairs in their own territories and ruled external interference in foreign countries off limits. For great powers, this represented a new foundation for interstate relationships and a measure of control lacking in the chaotic period of overlapping territorial jurisdictions and shifting borders in the Middle Ages. For weaker countries, sovereignty offered new assurances of security, potentially leveling the playing field of power politics.

However, as important as the sovereignty norm has been to defining the state system, it has faced countless challenges over time. Sovereignty has provided relatively little protection for some countries from interstate wars and territorial disputes, for example. It also has allowed leaders to rule with impunity inside their own countries. Some have orchestrated crimes against humanity, including genocide and ethnic cleansing, with little fear of outside intervention. These and other problems have led many to question the role of sovereignty in an era of globalization.

This study explores one part of this larger story: how innovations in satellite reconnaissance and communication technologies have enabled state and non-state actors to monitor human rights violations in foreign countries and appear to have influenced some decisions to engage in humanitarian interventions. New remote sensing capabilities have the potential to change the dynamics of foreign policy-making in Western governments, and in turn, facilitate critical diplomatic discourses on the evolution of a new "responsibility to protect" (R2P) humanitarian intervention norm. Nevertheless, the problems and limits of humanitarian operations today suggest that even after years of experimentation, norm entrepreneurs "have largely failed to entrench R2P as an undisputed feature of global governance."[3] This case explores the story arc of the relationship between technology innovations, state behavior, sovereignty, and humanitarian intervention.

The Traditional Norm: Sovereignty and Nonintervention

Absolute and exclusive state sovereignty has served as one of the most important standards of the international system. It became an ordering principle, a line of defense, and a force for stability that has shaped the course of global politics.

How and why did sovereignty emerge as a premier normative standard? One answer lies in the European struggle to overcome the chaos of the Dark and Middle Ages. According to Mark Zacher, "The medieval world did not have international boundaries as we understand them today; authority over territorial spaces was overlapping and shifting."[4] Geopolitical circumstances were complicated by ongoing disputes over the authority of the Catholic Church and the desire for political and religious autonomy manifest in the Protestant Reformation. An early attempt to resolve this dilemma, the 1555 Peace of Augsburg, established the principle of *cuius regio, eius religio*, meaning "whose rule, his the religion." While Augsburg raised the prerogative of the sovereign state by allowing different religious practices in German principalities, it also became a catalyst for further conflict. The Thirty Years' War (1618–1648) was a devastating series of conflicts in Europe that caused more than eight million deaths. The 1648 Treaty of Westphalia resolved the conflict in favor of sovereignty, creating a system of states with constitutional authority and legitimacy.

This represented a critical transition from the Middle Ages to the modern world of sovereign states and resolved the matter of territorial integrity as an ordering principle. The resulting system of delimited territorial states with exclusive authority over their domains defined the "basic rule of coexistence" for the modern state.[5] It also instituted a new legitimacy for international borders, while implying exclusive internal jurisdiction. A system where only government authorities would be entitled to create laws and politics could, at the same time, allow absolute rule for leaders but also create a norm that did not permit interference in other countries' affairs (much less permit forcible humanitarian intervention). For constitutional expert Louis Henkin, this new system became, quite simply, "how nations behave."[6]

Both realists and liberals have embraced sovereignty over time. Realists see it as a logical response to the anarchic international system; liberals tend to view it as a defining legal standard. As realists Robert Art and Kenneth Waltz argue, "States in anarchy cannot afford to be moral. . . . The preconditions for morality are absent in international politics. Every state, as a consequence, has to be prepared to do what is necessary for its interests as it defines them. Anarchy is the realm where all can, and many do, play 'dirty pool.'"[7] Sovereignty thus becomes an enabling instrument to promote global order, by force if necessary. It also has taken on legal connotations. Sovereign territorial authorities are those powers vested with the legitimacy to enter into treaties with other states, to participate in multilateral institutions, and to define the path for independence.

By the twentieth century, the concept of sovereignty and territorial integrity were hallmarks of the modern state system. The United Nations helped enshrine the principle of sovereignty in the post-1945 world order. The many rules and standards of the UN system operate on the assumption of state sovereignty; for example, the UN espouses a generalized commitment to nonintervention. Article II of the UN Charter grounds the United Nations in the "sovereign equality of all its Members." Article II(4) proscribes any use or even the threat of the use of force, and Article II(7) prohibits any form of external intervention in the domestic affairs of a state by any means. Taken together, these sections establish boundaries for the sovereignty norm and against forcible intervention.[8] The primary exception to this rule included in the UN Charter was Chapter VII, which references the power of the Security Council to use forcible means when it deems there is a fundamental threat to international peace and stability. This was a very high bar for intervention that helped undergird the plan for international order established by sovereignty.

Traditionally, the laws of armed conflict have included a principle of civilian protection—also known as the noncombatant immunity principle. This demands states avoid attacks against civilians and indiscriminate use of military force that threatens collateral damage. The 1899 and 1907 Hague Conventions on the Laws and Customs of War on Land further grounded this principle by establishing the so-called Martens Clause addressing crimes against humanity, prohibiting attacks against undefended or unfortified towns. The preamble to the 1907 Hague Conventions stated, "The inhabitants and the belligerents remain under the protection and the rule of the principles of law of the nations, as they result from the usages established among civilized peoples, from the laws of humanity, and the dictates of the public conscience."[9] Later, the tragic events of World War II and the Holocaust became a critical impetus for establishing clearer standards of state conduct. Polish legal scholar Raphael Lemkin coined the term "genocide" in 1944, defining it as "the coordinated and planned annihilation of a national, religious, or racial group by a variety of actions aimed at undermining the foundations essential to the survival of the group as a group."[10] In 1948, the United Nations issued the Universal Declaration on Human Rights, a bold statement of the rights of individuals and human security, as well as other conventions against genocide and other crimes of mass violence. Leaders also considered the creation of new institutions and rules that would protect basic security rights and insure justice, including the idea of an international war crimes tribunal.

Technological Innovations: Remote Sensing and Satellite Technologies

States have always been interested in looking "over the horizon" to gauge both threats and opportunities. The evolution of aerial reconnaissance for military intelligence purposes, also known as remote sensing, is a product of this curiosity, with its own rich history. When Pilâtre de Rozier, a French scientist, carried out the world's first successful hot air balloon flight in 1783, military strategists quickly recognized the potential of balloons as a platform for surveillance of battlefields. In the twentieth century, the U.S. Army adapted the next generation of aviation technology, airplanes, for use in the first aerial photographic reconnaissance missions in the Philippines and along the Mexican border from 1913 to 1915.[11] By World War II, this had become a regular practice to gain battlefield advantage, to identify military-industrial complexes for strategic bombing, and to conduct bomb damage assessments. During the Cold War, the U-2 spy planes carried imagery sensors including electro-optical reconnaissance systems, along with long-range image transmissions systems, for their high altitude overflights of targets. They provided unprecedented amounts of imagery of nuclear weapons storage sites, airfields, missile fields, and submarine bases in the Soviet Union.[12]

Government Satellite Programs

Satellites represented the next major advancement in reconnaissance technologies. Arthur C. Clarke, a young British Royal Air Force (RAF) officer, first conceived of satellites as a space-based mode of electronic transmissions for military and commercial purposes during World War II. Clarke published an article on the idea of using radio "relays" situated above the ionosphere to improve transmission of radio and television signals.[13] This idea presaged the development of thousands of satellites for commercial communication as well as scientific, military, meteorological, and intelligence-gathering purposes.[14] On October 4, 1957, the Soviet Union launched *Sputnik I*, the world's first artificial satellite, into orbit some 600 miles above the earth's surface. This spurred on the Eisenhower administration's own missile and satellite research programs, and ironically, helped catapult the United States to rapid and dramatic technological advantages in space. Indeed, in a matter of just twelve years, the United States went from basic research on ballistic missiles to landing men on the Moon (with live broadcast of their first steps on that celestial body beamed back to Earth via satellite). The *Sputnik* moment truly seemed to separate "the old from the new."[15]

Eisenhower approved a joint Central Intelligence Agency (CIA) and Air Force proposal to develop a space-based, satellite photo reconnaissance system in the late 1950s. The CORONA satellite program was designed to gather imagery of Soviet missile launch sites, production facilities, and military capabilities. Orbiting 200 miles above the earth, the satellite would take high-resolution photographs of ground targets using advanced cameras, then eject the film for processing using a small reentry "bucket" designed by General Electric (deploying a parachute to slow its descent over the Pacific Ocean).[16] Soon after the launch of the program in 1959 the CORONA missions were yielding more imagery of the Soviet Union than all U-2 flights in the late 1950s combined. More than a hundred CORONA satellites (also known by their series monikers KH-1 through KH-4) and follow-on systems ARGON and LANYARD were launched between 1960 and 1972.[17] The KH-11 (Keyhole) satellite program was developed in the 1970s to record and transmit near real-time images of a target area almost anywhere on the earth.[18] The expanded radius of surveillance and stereoscopic images greatly enhanced reconnaissance capabilities, and engineering improvements expanded the lifespans of KH-11 over time.

Modern reconnaissance satellites capture images using advanced cameras as well as infrared and light across a wide electromagnetic spectrum. Advanced satellite systems, which produce "hyperspectral imagery" (HSI) and "multispectral imagery" (MSI), allow modern satellites to do much more than simply track an object on the ground. They also can perform battle damage assessment, support special operations, analyze hostile terrain, and penetrate forest cover and camouflage.[19] Critically, these new remote sensing technologies may reveal dimensions of conflicts underway in remote regions of the world where governments have no other intelligence assets. Over time, government satellites have steadily improved in terms of reconnaissance capabilities, with better optics, thermal infrared imagery systems for nighttime photography, imaging radars to see through cloud cover, geo-location data for mapping purposes, longer dwell time over targets, and more rapid data transmission.[20] Satellite imagery certainly has proved its worth for U.S. management of foreign policy challenges over time—from its role in shaping U.S. strategies in negotiating an intermediate-range nuclear forces treaty in

Europe in the 1980s, to planning the 2011 raid on Osama bin Laden's compound in Pakistan.[21]

Commercialization and Democratization
of Information from Space

The 1990s and 2000s also saw significant advances in commercial satellite development for data gathering and communications. Many of these innovations were a product of the synergistic interests of government and industry. For example, the passage of the Land Remote Sensing Policy Act in 1992 was a milestone: it permitted private companies to enter the satellite imaging business and had a dramatic impact on space technology. WorldView Imaging Corporation, funded by Silicon Valley entrepreneurs, was an influential player in this early market. In 1993, the company received the first commercial sensing satellite license issued by the U.S. Department of Commerce for high-resolution space sensing, WorldView went on to launch a network of satellites that would allow it to collect and process imagery with very high resolutions (three meters at the time). By 1999, satellites capable of collecting very high-resolution imagery (one meter or better resolution) were in orbit. Today, WorldView's main subsidiary is DigitalGlobe, a commercial vendor of space imagery and geospatial content, and operator of civilian remote sensing spacecraft. High-resolution satellite imagery can be collected on contract and delivered to almost any desktop or web-based mapping platform. Many of its customers are private interests such as oil and gas exploration companies and engineering firms, plus nongovernmental organizations. Indeed, some high-resolution imagery for Google Earth and Google Maps is provided through DigitalGlobe contracts. Perhaps ironically, some of DigitalGlobe's largest customers today are U.S. federal agencies such as NASA, the State Department, and the National Geospatial-Intelligence Agency. In 2004, Google acquired the assets of Keyhole, Inc. (which was originally a CIA-funded company), to develop satellite-based imagery for virtual globes and maps, as well as geographical information systems for data management. Google Earth melds satellite imagery and aerial photography into a seamless platform for remote sensing and mapping.

Satellites also have revolutionized telecommunications. News networks and communications companies have recognized that satellites could be the future of their businesses, and they have committed tremendous resources to develop new means of electronic newsgathering in recent decades. Aided by other innovations, such as the transistor and miniaturized electronic circuits, telecommunications satellites were designed to be "mirrors" in the atmosphere, reflecting signals that originate from a ground transmitter to a ground receiver.[22] *Echo-1* was the first communications satellite launched by the U.S. government in 1960; *TELSTAR 1*, the first U.S. private commercial satellite, was launched for AT&T in 1962. The next year, the *SYNCOM II* satellite was the first launched into geosynchronous orbit. The 1964 Tokyo Olympics became the first major sporting event to be broadcast on television live via satellite. And in 1965, *Early Bird* (also known as *INTELSAT I*) became the first commercial communications satellite successfully launched into geosynchronous orbit. This marked the beginning of a wholesale rush to place communications platforms in space for use by private corporations and for newsgathering and reporting.

Today, with over a thousand operational satellites in orbit around the globe, the information landscape has clearly changed. Policy-makers in advanced industrialized states are able to monitor events as they happen around the world and shape their responses accordingly in real time. Information is received and monitored through multiple tracks. At the same, information provided by satellites powers the global economy. Global Positioning System (GPS) satellites and radio frequency identification systems (for satellite tracking of any object, including inventory on store shelves) represent profoundly new innovations with significant governmental and commercial applications. Combined with satellite-produced mapping (found in Google Maps today), these technologies have allowed a whole new level of navigation as well as identification of ground activity.[23] Consumers also have eagerly embraced the information age, as concerned citizens and groups have drawn on new volumes of information about the world around them to pursue different causes. In an era of dramatic innovations in technology, information itself may have become a form of power.

Stage I: New Technology Meets the Traditional Norm

As noted above, the global community had firmly established the principle of sovereignty in the United Nations Charter, but governments also began to pay greater attention to human security concerns in the post–World War II era. A series of technological developments in the twentieth century facilitated a new level of attention to human security. For example, expanding satellite technologies have provided governments with much greater awareness of the plight of various groups around the world as well as accounts of official efforts to solve such problems.

International engagement in the Persian Gulf War (1990–1991) and its aftermath seemed to illustrate these new dynamics at work.[24] Days after providing live coverage of the conduct and abrupt end to the war, satellite news channels began reporting on an emerging humanitarian catastrophe. In early 1991 Kurdish and Shiite groups in northern and southern Iraq rose up against Ba'athist party control. Saddam Hussein responded with a brutal crackdown. Given Iraq's history of repression of the Kurds, including its chemical weapons attack on the Kurdish city of Halabja in northern Iraq in 1988, hundreds of thousands of Kurds fled to remote areas in the wintry mountains to avoid attack in late March 1991. Western countries had their first major, post–Cold War humanitarian emergency on their hands—and this time, the international news media were there.[25]

The Bush administration's response to the crisis evolved very quickly. At first, the White House expressed caution, describing attacks on Shiites and Kurds as an "internal struggle," a civil war for the Iraqi people to resolve on their own. The president declared, "We're not going to get sucked into this by sending precious American lives into this battle."[26] However, international and domestic pressure for a response was building. British television coverage of the crisis was especially weighty: the footage was "overlaid . . . with an unremitting commentary" on the refugee crisis that pinned "responsibility simply and directly on Western leaders, especially Bush and [Prime Minister] Major."[27] Members of Congress also pressed the White House for action. In early April, an internal State Department report based on aerial reconnaissance and ground reports from refugees and human rights groups estimated that a thousand Kurds were dying every day.[28] "The suffering of the Kurds stood out from the others," given relentless media coverage, argues Daniel Schorr. "This was not a natural catastrophe, but a man-made disaster, and one that had a special claim on the American conscience."[29] Just days after saying the United States wanted Iraq to settle its internal affairs, the Bush administration announced it would soon start airdropping food, blankets, and clothing to Kurdish refugees. Bush explained, "No one can see the pictures or hear the accounts of this human suffering—men, women, and, most painfully of all, innocent children—and not be deeply moved."[30] UN Security Council Resolution 688 soon authorized a massive relief operation, involving

5,000 U.S. troops, supported by thousands of soldiers from key European countries.[31]

Western leaders also could not escape the relentless news coverage and intelligence reports of the crisis in the former Yugoslavia in the early 1990s.[32] Yugoslavia was a federation composed of six republics (Serbia, Montenegro, Croatia, Slovenia, Bosnia, and Herzegovina) and autonomous regions including Kosovo.[33] However, the federation dissolved on June 25, 1991, when the regional governments of Slovenia and Croatia declared their independence; in April 1992, Bosnian Muslims also declared their independence. Serbian leader Milosevic declared war on the secessionist republics, demanded a return to federation, and sent the Yugoslav National Army (JNA) to stop them.[34] The Bosnia War dragged on for more than three years. It was reported that 250,000 people were killed during the war in Bosnia and 2,000,000 more became refugees between 1992 and 1995.[35] Over time this conflict received extensive coverage by international news outlets, with nightly reports on the siege of Sarajevo and other battles broadcast on many major news networks. The Clinton administration pursued a number of diplomatic initiatives to attempt to bring the war to a close, and in 1995 the president hosted talks leading to the Dayton Peace Accords. To support the implementation of the Dayton agreements, a NATO-led Implementation Force (IFOR) peace operation was established in the former Yugoslavia.

Kosovo represented another potential ethno-political battlefront in the Balkans. Ethnic Albanians in Kosovo remained largely impoverished and disempowered by the Communist system, while Serbs controlled municipal governments, schools, and police forces (in spite of their presence as a distinct minority in the province). Groups that favored armed insurrection against Serb dominance formed the Kosovo Liberation Army (KLA) in 1996, a guerrilla movement that would target Serb paramilitary units and police in the province. The KLA rapidly gained support and began receiving secret shipments of military supplies across the border with Albania. The intensifying crisis in 1998 and 1999 raised important questions about humanitarian intervention, but for almost a year U.S. officials could not agree on how to respond.

Stage II: Norm Redefinition: U.S.
Humanitarian Intervention Debates

One sees signs of attempts to redefine U.S. foreign policy responses to humanitarian tragedies in the 1990s, though efforts by the Clinton administration immediately bumped up against questions of sovereignty. U.S. debates and policy actions in this period had the effect of raising the profile of crimes against humanity and emphasizing the "necessity" for a Western response. At the same time, greater information about and awareness of unfolding events in these crises catalyzed debates over whether sovereignty was effectively a shield allowing mass murder by despots.

Government intelligence and security reports along with satellite television coverage of the wars in the former Yugoslavia appeared to impact U.S. foreign policy regarding foreign interventions. In May 1993, U.S. ambassador to the United Nations Madeleine Albright spoke about the Bosnia crisis: "Every day we witness the challenge of collective security on television—some call it the CNN effect. Aggression and atrocities are beamed into our living rooms and cars with astonishing immediacy. No civilized human being can learn of these horrid acts occurring on a daily basis and stand aloof from them."[36] When asked to comment on factors that had changed foreign policymaking, former secretary of state Lawrence Eagleburger also spoke of the CNN effect: "The public hears of an event now in real time, before the State Department has had time to think about it. Consequently, we find ourselves reacting before we have had time to think. This is now the way we determine foreign policy—its driven more by the daily events reported on TV than it used to be."[37] Scholar Steven Livingston concurred, suggesting that media coverage of humanitarian crises effectively helped set the international agenda and pressure government action in interventions in Kurdistan, Somalia, and Bosnia.[38]

The crisis in Kosovo in the late 1990s represented a tipping point in the development of U.S. intervention policies. Faced with mounting evidence of systematic killings of ethnic Albanians in Kosovo through media reports and satellite reconnaissance analyses in 1998 and 1999, key officials in the Clinton administration felt a responsibility to act. The actual process of redefining U.S. policies on intervention was contentious, however. It produced serious disagreements among members of the president's inner circle, problems in Congress, and debates in international organizations. Secretary of State Albright lobbied for action, describing events unfolding in Kosovo as "ethnic cleansing."[39] In the wake of new attacks by Serbs in September 1998, President Clinton convened a meeting of top advisors at the White House to consider the U.S. response to the spiraling crisis. Sitting on the conference table in front of the participants that morning was a copy of the day's *New York Times* with a front-page story and photographs of one of the massacres. Albright reiterated her plea for the use of air strikes to bring Milosevic to the bargaining table. She insisted that Milosevic "understands only the language of force," and convinced the president to authorize planning for air operations.[40]

The international community also responded to this latest round of attacks. On September 23, 1998, the UN Security Council passed its strongest resolution on the crisis, Resolution 1199, which called for a cease-fire in Kosovo, a Serb withdrawal of forces, and the return of refugees. U.S. diplomats negotiated with their counterparts in NATO for a military intervention to stop the bloodshed in Kosovo. On March 4, 1999, President Clinton gave a nationally televised address to announce that NATO air strikes on Yugoslavia had commenced. Clinton portrayed the U.S. intervention as a moral imperative necessary to protect the Kosovars.[41] The Kosovo War lasted 78 days and ended with Milosevic accepting NATO's demands and withdrawing Serb forces from the province.[42]

Stage III: Constructive Norm Substitution

The United States and other great powers engaged in serious debates in multilateral institutions about the responsibility to protect in the post–Cold War era. A simplistic interpretation of this discourse would be that a combination of enhanced awareness of crises through satellite intelligence gathering and communication technologies and public pressure led governments to embrace modified sovereignty norm legitimizing humanitarian interventions. For example, President Clinton argued during the Kosovo crisis, "If somebody comes after innocent civilians and tries to kill them *en masse* because of their race, their ethnic background or their religion, and it's within our power to stop it, we will stop it."[43] Thus, seeing and knowing about international problems seemed to have become a catalyst for action. However, a more nuanced characterization of events in the past two decades suggests we may have witnessed both the dramatic rise and fall of this principle, and that R2P remains, at best, a contested norm frame.

The Development of R2P

R2P was growing in popularity in the 1990s based on discourse in international governmental organizations and among transnational advocacy networks. A number of voices began speaking out in support of protections of civilians. Sudanese scholar Francis Deng's articulation of a new way of viewing "sovereignty as responsibility" was especially impactful. Deng's ideas represented an opening in international diplomacy for governments to view protection of civilians as an obligation for sovereign states.[44] This perspective was embraced by many at the United Nations and was increasingly championed by nongovernmental organizations, as well. More sympathetic regimes shifted to embrace this view, fostering a new level of legitimacy in accountability for protection of citizens.[45]

In 2000–2001, the Canadian government seized on the momentum of this discourse by sponsoring a new International Commission on Intervention and Sovereignty (ICISS) to critically analyze a range of modern cases of crimes against humanity and government response. Its final report extended Deng's arguments that in the modern era, sovereignty includes a responsibility to protect citizens from harm. It also focused on the ethical and moral foundations of humanitarian intervention.[46] It stated: "The central normative tenet of R2P is that *state sovereignty entails responsibility and therefore each state has a responsibility to protect its citizens from mass killings and other gross violations of their rights.*"[47]

Among the many contributions of the ICISS Report to the international discourse on humanitarian intervention was the careful balancing of power and (redefined) concerns about sovereignty with the need for interventions for civilian protection. The study treaded rather carefully on power politics, affirming that the "international responsibility to intervene and halt mass killings and ethnic cleansing is located in the UN Security Council and that any intervention should be efficient and effective."[48] In the process, diplomats also attempted to change the discourse on the question away from the bold assertion of the right of intervention and toward the concept of protection.[49] Thus, the intent seemed to be that the international community would take on a new level of responsibility aimed primarily at protecting or insulating vulnerable civilian populations, with less of an emphasis on forcible military intervention meant to undermine state sovereignty.

The UN World Summit in September 2005 provided another institutional forum to advance R2P—and another setting in which the United States had to tread a delicate diplomatic course. Many world leaders provided ringing endorsements of R2P at the summit, characterizing it as a new declaratory commitment to protect endangered populations.[50] Participants recognized the contributions of the 2001 ICISS report and the emerging consensus on the need to respond to egregious violations of human rights. UN member states sought to forge collective responses to genocide, war crimes, ethnic cleansing, and crimes against humanity. Notably, the discourse at the World Summit continued the shift away from an embrace of "humanitarian intervention" and toward broader responsibilities. U.S. ambassador to the UN John Bolton supported the potential norm evolution, yet only if the Security Council approved operations undertaken. He said, "For its part, the United States stands ready to take collective action, in a timely and decisive manner, through the Security Council under Chapter VII of the UN Charter, and as appropriate, in cooperation with relevant regional organizations, should peaceful means be inadequate and national authorities be unwilling or unable to protect their populations."[51] The summit Outcome Document allowed that military force would be an option to respond, but only after other alternatives had been considered and failed, and only for cases of "genocide, war crimes, ethnic cleansing, and crimes against humanity." Subsequent government statements and policy actions displayed the caution and circumspection of the U.S. position, maintaining that the authority for R2P should remain firmly in the Security Council where it held the veto.

The World Summit Outcome Document quickly became part of the canon of the emerging norm. Diplomats have regularly invoked the responsibility to protect in relation to intervention in countries like the Ivory Coast, Libya, and Syria over the years that followed. And in 2006, the UN Security Council made specific references to R2P in Resolution 1706 on the need to respond to the crisis in Darfur, western Sudan. UN Secretary General Ban Ki-moon appointed Francis Deng as a special UN advisor for the prevention of genocide. In January 2009, the secretary general released a report entitled *Implementing the Responsibility to Protect* that detailed specific guidelines on the responsibilities of individual states, international assistance and capacity building, and emphasized the need for timely and effective international responses.[52]

Getting in the Game: NGOs and Satellite Activism
Even as U.S. support for the ICISS and humanitarian intervention seemed to waver, more international governmental organizations (IGOs) and nongovernmental organizations (NGOs) became determined to "get in the game" of informed, empowered activism using satellite technology. The proliferation of technical means to collect and disseminate evidence of past, ongoing, or even imminent crimes against humanity also helped create pressures for evolution of the norm frame. For example, in 2000, the United Nations implemented a new satellite reconnaissance program, the Operational Satellite Applications Programme (UNOSAT), to provide "satellite solutions" to humanitarian crises and sustainable development challenges. UNOSAT staff included satellite imagery experts, programmers, Internet communications experts, and scientists trained in geology and geographic information systems. In 2003, the program implemented a new Humanitarian Rapid Mapping Service designed to provide the humanitarian community with satellite imagery analysis and mapping of crisis situations; this mission was expanded in 2010 with a grant from the MacArthur Foundation. UNOSAT officials stress that their program is different from classified government data collection using remote sensing given their commitment to widespread dissemination of the data collected for purposes of human security and development planning. The program has been so successful, UN officials said, that they are seeking to develop more integrated information awareness programs to involve volunteer mappers and citizens on the ground, offering a more panoramic picture of the challenges at hand.[53]

Nongovernmental organizations also boldly entered into the field of satellite imagery. For example, policy directors at Human Rights Watch (HRW) determined they might gain more leverage in political debates through collection and interpretation of satellite imagery. HRW hired a former analyst from UNOSAT, Joshua Lyons, to run a new program that involved contracting images of crisis zones from DigitalGlobe satellites for enhancement of other reconnaissance information. In an interview, Lyons said that he saw tremendous potential advantages to gaining exclusive knowledge of developments on the ground in humanitarian crises. But he warned that because technology has been evolving very quickly, it is incumbent upon all participants in the political discourse over human rights to figure out how to apply it in critical and creative ways. He also pointed out that HRW relied upon commercial and scientific data, some of which are free, and high-resolution photographic images could be purchased for less than $200.[54] In the past decade HRW and other NGOs have become very interested in the use of new technologies to promote awareness and understanding of mass atrocities. They have sought to incorporate the latest in satellite technology and imagery analysis to detect and expose human rights abuses, with the ultimate goal of protection of innocents.

Another major program in this tradition, the Satellite Sentinel Project (SSP), was launched in December 2010 through collaboration between Harvard University's Humanitarian Initiative and the Enough Project, a nongovernmental organization cofounded by movie actor George Clooney. The goal of the SSP was lofty: to focus world attention on mass atrocities by using cutting-edge technologies and intelligence gathering to prevent or forestall genocide. Project directors also hoped to deter a full-scale civil war in Sudan by documenting threats to civilians along both sides of the border. Specifically, the SSP Crisis Mapping and Early Warning System was designed to collect and analyze imagery purchased by contract from DigitalGlobe satellites passing above the Darfur region. Staff experts would monitor events on the ground such as possible threats to civilians, identify bombed and razed villages, and note other evidence of mass violence. The work combined satellite imagery, field reporting, and crisis mapping systems into a unified monitoring program designed "to detect, deter, and document threats to vulnerable populations." When SSP analysts detected troop movements on the ground suggesting pending attacks, they worked with the Enough Project to issue alerts to the media and policy-makers, as well as mobilize a network of activists on Twitter and Facebook to call on the Sudanese government to halt operations. SSP directors billed this new use of technology as a "substantial paradigm shift from traditional, often retrospective, collection of evidence corroborating alleged human rights violations."[55] Its motto became "The world is watching because you are watching." Together, the advances suggest a significant uptick in the use of satellite imagery by international governmental organizations and nongovernmental organizations, with the potential to truly crystallize a new norm frame in R2P.

A New Norm? Darfur, Satellites, and Sovereignty

The challenge of genocide in Darfur, the western region of Sudan, presented a modern test of the evolution of the responsibility-to-protect norm that demonstrated the complexities of attempted norm substitution through contestation. Non-Arabs in Darfur and elsewhere in the country have long held claims against the central government in Khartoum for their economic underdevelopment and marginalization. Conflict erupted over discrimination against non-Arabs between rebel groups based in Darfur—the Sudan Liberation Army (SLA) and the Justice and Equality Movement (JEM)— and the Sudanese government. In response, the Sudanese armed forces and a government-backed militia known as the Janjaweed, composed mainly of fighters of Arab background, attacked these groups along with civilian populations suspected of supporting the rebels in the Darfur region. The Janjaweed and Sudanese military carried out raids, which included extrajudicial killings, on villages in the region. The crisis has produced hundreds of thousands of casualties and millions of refugees. Many believe that Sudanese president Omar al Bashir is responsible for crimes against humanity, including genocide, and in 2009, he became the first sitting president to be indicted by the International Criminal Court for directing a campaign of mass violence against civilians.

Western media coverage of the crisis increased in 2004 when news organizations began to cover the refugee crisis in neighboring Chad.[56] Human rights organizations also took up the cause. Human Rights Watch published two major reports in 2004 designed to call attention to the crisis and challenge international non-responses. That same year, a young candidate for the Senate from Illinois named Barack Obama spoke out on the matter, declaring: "Genocide is underway in Darfur. . . . We cannot, in good conscience, stand by and let this genocide continue. . . . The international community has failed to do enough. . . . The United States, along with the UN, must take immediate steps to halt this dire situation."[57] In July 2004, UN Security Council Resolution 1556 described the conflict as a "threat to international peace and security." One year later, a Security Council investigation concluded that the Sudanese government and Janjaweed were responsible for "crimes against humanity and war crimes that may be no less serious and heinous than genocide," and it referred the matter to the International Criminal Court.[58]

When a tentative cease-fire agreement was signed in 2004, the African Union established a Mission in Sudan (AMIS)—a peacekeeping force for the Darfur region that grew to more than 7,000 troops in 2005. UN Security Council Resolution 1564 authorized close coordination with the United Nations Mission in Sudan (UNMIS). Conflicts continued across remote regions of Darfur, and AMIS peacekeepers were not successful in stopping the violence. UN Security Council Resolution 1706 on Darfur was the first resolution of its kind linking R2P to intervention in a specific conflict.[59] And in 2007 the Security Council unanimously adopted Resolution 1769, which authorized the hybrid AU-UN Mission in Darfur (UNAMID). This resolution explicitly invoked the responsibility to protect and authorized a robust military force to operate under Chapter VII powers of the UN Charter. As IGOs and NGOs continued to try to rally support for a stronger response to the crisis from Western countries, Sudanese diplomats countered the Darfur crisis was an "internal matter" and that the government had sovereign rights that must be respected.

The Satellite Sentinel Project and Darfur

The Satellite Sentinel Project was launched in December 2010 with the goal of focusing world attention on mass atrocities by using cutting-edge technologies and intelligence gathering to prevent or forestall genocide in Darfur. More broadly, the project was certainly inspired by the optimism of the 2005 World Summit and attention to human security concerns in the twenty-first century. Technology experts like Robert Latham characterize these types of projects as part of a revolutionary change—the empowerment of non-state actors to use advanced technologies to pressure governments to act.[60] New technologies provide new types of transnational actors with independent information they need to try to leverage decision-making. The result can be a changed normative frame where non-state actors help promote greater community awareness and actions for the common good.

Using a combination of imagery from DigitalGlobe satellites passing above the Darfur region, field reports, alerts from ground observers by satellite phone, and crisis mapping, the SSP would provide nongovernmental organizations with unprecedented reach and influence. After a two-year "experiment," project directors began to assess its outcomes. Generally speaking, they concluded the program was successful in raising public awareness, which made it necessary for policy-makers to pay attention. SSP's published reports became recognized as an otherwise unavailable, contemporaneous source of information about the conflict in Sudan for both policy-makers and the concerned public. SSP's ability to collect, analyze, and release information in near real time about potential threats to civilians did alert authorities to actions by the Sudanese military that should be condemned. SSP reports "became a widely cited resource on the evolving situation in Sudan by a range of policy actors, including the International Criminal Court, the U.S. Congress, UN agencies and others."[61] SSP concluded that its mapping and early warning systems provided the first sustained public program to systematically monitor and report on potential hotspots and threats to security along a border. It called this "a watershed moment in the development of 'protective humanitarian' technologies by employing the strategic collection and targeted presentation of data to deter and prevent mass atrocities."[62]

The SSP project actually exceeded some expectations. In essence, it represented one of the first, large-scale reproductions of classified government intelligence remote sensing operations for data collection and analysis. A staff report explained that "SSP's work was initially conceived as mostly gathering evidence that might be used in any future war crimes tribunal for Sudanese leaders. But the imagery was so accurate that it could also be used to monitor claims about massacres and mass graves."[63] Its coverage became so good that SSP analysts gradually moved from "a traditional 'documentation posture' into a more predictive 'detection posture.' Analysts were thus able to better target their collection of imagery to be more relevant to the real time security of vulnerable populations." By developing a new set of systems and analytics, project director Nathaniel Raymond said, the SSP system helped analysts "take a firehose flow of information and turn it into dixie cups" of usable data.[64] The staff found useful ways to "get the right tempo on the right task . . . combined with the analytic carriage, to make use of it with open and closed source intelligence."[65]

Furthermore, Raymond and his colleagues maintain that SSP intelligence information reached the highest levels, including appearing in the Presidential Daily Briefing. With SSP data, he claimed, "at the National Security Council level and UN Security Council level we have been able to foster a differential intelligence narrative of events."[66] The Enough Project also served to raise the visibility of the Darfur crisis and intensified demands that Western governments respond forcefully to human rights violations in western Sudan. According to project analyst Akshaya Kumar, "We know that this information is being used" at the highest levels, including by the Security Council and government officials, even when the organizations have their own, independent satellite data.[67] Meanwhile, dozens of members of Congress signed a letter to President Obama that cited SSP's work on monitoring human rights abuses and called for a shift in U.S. foreign policy toward the Sudan.[68]

Finally, while the Darfur crisis generated significant debate over the best international responses to genocide, it also appears to have been formative for the Obama administration's foreign policy. Indeed, there was a sharp uptick in administration initiatives to address crimes against humanity in 2011 and 2012. At a major convention of the UN supporter states for responsibility to protect, a U.S. representative stated: "The United States was then [2005] and is now a strong supporter of the concept of the Responsibility to Protect, and we are committed to working with international partners at the Human Rights Council to focus on pillar two, prevention and capacity building, in order to develop more effective strategies to protect populations from atrocities."[69] In August 2011, the Obama administration released Presidential Study Directive 10, which stated that "preventing mass atrocities and genocide is a core national security interest and a core moral responsibility of the United States."[70] Citing the problem that international engagement on genocides might come too late, Obama established a new Interagency Atrocities Prevention Board with the mission of articulating a more forward-leaning posture to detect and head off potential mass atrocities and genocide using networks of public and private sources. The object would be to "coordinate a whole of government approach to preventing mass atrocities and genocide."[71] The administration called for a new system of intragovernmental reporting that would properly allow "'red flags' and dissent to be raised to decision makers." President Obama declared that by "institutionalizing the coordination of atrocity prevention" the West could "increase the capacity and develop doctrine for our foreign service, armed services, development professionals, and other actors to engage in the full spectrum of smart prevention activities."[72] By demonstrating resolve to act for the international community, President Obama appeared to be signaling that the U.S. government was "all in" on genocide prevention.

A Failed Experiment? SSP and the Limits of R2P

At the same time, however, many have identified limits of the non-state satellite monitoring of potential genocides. SSP director Raymond noted that the project highlighted some of the challenges of gathering and using remote sensing and data collection technologies for any entity outside of government. For example, there were significant technical challenges to overcome in the project: even though they contracted with DigitalGlobe for imagery, SSP staff still had to collect and interpret high volumes of satellite and non-satellite data. This required them to develop their own software for geocoding and data interpretation—a significant innovation in its own right. Thus, this was an innovative private experiment that contrasted with government geospatial analysis in many ways. SSP staff had to develop a hybrid set of assessment mechanisms for military movements, humanitarian tragedies, and potential policy solutions. In a 2013 report, program directors concluded, "the experience of the Satellite Sentinel Project (SSP) suggests that attempting to enhance the situational awareness of policymakers and the public does not appear by itself at least in the case of Sudan to affect whether and to what degree governments respond to mass atrocities as they occur."[73] Ultimately, Raymond and his colleagues conclude pessimistically that the impact of the project was actually limited: "Regardless of the publicity resulting from its reports, SSP was unable to catalyze timely or robust action within policy communities."[74] When pressed on this question in an interview, Raymond added:

> Well, the needle didn't move. What we were going for is what we term an ambient protective effect or APE. Could we cause a higher level of human security protection because of the monitoring act itself, denying advantage and impunity to perpetrators, and catalyzing international response because we have the tempo and systems and volume? . . . The answer was "no." What happened was we were able to force the international community to say yes . . . but they still didn't engage. They just stopped denying it.[75]

Other experts have drawn similar conclusions about whether the democratization of information over the past two decades has actually changed the policy environment. Even though there are innovations in remote imaging seemingly every few months—with new companies planning to launch constellations of dozens of microsatellites for continuous monitoring of the earth through still and even moving pictures—director of satellite imagery at HRW Joshua Lyons warns it is easy to oversell the value of this technology. When asked about the direct impact of imagery on foreign policy decision-making he replied that there simply are no "smoking gun" cases where satellite evidence of atrocities have directly changed Western policy. He added, "Certainly U.S. intelligence imagery directly informs policy makers and often they release restricted and commercial sat imagery to justify a new course of action (for example, Bosnia, Kosovo, Iraq, etc.) after the fact." But it is important, he added, to distinguish between internal imagery as a trigger for decisions and external, public-release imagery evidence of mass atrocities that might shame or force a government to respond. Lyons is skeptical that such images can have that effect, especially following the case "where videos of dead children from the chemical attack in Damascus in 2013 did not trigger a U.S./EU intervention." He concludes, "it's hard to imagine that satellite imagery would either."[76]

Cameron Hudson, former chief of staff of U.S. ambassador Princeton Lyman, the U.S. special envoy to Sudan, and former director of African affairs at the National Security Council at the White House, 2005–2009, agreed with these assessments. He said in an interview that there were real limits in linking technology innovations and norm change. In relation to specific decision-making contexts for responses to genocide and other major challenges around the world, Hudson said that satellite imagery was helpful only in general terms. However, he argued, "satellite imagery is hardly ever a smoking-gun link to events or circumstances on the ground, but can be used to detect general patterns in the flow of conflicts."[77] Hudson was especially critical of the potential for nongovernmental organizations to use satellite imagery to promote a cause. Reflecting on the question of whether there has been a significant advance or an evolution of R2P, Hudson concluded, "many governments provide a rhetorical commitment to the evolution of R2P . . . but there's no empirical evidence for 'if they know we are watching they will behave better.'" "True normative change," he added, "probably moves more like tectonic plates—very, very slowly."[78]

Outcome

This case study suggests that the international community has made some progress in the evolution of the sovereignty norm and acceptance of the responsibility to protect, yet the process of norm change remains contested. Technological advancements in remote sensing and communications by satellites have helped to redefine the stance of the United States and other great powers on preventing mass atrocities. But they represent only a first step, as governments have tried to shift to embrace humanitarian interventions in select circumstances and build domestic political coalitions in support of the legitimacy of such actions. Attempting norm substitution through contestation has been much more complicated, though. While many states, international governmental organizations, and nongovernmental organizations have endorsed a new R2P doctrine as a legitimate alternative to traditional sovereignty, they sometimes have been reluctant to act.

Much of the evidence examined here suggests R2P remains a work in progress. Optimists believe that the responsibility to protect, based on the fundamental principle of "seeing and knowing," represents a legitimate new way of operating in twenty-first-century international relations.[79] Former UN secretary general Kofi Annan concluded that in the face of revolutionary technological and political changes, "state sovereignty, in its most basic sense, is being redefined . . . by the forces of globalization and international cooperation."[80] Numerous heads of state from around the world have endorsed the value of an R2P posture and have spoken out in favor of protection of human rights in the face of political violence. Meanwhile, nongovernmental organizations continue their campaigns for activism in global politics and seek ways to exploit remote sensing technologies to promote human rights around the world.

However, this study shows that even with increased information and awareness, as well as grassroots pressure for action, there has been little bandwagoning behavior in response to recent tragedies. Great-power resolve to intervene in all humanitarian crises has seemed to waver based on concerns about legitimacy. While experts contend that sovereignty in the twenty-first century implies a standard of reasonable treatment of citizens, government officials are hard pressed to account for these standards. There remain fundamental obstacles to debates over sovereignty and humanitarian intervention, which are difficult to overcome in many dialogues. Even when Western powers determine that action is required, they appear to prefer limited operations such as air strikes on select targets or airdrops of humanitarian relief supplies, rather than comprehensive ground operations to separate warring factions or provide safe haven. At this writing, the evidence seems to suggest that the broader process of constructive norm substitution continues, fostering significant debate and contestation in multilateral institutions.

6 Armed UAVs and the Norm against Assassination of Foreign Adversaries

> Attached to force are certain self-imposed, imperceptible limitations
> hardly worth mentioning, known as international law and custom, but they
> scarcely weaken it. . . . To introduce the principle of moderation into the
> theory of war itself would always lead to logical absurdity.
> —*Carl von Clausewitz*[1]

> From the Civil War to our struggle against fascism, and on through the
> long twilight struggle of the Cold War, battlefields have changed and
> technology has evolved. . . . As was true in previous armed conflicts,
> this new technology raises profound questions—about who is targeted,
> and why; about civilian casualties, and the risk of creating new enemies;
> about the legality of such strikes under U.S. and international law; about
> accountability and morality. . . . For the same human progress that gives
> us the technology to strike half a world way also demands the discipline to
> constrain that power—or risk abusing it.
> —*Barack Obama*[2]

THE DEVELOPMENT OF UNMANNED AERIAL VEHICLES
(UAVs, or drones) armed with missiles to strike ground targets
raises critical questions about modern warfare and the norm against assassination of foreign adversaries. Contractors in the United States and Israel
developed modern military drones in the 1980s and 1990s. These systems
could be flown remotely at high altitudes for long periods of time and provided ideal platforms for reconnaissance operations. In 2001, the George W.
Bush administration took these weapons to the next level, authorizing the
first drone air strikes in Afghanistan by an MQ-1B Predator affixed with

Hellfire missiles. The Pentagon and the CIA embarked on a vigorous drone war in Afghanistan and the tribal regions of Pakistan. President Obama actually expanded the drone campaign against al Qaeda and Taliban targets and authorized operations in Somalia and Yemen. And in 2014, Obama employed armed drones in strikes against Islamic State of Iraq and Syria (ISIS) terrorists in northern Iraq.

Experts and policy-makers agree that drones represent innovative technologies that have the potential to change the international security order. At the same time, these new technologies and their rapid proliferation around the world prompt questions about ethics, legality, and efficacy. The United States has engaged in rich yet quiet, diplomacy in the past decade to convince critics at home and allies abroad to accept the legitimacy of this new weapon of war. This study tells the story of a successful U.S. campaign to redefine and substitute a modified norm frame.[3]

Traditional Normative Standards: Sovereignty and Assassination Bans

The technological innovation of UAVs impacts at least two fundamental normative standards: sovereignty and the norm against assassination of foreign leaders. As noted in Chapter 5, sovereignty has served as the cornerstone of the international system from the Peace of Westphalia to the present. This emerged from centuries of diplomatic efforts to overcome seemingly enduring conflicts in Europe. The 1555 Peace of Augsburg and the 1648 Treaty of Westphalia helped establish sovereignty as an ordering principle, founded on a system of states with constitutional authority and legitimacy. Critically, Westphalia also settled the matter of territorial integrity—a new arrangement that defined the "basic rule of coexistence" for the modern state system.

Sovereignty came to be embraced by both realists and liberals, as well as take on legal connotations in defining legitimacy of the state system. The United Nations helped enshrine the principle of sovereignty in the post-1945 world order. The many rules and standards of the UN system operate on the assumption of state sovereignty; for example, the UN espouses a generalized commitment to nonintervention. The system expects that if force need be used, it would be to reestablish a political order, not a social one. Article II of the UN Charter grounds the United Nations in the "sovereign equality of all its Members," and its sections establish boundaries for the sovereignty norm and against forcible intervention. These and other UN principles helped set a high bar for intervention in a system of sovereign, stable nations.

The laws of armed conflict also outlined principles for civilian protection, or the noncombatant immunity principle. The principle of civilian protections, which demands that states avoid indiscriminate uses of military force that threaten civilians, had been an ancient and widely accepted rule of the law of armed conflict. These rules were originally grounded in treaties that prohibited attacks directed against undefended or unfortified towns. A 1923 Hague agreement prohibited "aerial bombardment for the purpose of terrorizing the civilian population, of destroying or damaging private property not of a military character, or of injuring noncombatants."[4] Later, the 1948 United Nations Universal Declaration on Human Rights and the Geneva Conventions also established ordering principles that helped define the modern human rights regime.[5] Article 48 of the 1977 Additional Protocol to the Geneva Conventions articulated a more detailed commitment by states to protect civilians: "Parties to the conflict shall at all times distinguish between the civilian population and combatants and between civilian objects and military objectives, and accordingly shall direct their operations only against military objectives."[6]

The norm against assassination of foreign adversaries evolved in a somewhat parallel fashion to that of sovereignty. Political assassinations were almost routine in the ancient world, and this continued into the Middle Ages, where the "killing of kings" was considered fair game.[7] Public officials faced the real possibility that adversaries inside and outside a principality might kill them as a route to power or influence. The practice was so widespread that it became embedded in the foundations of international law: "In 1516, Thomas More extolled the use of assassination both as a useful tool of statecraft and as a means of sparing ordinary citizens the hardships of wars for which their leaders were responsible."[8] Thus, not only was assassination considered an instrument of statecraft, it was seen as a desirable alternative to war in some circumstances. Hobbes described the world in this period as one of extreme conflict where there was no room for morality, arts, and letters. Clausewitz asserted that "to introduce the principle of moderation into the theory of war itself would always lead to logical absurdity."[9]

The development of the modern norm against assassination dates back to the establishment of the Westphalian system of sovereign states in the 1600s. By then, attitudes had begun to shift away from attacks on foreign heads of state and toward a system of sovereignty and balances of power that might grant more stability and order to Europe. In fact, the Thirty Years' War included very few assassinations. Philosophers and kings began to argue that such actions were immoral—out of bounds for respectable nations. For example, Hugo Grotius called for a strict ban on assassination, what he termed killing "by treachery."[10] In a famous treatise in 1758, Emmerich de Vattel wrote: "I find, then, the name of assassination to treacherous murder. . . . The sovereign who makes use of such execrable means should be regarded as an enemy of the human race."[11] Later, Thomas Jefferson opined, "Assassination, poison, perjury. . . . All of these were legitimate principles in the dark ages which intervened between ancient and modern civilization, but exploded and [were] held in just horror in the 18th century."[12]

The development of international law further contributed to limits on the practice of assassination. Emerging "laws of war" included standards of behavior that called for restraints on the use of force in a number of categories. One of the first attempts at codification of new standards was the U.S. Army's Lieber Code of 1863. The Lieber Code defined assassination as antithetical to the modern era, stating: "Civilized nations look with horror upon offers or rewards for the assassination of enemies as relapses into barbarism."[13] The Hague Convention of 1907 took this a step further, establishing a customary prohibition on assassination as "treacherous killing." This was to be a definitive statement of the laws of war on the matter, and it has appeared in numerous international agreements in the years since. States advanced laws and regulations governing the use of force and questions of intervention in the internal affairs of sovereign states, forbidding actions such as assassination. The 1937 Convention for the Prevention and Repression of Terrorism codified the illegality of the assassination of foreign leaders, their families, and other "protected persons."[14]

Major conflicts in the twentieth century highlighted the push and pull of the norm against assassination. The norm proved surprisingly resilient during World War II, for example. In one instance in the late 1930s, the British government rejected a proposed plan to support a coup against Hitler as "unsportsmanlike," even though it offered hope for averting an imminent war in Europe.[15] The British Special Operations Executive only undertook "a deliberate and continuous effort to try and liquidate Hitler" at the time of the Allied invasion of Normandy in June 1944.[16] After World War II, the U.S. *Army Field Manual* noted that anyone who carried out political assassinations would be committing a war crime and would be punished for violating clear standards. Cold War dynamics changed these calculations, however, and U.S. intelligence agencies sponsored a number of covert operations to assassinate foreign adversaries whom they believed were sympathetic to Communism. In 1975, an independent Senate committee exposed many of these operations and recommended that the United States oppose the use of assassinations because it "violates moral precepts fundamental to our way of life . . . [and] traditional American notions of fair play."[17] In response to congressional and public pressure, President Gerald Ford issued Executive Order 11905, prohibiting U.S. involvement in assassination plots. It stated, in part, "No employee of the United States Government shall engage in, or conspire to engage in political assassination."[18] At this writing, the United States is the only state that has enacted a clear declaratory policy renouncing assassination by executive order.

Technology Innovation: The Meteoric Rise of Drones

Drones clearly have the potential to revolutionize warfare. The history of UAV research and development has been shrouded by government secrecy, though information has emerged slowly over time through statements by government officials, public records, corporate reports, sightings by aviation buffs, and investigative journalism.[19] In May 2013, President Obama offered the first official, public acknowledgment of the drone war—and the clearest indication yet of administration thinking about the use of UAVs in relation to domestic and international law.

The development of unmanned aerial systems for reconnaissance was inspired by manned flight. That is, the idea of building flying platforms for long-distance photography and the gathering of intelligence on enemies dates back to flights by hot air balloonists in wartime and the use of aircraft for similar purposes in the early twentieth century (see Chapter 5). The U.S. Army began experimenting with UAVs—in effect, small, radio-controlled planes—as early as World War I. During World War II, Reginald Denny, a British pilot and Hollywood actor, developed a hobby radio-controlled plane and sold thousands to the Army by marketing it as the OQ-2 Radioplane for use in aerial gunnery practice. Nazi Germany also advanced drone technology with its V-1 "buzz bombs," which were effectively unmanned aerial torpedoes launched from northern Europe and flown on autopilot toward military targets and population centers in Great Britain. As technologies advanced, the U.S. military began to work more closely with aerospace companies to develop new, unmanned reconnaissance planes. The 1960s saw the advent of the Fire Fly and the Firebee systems, descendants of radio-planes for aerial gunnery targeting, which flew thousands of reconnaissance missions during the Vietnam War.[20] The CIA, National Reconnaissance Office, and Boeing collaborated on research on high-altitude observation drones that might someday replace the U-2 spy plane. The Pentagon also became very interested in the Israeli Defense Forces' success in using Pioneer drones to scout Syrian radar sites in the Bekaa Valley during the 1982 Israeli invasion of Lebanon. U.S. secretary of the navy John Lehman ordered the purchase of more than seventy Pioneer drones from Israel, and the Reagan administration ramped up spending for national drone research and development.[21]

Israeli aeronautical engineer Abraham Karem, a designer of drone aircraft who emigrated to the United States in the 1970s, was the father of the modern Predator drone. Karem started his own drone design company, Leading Systems, working from a garage in California. His designs eventually drew the attention of other entrepreneurs and the government. Leading Systems received seed money from the Pentagon and the Defense Advanced Research Projects Agency (DARPA) to develop an unmanned drone aircraft for possible use in the war on drugs.[22] His UAV, known as Amber, exceeded its contract's specifications, offering ready surveillance of ground activities through a camera mounted in its nose, and test flew for hundreds of hours without a crash. Indeed, the Amber system had many of the elements that would later become part of the Predator design. In 1988, Karem sold Leading Systems to General Atomics in San Diego, California. He continued working on an improved version of his drone, the Gnat-750, which made its first flight in 1989. The CIA and the Turkish government bought multiple Gnat-750s, and the drones were used in Bosnia in 1995.[23]

The first Predator drones (designated RQ-1) were designed solely for reconnaissance. They employed the latest advances in avionics and composite materials. Drawing lessons from the Amber and Gnat systems, the Predator went from the drawing board to the skies in less than fifteen years. The RQ-1, twenty-seven feet long, with a wingspan of forty-eight feet, and weighing only 10,000 pounds, could be launched from small airfields and fly at medium to high altitudes (around 30,000 feet) for twenty-four hours.[24] The remotely piloted RQ-1 exhibited what has become a fairly standard, modern drone design: shaped like a cross between an airplane and a cruise missile, it is fitted with a small turret under its nose, known as "the ball," which carries surveillance and targeting equipment. Critically, this new drone would be controlled remotely via satellite—an advantage that few other nations had at the time.[25] U.S. drone pilots could sit at consoles thousands of miles away and fly the UAVs using a keyboard, steering device, and computer data.

As impressive as the first-generation Predator systems were, they also faced limitations in design and capabilities. For example, they were underpowered (by a modified Rotax snowmobile engine), were not equipped with radar to see through clouds, had no de-icing equipment, and were difficult to land. A skeptical Air Force acquired its first Predator systems only when a congressional earmark forced it to do so in the mid-1990s.[26] Other government agencies including DARPA and the CIA saw Predators as a ready solution to their need for more remote surveillance following terror attacks by al Qaeda in bombings of U.S. embassies in Africa in 1998 and the USS *Cole* in Yemen in 2000.

In the late 1990s, the CIA supported development of a modified Predator, known as Predator B (also known as RQ-1B). The Predator B has greater surveillance capabilities, including a video camera for real-time surveillance of ground targets and another to detect infrared signals in the nose ball. The ball also houses a laser pointer for target designation and a radar system known as the vehicle and dismount exploitation radar (VADER), which allows the drone to "see" through smoke, clouds, or dust.[27] Predator B's acquired by the CIA were at the heart of a new reconnaissance operation, known as Afghan Eyes, that flew drones from Uzbekistan over bases in Taliban-controlled southeastern Afghanistan in an effort to locate Osama bin Laden. On at least one occasion in 2000, experts believe they observed bin Laden gathered with his advisors at a camp in Afghanistan. Officials were reportedly frustrated, though, that while they could locate a high-value target using a drone, too much time was required to report this back to commanders who might then dispatch a jet fighter or launch a Tomahawk missile to hit the target. As a CIA operative later put it, "If we had developed the ability to perform a Predator-style targeted killing before 2000, we might have been able to prevent 9/11."[28]

Stage I: Technology Meets the Traditional Norm

The George H. W. Bush administration authorized the first deployment of modern U.S. reconnaissance drones during the Persian Gulf War in 1990–1991 to aid in targeting naval bombardments and to conduct bomb damage assessments. Drones also were used to help plot routes for the terrain-contour guidance system of the new Tomahawk cruise missiles.[29] Notably, this embrace of innovative new technologies for warfare generated no major public debates at the time. The drones were used in conflict zones by the commander in chief and operations remained highly classified. The Clinton administration's deployment of first-generation Predator drones in two instances in the Balkans in the 1990s showed that these were valuable systems. Drones provided information about Serb artillery unit placements during the late stages of the Bosnia War in 1995, and later during the Kosovo War of 1999 they were used to provide information for U.S. and NATO military commanders on Serb air defenses and on refugee patterns.

Origins of the Drone War

The events of September 11, 2001, prompted an intense new level of focus and interest in innovative defense technologies. Air Force Chief of Staff General John Jumper and other commanders began to view UAV technologies as force multipliers. They determined drones could enhance U.S. operations on the modern battlefield, but also keenly felt the limits of the Predator as reconnaissance-only platforms. Cofer Black, the head of the CIA's Counter Terrorism Center, and Richard Clarke, the chief counterterrorism advisor for the National Security Council, pushed the issue of arming UAVs, and in early 2001 General Atomics began upgrading the Predator to carry air-to-ground missiles and improving its targeting capability.

The executive branch supported the development of a system that could both provide up-to-the-minute intelligence on enemy activities on the ground *and* target them with missiles or bombs. This, it believed, would offer an effective, immediate, and discriminate use of force. With the capability in hand in the form of the Predator B, President Bush signed a finding that sanctioned armed strikes on al Qaeda leaders as a defensive measure in the global war on terrorism. The intelligence community and the military was at war, Bush believed, and had the right to execute enemies. At the same time, internal documents also show some of the first debates underway inside the administration about the new killing technology and the ethics and legality behind its use.[30]

Some Predator systems were modified to become hunter-killer drones (labeled MQ-1B). On February 16, 2001, Predator 3034 took off on a secret flight test and successfully hit a ground target with a Hellfire missile. These missiles, which were originally developed as anti-tank systems for launch from helicopters, were able to strike at a range up to eight kilometers. The Predator B was modified by installation of a laser target designator and advanced avionics and its wing pylons were strengthened to carry and launch missiles.[31] The missiles themselves also had to be reconfigured for use to explode with shrapnel on soft targets rather than penetrating armor as they had originally been designed to do. Expert Brian Glyn Williams calls the advent of armed Predator drones "a revolutionary moment in the history of aerial warfare. The unmanned reconnaissance drone had become a killer."[32]

Armed drones quickly became a centerpiece of the war on terror. The first known use of a military Predator to successfully hit an enemy target with a missile occurred in Afghanistan in October 2001. In November 2001, a UAV killed Mohammad Atef, the third-ranking commander of al Qaeda, and one year later a UAV killed one of the al Qaeda plotters of the USS *Cole* bombing in Yemen. This generated excitement inside the corridors of power about the potential lethality of this new system. A senior U.S. official later summarized the new attitude of the government regarding the use of drones, stating, "The gloves are off. Lethal operations that were unthinkable pre-September 11 are now underway."[33] By 2004, drones were raining missiles down on al Qaeda and Taliban operatives hiding in the Federally Administered Tribal Areas (FATA) region in Pakistan.[34] In a rare public statement on UAVs, the Air Force announced in 2007 that it had established its first unmanned aircraft wing with sixty Predators and six Reapers (a newer, heavier platform design). The modern drone war had begun.

The Obama Administration and Drones

Soon after taking office, Barack Obama secretly expanded the CIA drone campaign to target groups seeking to destabilize the Pakistani government and authorized further drone uses in other countries, including Yemen and Somalia. In late 2009, when President Obama announced his decision to send a "surge" of 30,000 troops to Afghanistan, he also secretly authorized expansion of the drone program in Pakistani tribal areas. The year 2011 saw very significant uses of drones, including the first confirmed drone strikes against a terrorist group in Somalia, a strike in Yemen that killed al Qaeda member and cleric (and also a U.S. citizen) Anwar al-Awlaki, and aerial surveillance over the Abbottabad compound of Osama bin Laden in Pakistan during the U.S. Navy Seal raid.[35] Drones appeared to provide revolutionary levels of information about activities on the ground, and by arming these systems the U.S. had extended its reach in a profound, new way.

Military and intelligence agencies expanded their development of drones. According to the Department of Defense's 2011 aircraft procurement plan, the number of aircraft in the unmanned system category was to triple between 2011 and 2012, coupled with a slight overall decrease in the aviation force structure. At this writing, the Pentagon possesses large numbers of five types of UAVs: the Air Force's Predator, Reaper, and Global Hawk, and the Army's Hunter and Shadow. The Reaper is much larger than the Predator, with a powerful engine designed for high altitude flight (up to 50,000 feet) and endurance (flying for up to thirty-two consecutive hours before returning to base).[36] What really differentiates it from the Predator, though, is its ordinance capacity: experts suggest the Reaper can carry as many as sixteen Hellfire missiles or a mix of 500-pound bombs, Sidewinder missiles, and smaller bombs. Other drones in the arsenal include the MQ-1C Gray Eagle, which is a slightly larger, longer endurance version of the Predator deployed by the Army with more surveillance equipment; the Navy's Unmanned Carrier-Launched Airborne Surveillance and Strike (UCLASS) vehicle; the MQ-8 Fire Scout; the Broad Area Maritime Surveillance (BAMS) UAV; and the Marine Corps' Small Tactical Unmanned Aerial System.[37]

At this writing, the United States is experimenting with even more advanced systems, such as the RQ-170 Sentinel, which has a flying wing design for maximum stealth.[38] The Sentinel is reported to have performed surveillance and data relay related to the operation against Osama bin Laden on May 1, 2011. Meanwhile, DARPA is working with defense contractors to build other types of advanced UAVs, including jet-powered systems and new designs capable of takeoff and landing on aircraft carriers. Research is also underway on more autonomous capabilities for drone systems. One program, the Joint-Unmanned Combat Air System (J-UCAS) program, initiated in 2003, was designed to produce a "collection of unmanned, weaponized, high performance aircraft equipped with the latest contemporary autonomous capabilities."[39] Critics at a 2014 UN meeting on the implications of "lethal autonomous weapons systems" warned that the United States and other great powers were creating a new generation of "killer robots."[40]

Given the success of UAV operations, it is not difficult to understand how these systems enjoyed their meteoric rise from concept to weapon of choice in the war on terror. Not only did drones eliminate threats to pilot lives, they also could perform much beyond the limits of human endurance. Advanced navigation and communications technology, and increases in military communications satellite bandwidth made remote operation of these systems more and more practical. Drones could carry out tasks often considered complicated and dangerous, such as missions to suppress enemy air defenses or behind enemy lines.[41] In many ways, UAVs seemed ideal weapons system for the shadowy global war on terror, and few officials were publicly willing to question U.S. policies.

Stage II: Armed Drones and the War on Terror

As noted above, long-standing official U.S. policy prohibited targeting foreign leaders for assassination. A gap emerged between rhetoric and reality by the 1980s, though. For example, the U.S. air strikes on Libya in 1986 included the bombing of a presidential palace in Tripoli, but officials maintained it was a "command and control" facility. In a presidential finding from the Persian Gulf War (1990–1991), George H. W. Bush signed secret orders for the CIA to spend more than $100 million on covert operations to "create the conditions for removal of Saddam Hussein from power."[42] A *Los Angeles Times* investigation later revealed that high-ranking U.S. officials had secretly deliberated on operations to assassinate Saddam Hussein during the war but decided against them.[43]

More policy-makers, researchers, and concerned citizens seemed willing to debate whether assassination ever might be considered a legitimate foreign policy tool in the war on terror. Al Qaeda bombings of two U.S. embassies in Africa in 1998 represented an important turning point. Members of Congress on both sides of the aisle began to speak up about whether the executive order banning assassination was necessary and whether presidents and military commanders should be given wider latitude in this area. Critics charged that the language of Executive Order 12333—"No person employed by or acting on behalf of the United States shall engage in, or conspire to engage in, assassination"—was simply too vague to be effective.[44] In 1998, a bipartisan group of senators asked FBI Director Louis Freeh to research the legality of assassinating terrorist leaders. They asked for clarification as to whether Executive Order 12333 and its amendments prohibiting assassinations of heads of state also applied to terror groups.[45]

International Terrorism and Norm Redefinition

The George W. Bush administration set about redefining the U.S. approach to normative constraints on state behavior in the aftermath of the terror attacks of September 11, 2001. The White House interpreted the attacks as a serious challenge to security, but also a "moment of destiny" for the nation that dictated bold and decisive action. Officials determined that past defense strategies, as well as traditional norm stewardship, were no longer adequate to guarantee security. The administration attempted to redefine the U.S. position on the norms through doctrinal statements and pressure on Congress, and it demonstrated this commitment in actions in the Iraq War. At the time, National Security Advisor Condoleezza Rice said 9/11 had "shifted the tectonic plates" of global politics. In the circumstances, she argued, it was "important to try to seize on that and position American interests and institutions and all of that before they harden again."[46] President Bush made clear in a national address on September 12 that in the wake of the attacks the United States would "make no distinction between the terrorists who committed these acts and those who harbor them."[47] This was a broadening of potential challenges to include state sponsors of terrorism such as the Taliban regime in Afghanistan and other rivals. The effect of this was to blur the distinction between state and non-state actors, with implications for the use of force.

The Bush administration enjoyed an unprecedented level of popular support for these policy changes from the American public at the time. Approval ratings for President Bush rocketed to the highest level for any president on record after the attacks (92 percent). Within days, Congress passed a broad resolution that authorized the president "to use all necessary and appropriate force against those nations, organizations, or persons he determines planned, authorized, committed, or aided the terrorist attacks that occurred on September 11, 2001, or harbored such organizations or persons, in order to prevent any future acts of international terrorism against the United States." Many interpreted this resolution, plus related legislation (such as the USA Patriot Act), as providing a blank check for the White House to take extreme actions in the name of defense and homeland security.

President Bush advocated the exercise of American power, even unilaterally if necessary, to achieve security objectives. In 2002, he articulated "a proactive doctrine of preemption" that would differ dramatically from deterrence
or a purely defensive orientation.[48] Bush stated in a high-profile speech at
West Point on June 1, 2002: "The gravest danger to freedom lies at the perilous
crossroads of radicalism and technology. . . . They want the capability to black-
mail us, or harm us, or to harm our friends—and we will oppose them with
all our power."[49] The decision to go to war with Iraq in 2003 demonstrated that
conflating the problem of revisionist or rogue states with the threat posed by
terror organizations was more than a rhetorical device. President Bush's 2002
National Security Strategy document had explained: "Given the goals of rogue
states and terrorists, the United States can no longer solely rely on a reactive
posture as we have in the past. . . . We cannot let our enemies strike first."[50]
While the new doctrine was better described as prevention rather than preemption, since it envisions military action against threats that are prospective
rather than imminent and inevitable, the result was an action that redefined
U.S. policies relative to existing norms. The United States would claim the
right to act preventively and use military force to target even potential threats.
This could undermine the principle of sovereignty and nonintervention, as
well as potentially push the normative envelope on assassination of foreign
leaders.

Drones in the War on Terrorism
Drones became a centerpiece of the new war on terrorism and fostered a
whole new dialogue in the Bush administration about "targeted killings" and
even "decapitation strikes" on leaders of terrorist groups or rogue states.[51] U.S.
leaders began adopting these tactics, which had long been used by the Israeli
Defense Forces and the Mossad, with the goal of reducing a state or group's
operational capability, eliminating its leaders or skilled members of the group,
and forcing it to divert valuable time and resources.[52] U.S. intelligence officials
considered how new technologies might change the decision calculus and
potentially offer a much more efficient route for achieving strategic objectives.

Bush signed a secret finding in the fall of 2001 that "concluded that executive orders banning assassination do not prevent the president from lawfully
singling out a terrorist for death by covert action."[53] Where there had been
doubts, the CIA and the Defense Department now seemed to embrace aggres-
sive counterterrorism operations. Drone strikes soon were employed in the

killing of al Qaeda leaders in Afghanistan. U.S. drone operations in the FATA region in Pakistan began in late 2003. Though the U.S. and Pakistani governments maintained a veil of secrecy for these operations, experts believe that from 2003 to the fall of 2013, approximately 344 drone strikes had taken place in Pakistan's FATA region, killing an estimated 2,540 Taliban and al Qaeda operatives and several hundred civilians.[54] The Bush administration also extended the use of Predator drones and other UAVs in the war on terror in Yemen and Somalia.

By the late 2000s officials seemed ready to make a broader case for legitimacy of drone strikes. National Security Advisor Condoleezza Rice commented, "The president has given broad authority to U.S. officials in a variety of circumstances to do what they need to do to protect the country. We're in a new kind of war, and we've made very clear that it is important that this new kind of war be fought on different battlefields." She added, "I can assure you that no constitutional questions are raised here."[55] Later, in response to greater public scrutiny and criticisms of the drone war, former CIA director Panetta said that when it came to the Predator and Reaper campaigns, they were "the only game in town in terms of confronting or trying to disrupt the al Qaeda leadership."[56] Harold Koh, a leading State Department lawyer and former dean of the Yale Law School, declared in a 2010 speech to the Annual Convention of the American Society of International Law that "U.S. targeting practices, including lethal operations conducted with the use of unmanned aerial vehicles comply with all applicable law, including the laws of war."[57]

Congress provided a broad mandate to the president in the war on terrorism through its September 2001 Authorization for the Use of Military Force (AUMF). It also supported the redefinition of U.S. foreign policy ends and means relative to international security norms in the war on terrorism. Administration representatives engaged in numerous private consultations with leading members of Congress on the drone program in the 2000s related to both the value of the operations and continued funding. With the tacit approval of Congress, the CIA and Pentagon followed executive orders to expand the drone war from 2001 in Afghanistan to operations in Yemen and the FATA region of Pakistan. By 2007, reports indicated drones were being used for reconnaissance roles against the al Shabaab terrorist organization in Somalia (a group that did not exist before 9/11). When pushed by outside critics on their authority, Obama administration officials cited the AUMF as authorizing the use of drones to target al Qaeda elements in Yemen. By March

2009, U.S. officials were claiming that drone strikes had killed nine of al Qaeda's top twenty commanders. A year later the administration acknowledged they had killed more than 800 al Qaeda and Taliban fighters in Pakistan.[58]

Finally, nongovernmental organizations did rise up to challenge the ethics and legality of the drone program. Human Rights Watch and other NGOs began to speak out against it in the mid-2000s, citing evidence of targeted killings causing collateral damage in Afghanistan. NGOs raised critical questions about the practical and moral grounds of the operations. More broadly, these groups questioned under what circumstances drones might be considered an appropriate means to achieve objectives. Critics on the left saw the use of armed drones as something wholly incompatible with how the U.S. polity and other countries understood the existing norms governing international intervention for self-defense, and this set up a conflict over the content of important international rules. This policy, critics charged, was profoundly revisionist. It was "expressly designed to delegitimize the existing practices around preemption and institutionalize a new norm based on a different understanding of imminence" of threats.[59] More and more voices suggested that the use of drones might be metastasizing into a reckless campaign that was killing too many innocents and fanning the flames of insurgency.

Stage III: Constructive Norm Substitution

Governments around the world recognized that in the twenty-first century the United States was willing to engage in preemptive actions that included targeting foreign leaders and attempts to remove them from office. Decapitation strikes could occur, and in some circumstances they might be seen as legitimately in the interest of global security. The Bush administration continued to coordinate its activities with scores of governments around the world in a broader war on terrorists and insurgents. When the Russian government faced serious threats from terrorist groups based in the Caucasus, for example, it sought intelligence cooperation with the United States. Russian authorities, in turn, provided basic information on the movements and activities of individuals monitored by the United States (including those of Tamerlan Tsarnaev, an ethnic Chechen and U.S. resident who was one of the alleged Boston Marathon bombers in 2013). The Bush administration also worked closely with authorities in friendly regimes around the world including Turkey, Peru, and Colombia, on combating insurgency. Surveillance, apprehension, and even targeted killings of leaders of terrorist groups and drug cartels had the effect of creating organizational turmoil (not to mention the end of major movements such as the Shining Path and the Tamil Tigers).[60] The result was a seemingly broad endorsement by the international community of the evolution of the traditional interpretation of the sovereignty norm and standards against preemption. This also marked a move away from considering the threat of imminent attack as a necessary condition to justify legitimate and legal preemption by force.

Thus, it appears that American technology innovations coupled with prevailing balances of power and a confluence of great-power interests allowed the United States to push the international community to broaden the understanding of "imminence" of threat as well as acceptable actions to target the threat. The net effect of these developments was the revisiting of the customary-law understanding of the terms of imminence. Ultimately, the U.S. effort to ascribe legitimacy to this new area of focus constitutes an evolution of the rules on the use of force.

The Obama Administration and
Constructive Norm Substitution

As a constitutional lawyer, Barack Obama pledged during his campaign for the presidency that he would pursue greater openness in the war on terrorism and revisit major parts of the Bush doctrine. However, he appeared to encounter significant cross-pressures in his drive to reform the system. Bush personally asked Obama during the presidential transition to consider the extension of several critical programs for U.S. national security, including the successful armed drone program in the tribal regions of Pakistan. Once in office, the new president oversaw a dramatic expansion in the global war on terrorism, including an expanded use of armed drones and increased funding for the Joint Special Operations Command and intelligence surveillance.

One of Obama's first orders as president was to significantly ramp up the search for Osama bin Laden. U.S. Special Forces killed bin Laden on May 1, 2011.[61] In a national address, the president called the achievement "a testament to the greatness of our country and the determination of the American people," and added that the cause of securing the country would continue.[62] In an addendum to the events of the day, large crowds gathered outside the White House to cheer the action and across the country there were spontaneous celebrations and public rallies. The domestic audience for the achievement—a successful targeted killing—seemed exuberant, suggesting a latent shift in attitudes on the question over time. According to a May 2011 New York Times/CBS News poll, support for Obama's performance as president rose sharply after the killing of bin Laden, from 46 percent to 57 percent. Eighty-five percent of Americans surveyed supported the way Barack Obama handled the pursuit of Osama bin Laden (with only 7 percent disapproving).[63] As the president subsequently elaborated, "We obviously believe that we were absolutely within our rights to go after the most wanted man in the world, the most wanted terrorist in the world—the man who ordered the attacks on so many Americans and killed so many Americans."[64]

Within his first ten months in office, President Obama authorized twice as many targeted killings using drones as George W. Bush had during his entire presidency.[65] Obama saw the program as a way to keep the pressure on a dangerous enemy that was continuing to plot and plan attacks from its safe havens in Pakistan, while lessening the U.S. footprint in the region. And the drone program had the desired effect of degrading the core organization of al Qaeda in Pakistan, potentially raising the possibility of ending the larger war effort in favor of more intense counterterrorism and intelligence operations aided by pinpoint strikes. Just five months after the bin Laden operation a U.S. drone fired a Hellfire missile in Yemen to kill Anwar al-Awlaki.

Building Political Legitimacy at Home and Abroad
President Obama also recognized the importance of establishing a foundation of political legitimacy for carrying out drone strikes within proscribed limits. This began at home. Obama changed the procedure for approval of strikes, shifting authority to the White House and counterterrorism advisor John Brennan. Administration officials also began to outline a new set of rules for conducting lethal operations abroad—what the White House termed "institutionalization"—with the president's expressed goal to turn the country away from "perpetual war" and toward a counterterrorism policy that better balanced security and rights. Counterterrorism advisors developed a comprehensive database, which they called the "disposition matrix," with information on suspected terrorists and militants that would provide options for killing or capturing targets.[66] Department of Justice white papers also outlined criteria for the possible assassination of American citizens that represent an "imminent threat" to the United States (partially in response to the al-Awlaki killing). The president also worked to try to standardize the

targeted-killing program by transferring CIA operations to the control of the U.S. military. While Obama had signed a presidential finding in support of the CIA's targeted-killing program, he sought greater authority over the final decision on the military's kill-or-capture orders, so-called direct action operations. He ordered other policy changes including a ramping down the controversial practice of "signature strikes," where groups of suspected terrorists have been targeted even though their identities were not known. Ultimately, the standards for the president to authorize lethal force would be that targets represent a "continuing, imminent threat," and where "capture is not feasible."

Near the end of President Obama's first term, the administration also issued a series of statements and policy declarations that effectively outed drones as a critical instrument in the war on terrorism in the process of defining policies. This appears to have been a conscious initiative designed to influence both domestic and international audiences regarding the legitimacy of these operations. For example, on May 1, 2012, Brennan gave an address at the Woodrow Wilson Center on the ethics and legality of drone operations. He maintained that drone strikes were completely consistent with international standards, including domestic law and the Constitution, which, he said, gave the president powers to protect the nation from imminent threats of attack. He went on to make the case: "As a matter of international law, the United States is in an armed conflict with al-Qaida, the Taliban and associated forces, in response to the 9/11 attacks, and we may also use force consistent with our inherent right of national self-defense. There is nothing in international law that bans the use of remotely piloted aircraft for this purpose."[67] Thus, drone strikes were ethical and consistent with the laws of war, Brennan argued, in addition to meeting the basic tenets of just-war theory. Strikes would conform to the principles of necessity, discrimination, and proportionality. Brennan added, "It is hard to imagine a tool that can better minimize the risk to civilians than remotely piloted aircraft. . . . For all these reasons, I suggest to you that these targeted strikes against al-Qaida terrorists are indeed ethical and just."[68]

Brennan had another reason for outlining U.S. policies in these ways: promoting international standards to regulate the behavior of all countries that were experimenting or considering acquisition of drones in the future. Calling targeted strikes by unmanned aerial vehicles "a wise choice," Brennan was urging the international community to accept that with great power comes great responsibility. He said that given the fact "other nations also possess this technology, and many more nations are seeking it, and more will succeed in acquiring it," the United States was "establishing precedents that other nations may follow. . . . If we want other nations to use these technologies responsibly, we must use them responsibly. If we want other nations to adhere to high and rigorous standards for their use, then we must do so as well. We cannot expect of others what we will not do ourselves."[69]

In May 2013, President Obama gave a high-profile speech on counterterrorism at the National Defense University in which he publicly acknowledged U.S. drone strikes for the first time and made clear that he was ordering "reforms" that would regularize and curtail such operations. Obama sought to place these activities in context, arguing:

> Our operation in Pakistan against Osama bin Laden cannot be the norm. . . . It is in this context that the United States has taken lethal, targeted action against al Qaeda and its associated forces, including with remotely piloted aircraft commonly referred to as drones. As was true in previous armed conflicts, this new technology raises profound questions—about who is targeted, and why; about civilian casualties, and the risk of creating new enemies; about the legality of such strikes under U.S. and international law; about accountability and morality. . . . America's actions are legal. We were attacked on 9/11. Within a week, Congress overwhelmingly authorized the use of force. Under domestic law and international law, the United States is at war with al Qaeda, the Taliban, and their associated forces. We are at war with an organization that right now would kill as many Americans as they could if we did not stop them first. So this is a just war—a war waged proportionally, in last resort, and in self-defense. . . . And yet as our fight enters a new phase, America's legitimate claim of self-defense cannot be the end of the discussion. To say a military tactic is legal, or even effective, is not to say it is wise or moral in every instance. For the same human progress that gives us the technology to strike half a world way also demands the discipline to constrain that power—or risk abusing it. That's why over the last four years, my Administration has worked vigorously to establish a framework that governs our use of force against terrorists—insisting upon clear guidelines, oversight and accountability that is now codified in Presidential Policy Guidance that I signed yesterday.[70]

The president's speech was designed to both acknowledge government actions and make the case for their legitimacy in the context of customary law. As such, it was clearly intended to influence audiences both at home and abroad.

Obama maintained that the 2001 AUMF, updated in the 2012 National Defense Authorization Act, gave the executive branch war powers against al Qaeda. War powers include the power to kill, to capture, to detain, to interrogate, to engage in surveillance. He also acknowledged limits and the importance of moderation in the use of force. An editorial observed that Obama's speech "was the most important statement on counterterrorism policy since the 2001 attacks, a momentous turning point in post-9/11 America. For the first time, a president stated clearly and unequivocally that the state of perpetual warfare that began nearly twelve years ago is unsustainable for a democracy and must come to an end in the not-too-distant future."[71]

The White House also released a document in conjunction with the president's speech outlining the counterterrorism policy standards and procedures that were either already in place or would be implemented over time. Among its central tenets was the statement that in counterterrorism, "the policy of the United States is not to use lethal force when it is feasible to capture a terrorist suspect, because capturing a terrorist offers the best opportunity to gather meaningful intelligence and to mitigate and disrupt terrorist plots." Lethal force would be used "only to prevent or stop attacks against U.S. persons, and even then, only when capture is not feasible and no other reasonable alternatives exist to address the threat effectively." The policy statement outlined a number of additional criteria, including that there must be a legal basis for using lethal force and that the target must pose "a continuing, imminent threat to U.S. persons." Critically, the policy document also stressed, "whenever the United States uses force in foreign territories, international legal principles, including respect for sovereignty and the law of armed conflict, impose important constraints on the ability of the United States to act unilaterally— and on the way in which the United States can use force. The United States respects national sovereignty and international law."[72]

Taken together, these statements and policy declarations represented an attempt to shift the norm frame from a reactive stance to a proactive one. A key emphasis in this revision was to change the way the "imminence" of an attack might be defined. A broadened interpretation would provide the necessary condition to justify legitimate and legal preemption by force. Thus, these rules both regulated state behavior by limiting the acceptable use of force and helped to reconstitute state sovereignty by defining the terms of intervention and statehood. Because customary international law suggested that states had the right of self-defense in situations where it was clear the enemy was preparing to attack a country, the Obama administration was pressing its allies to accept a broadened frame of legitimate anticipatory self-defense. U.S. diplomats argued to the international community that given technological advances and the nature of the asymmetric conflict, the use of preemptive drone strikes should be considered legitimate.

The Obama administration had for the first time publicly acknowledged its actions might challenge existing standards and sought to publicly justify its policies in accord with international norms.[73] Some diplomats at the United Nations countered that targeted killing was a form of preemption, and as such would require the authority of the UN Security Council. Critics cited Article 51 of the UN Charter, which required justification of the right of self-defense and notification of military actions to the international community. Some member states saw these stipulations as the foundation of their sovereign right to self-defense. In a high-profile report to the UN Human Rights Council, Philip Alston, the United Nations special representative on extrajudicial executions, warned that the use of armed drones by the United States to kill terrorism suspects threatened to undermine global constraints on the use of military force. He added, "I'm particularly concerned that the United States seems oblivious to this fact when it asserts an ever-expanding entitlement for itself to target individuals across the globe. But this . . . ill-defined license to kill without accountability is not an entitlement which the United States or other states can have without doing grave damage to the rules designed to protect the right to life and prevent extrajudicial executions." The report concluded that a targeted killing outside of an armed conflict "is almost never likely to be legal" and contradicted international law.[74] Diplomats continued to question the broader U.S. interpretation of the legitimacy of preemptive strikes and targeted killings, even as more nations began to develop and use drones in warfare.

Outcome

Many experts contend that U.S. actions in the global war on terrorism norm have effectively redefined standards of self-defense in an age of complex threats and asymmetric warfare. There is some evidence to suggest that a selective (and perhaps illiberal) norm of targeted killing of foreign adversaries has been successfully substituted for traditional standards opposing such actions. Promoted by norm entrepreneurs, including states, some experts conclude that the targeted-killing norm "has been legitimated and rationalized by policy briefs, learned tracts, and media events. Politicians, scholars, and pundits have supported it. And a number of key states have put it into practice."[75]

Evidence for an assessment of successful norm substitution through contestation can be found in evolving standards regarding the legitimacy of these actions as well as bandwagoning behavior. First, government officials maintain that assassination as defined in past international statutes remains a violation of U.S. and international law. But broader framing of the global war on terrorism and government statements defending its drone operations focus on individuals who are *not* protected by traditional statutes. In a global war on terrorism, officials maintain that UAV strikes represent legitimate acts of self-defense and are consistent with international legal standards, international institutions, and regulations. Though few are willing to speak at length about these issues, former U.S. State Department legal advisor Abraham Sofaer has argued that targeted killings are not prohibited by Executive Order 11905 banning assassinations: "killings in self-defense are no more 'assassinations' in international affairs than they are murders when undertaken by our police forces against domestic killers."[76]

Other countries have made similar claims of legitimacy. In the 1990s during the first Intifada, Palestinian human rights activists began claiming that the Israeli Defense Force (IDF) systematically targeted individual leaders of the uprising for assassination, but Israel did not publicly confirm its use of "targeted assassination" until early 2001 during the second Intifada.[77] But in the most important decision, a 2006 case brought by Israeli and Palestinian NGOs, the Supreme Court of Israel generally affirmed the government's and military's assassination and targeted-killing policies.[78] Daniel Reisner of the International Legal Division of Israel's Military Advocate General's Office contends that "international law progresses through violations. We invented the targeted assassination thesis and we had to push it. At first there were protrusions that made it hard to insert easily into the legal moulds. Eight years later it is in the center of the bounds of legitimacy."[79] Meanwhile, the governments of China, Russia, Sri Lanka, and other countries have conducted operations against suspected leaders of terrorism and insurgency. When pressed, these and other governments have used similar arguments to rationalize and promote the practices.

Beyond debates about legitimacy, what we are clearly witnessing are strong patterns of bandwagoning behavior on drones. The global war on terrorism appeared to create a significant opening for states around the world to reframe their actions against insurgency and terrorism as sovereign self-defense. Actions by great and lesser powers alike—from Russia's crackdown on Chechen separatists to the Sri Lankan military's ruthless drive against the Tamil Tigers in 2009 that wiped out its leadership—suggest a newfound attention to the potential "benefits" of selective targeted killing. Israel announced that it was engaging in systematic "targeted assassination" of individual leaders of the Intifada in the 2000s, and the British government grudgingly acknowledged it had used targeted-killing strategies in its war against the Irish Republican Army in Northern Ireland decades earlier.[80]

Today, the world stands on the cusp of a new age of drone development and use. The United States' military and intelligence agencies have greatly expanded their use and development of drones in the past fifteen years. Pentagon spending on UAVs increased more than tenfold from 2000 to 2010 (to $3.3 billion in FY2010).[81] The number of aircraft in the unmanned system category more than tripled between 2011 and 2012.[82] And at least eleven governments were known to possess armed UAVs in 2011, including the United States, Israel, the United Kingdom, China, France, Germany, India, Italy, Iran, Russia, and Turkey.[83] Meanwhile, the number of countries that have acquired UAVs has doubled in the past decade to around seventy-five. With the expansion of capabilities such as different ways of arming drones and miniaturizing technologies, more and more countries are seeing potential civilian and military uses for these systems.[84] As expert Peter Singer concludes, drone technology is here, "and it isn't going away. It will increasingly play a role in our lives. . . . The real question is: How do we deal with it?"[85]

7   The Final Frontier? Weaponizing Space

More than by any other imaginative concept, the mind of man is aroused
by the thought of exploring the mysteries of outer space. Through such
exploration, man hopes to broaden his horizons, add to his knowledge,
improve his way of living on earth.
     —*Dwight D. Eisenhower*[1]

The United States and the international community face a fundamental
choice in the years ahead. That choice is between space assurance or
space weapons. . . . By advancing the peaceful uses of space rather than
weaponizing this realm in previous decades, the United States and other
countries have reaped extraordinary rewards. . . . Among the extraordinary
powers that the United States now enjoys is the power to shape the agenda
for the use of space in the twenty-first century.
     —*Michael Krepon*[2]

THIS CHAPTER EXPLORES HOW SPACE TECHNOLOGY
innovations have emboldened states to seek dominance in a realm
beyond terra firma and to attempt to change the normative architecture to
legitimize their actions. The Cold War "space race" officially began in the
1950s when the Soviet Union launched *Sputnik I* into orbit in October 1957,
and the United States sent its first satellite, *Explorer I*, into space four months
later. Meanwhile, policy-makers, scientists, and military leaders attempted to
head off the potential dangers of weaponization of space through multilateral
diplomacy. The 1967 Treaty on Principles Governing the Activities of States
in the Exploration and Use of Outer Space outlined measures to protect the
region from becoming an "area of international conflict." Subsequent agreements emphasized how space activities should be undertaken in accord with

international law and the Charter of the United Nations, forbade claims of sovereignty on the moon, and banned the introduction of weapons of mass destruction into space. Universality and peaceful uses were critical common denominators in all these agreements.[3]

Today, we are witnessing an evolution of the normative architecture of space in the face of new challenges and opportunities. The number of countries capable of launching weapons or objects into space has grown dramatically, and the types of actors involved have diversified (e.g., private companies and multilateral consortia). New anti-satellite technologies and ballistic missile defense research raise important questions about weaponization of space. Experts also have identified orbital debris as a serious, low-technology threat to space exploration. As more spacefaring nations acknowledge these problems, multilateral negotiations are underway to establish a new international code of conduct for activities in space.

Traditional International Norms: Peaceful Uses and Universal Access

Space technology innovations have impacted several different dimensions of traditional norms. Many policy-makers view outer space as a "common heritage area" or "sanctuary"—a universal resource in need of preservation. Some favor prohibiting deployment of weapons in space and call for peaceful settlement of rival claims over space or celestial bodies. However, others counter that state interests may extend to space, and they view the deployment of defensive weapons systems or satellites as a natural extension of sovereignty.

The principle of freedom of access and navigation through the global commons is grounded in customary and international law as well as agreements formulated through international organizations. For decades, diplomats have endorsed defining some regions as "common heritage" areas that would imbue them with special qualities. On a philosophical level, this characterization accords special protections and ensures equal access for all players. Not only does this protect resources in the global commons, it opens the possibility of joint endeavors such as international scientific programs to advance universal understanding of issues such as biodiversity loss and climate change.[4] Practically speaking, demarcating areas of global commons offers a diplomatic balance between state sovereignty and universalism.

The cases of the world's oceans and Antarctica are illustrative of the types of challenges faced when trying to regulate state behavior in commons areas.[5] Oceans have served as the primary route of international commerce and exchange for centuries. International waters have become superhighways for trade. Modern international law grants ships the right to freedom of navigation of the oceans, as well as "expeditious" passage through territorial waters in certain circumstances.[6] This traditional norm has its roots in the Westphalian system of sovereign states and fundamental tenets of international law.[7] The 1982 United Nations Convention on the Law of the Sea (UNCLOS) underscores legal standards governing international waters, especially the principle of freedom of universal usage. Like space, Antarctica is uninhabited, remote, and a hostile setting for human activity. Antarctica contains vast untapped resources, including nearly 70 percent of the world's fresh water frozen in ice and a surprising array of biodiversity. Great powers arrived at a consensus in the 1950s that Antarctica should be shared by all. The 1959 Antarctic Treaty was the first of what became known as "non-armament" treaties for a commons area. It installed a normative framework of universalism and peaceful purposes for the continent, placing all competing political claims of sovereignty in abeyance and established the continent as a common heritage site for interests, especially international scientific cooperation. Military activities, such as the establishment of military bases or weapons testing, were specifically prohibited.[8]

Experts and policy-makers have championed competing visions for international engagement in outer space. At one end of the spectrum, many believe space should be treated as a global "sanctuary" or commons, with access and potential gains to benefit all players in the global community.[9] Establishing a set of multilateral agreements to promote mutual understanding and outlaw the militarization of space would help balance many different interests and short-circuit the potential for conflict. Conversely, some argue that the only way to protect humanity's engagement in space is to control it.[10] They view outer space as an arena for potential dominance and exploitation. Great powers with the capability to reach space should be allowed to plant the flag there, establish their presence, and reap the rewards associated with their technological prowess.[11]

The development of a normative architecture for space actually began in utilitarian (or realist) terms. The early space race was less a noble, civilian pursuit of common objectives, and more an intense, militarized competition for hegemonic dominance of this new frontier.[12] For example, early research programs on missile and rocket technology development appeared virtually interchangeable in the Soviet Union, and to some degree in the United States as well.[13] Any rocket that was capable of delivering a satellite to space could be modified to launch nuclear warheads. The U.S. government also commissioned studies of satellite and anti-satellite capabilities very early on, with the plan to develop the capability to shoot down enemy satellites at will.[14] In fact, President Kennedy's plan to send a manned mission to the moon only advanced as quickly as it did because the United States had conducted a decade of secret military research on missile technology.

At the same time, world leaders appeared to embrace a normative architecture emphasizing universality and peace. Many governments expressed the view that universality would provide necessary constraints on state behavior. The United Nations offered its good offices for management and conflict resolution in space, including the early formation of the Committee on the Peaceful Uses of Outer Space (COPUOS, founded in 1959), an ad hoc group of concerned states that would help negotiate an outer space regime. This has since become a permanent part of the United Nations, affiliated with the UN's Outer Space Affairs Division, and its membership has grown dramatically. COPUOS is the only formal body empowered to negotiate new international space laws, and decisions in the committee are taken by voting by member states. Space security issues also have been addressed in the UN First Committee and the Conference on Disarmament based in Geneva (established in 1979).

Members of the exclusive club of spacefaring nations came to support international conventions and treaties to establish foundations for a space norm. The 1963 Limited Nuclear Test-Ban Treaty prohibited future testing of nuclear warheads in outer space, in the atmosphere, and underwater. The UN General Assembly passed the 1963 Declaration of Legal Principles Governing the Activities of States in the Exploration and Use of Outer Space, representing a broader, multilateral action designed to create a set of standard behaviors for outer space.[15] The 1967 Treaty on Principles Governing the Activities of States in the Exploration and Use of Outer Space, including the Moon and Other Celestial Bodies was the first official treaty to deal exclusively with outer space.[16] Article III forbids hostile acts in space or engaging "in any such threat in relation to the Earth, Moon, spacecraft, the personnel of spacecraft or manmade space objects." It also prohibits any objects being launched into orbit with nuclear weapons or other forms of weapons of mass destruction, as well as any attempt to establish military bases, installations, and fortifications in space. Later, the Outer Space Treaty was the foundation for other agreements negotiated under the auspices of the UN COPUOS, including the 1968 Agreement on the Rescue and Return of Astronauts and Objects Launched into Outer Space, the 1976 Convention on Registration of Objects Launched into Outer Space, and the 1982 Principles Governing the Use by States of Artificial Earth Satellites for International Direct Television Broadcasting.

Technology Innovations: Filling Up Space

Advances in Rocketry and Satellites

Several different types of space technology innovations—including rockets, satellites, and anti-satellite and missile defense systems—have impacted the development of international norms.[17] Early origins of the science of rocket propulsion included the invention of black powder (later known as gunpowder) in the eighth-century Tang dynasty of China and experiments with rockets in Europe during the Renaissance and the early modern period. In 1650, a Polish artillery expert, Kazimierz Siemienowicz, published a series of drawings for a staged rocket that would allow it to travel longer distances. English scientist Isaac Newton's treatise *Philosophiae Naturalis Principia Mathematica* (1687) described basic physical principles in nature. Newton's laws of motion became the building blocks of advanced physics, engineering, and rocket design.

Advances in the twentieth century made possible the development of much larger rockets that could deliver a satellite into orbit or a warhead to an enemy's capital—making rockets both objects and symbols of great-power competition. Robert Goddard was the leading innovator of rocket technology in the United States during the first half of the twentieth century. He is credited for the invention of a workable liquid-fueled system for rockets as well as a multistage system for rockets to punch through the atmosphere and reach outer space. Goddard's writings also influenced the work of a young scientist in Germany, Wernher von Braun.[18] Von Braun worked for the German army developing ballistic missiles and rockets in the 1930s and later directed the V-2 rocket project at a secret laboratory at Peenemünde, Germany. This rocket was a watershed achievement: a 45-foot-long ballistic missile that could deliver a 2,000 pound warhead to a target up to 500 miles away using a sophisticated guidance system. German forces launched the first V-2 rockets against targets in Belgium, France, and London in the fall of 1944.

World War II and the Cold War became catalysts for advances in rocket design. Goddard was commissioned by the military to return to government work on the development of a liquid-fueled, multistage rocket after Pearl Harbor. During the Allied assault on Germany in 1945, U.S. troops captured launch sites and unused V-2 rockets and equipment. Von Braun himself orchestrated a surrender to the Western Allies for hundreds of his scientists, along with giving up the rockets, components, plans, and test vehicles at their facility. U.S. Operation Paperclip, a clandestine mission at the end of the war, apprehended more than a thousand additional German rocket engineers and scientists to work for the West.[19] In the 1950s, von Braun helped develop the Army's Jupiter ballistic missile and oversaw significant advances in research on multistage rocketry.[20]

The National Aeronautics and Space Act of 1958 formally established the U.S. civilian space program. Among other things, it called for the creation of a new National Aeronautics and Space Administration (NASA). Section 102 of the Space Act outlined the objectives of NASA research, included expanding human knowledge of space, improving space vehicles, studying the benefits of space activities, and making the United States a leader in space science and technology. One of the first successful NASA programs, headed by von Braun and his research team, was development of much larger Saturn rockets for the NASA space program in the 1960s, versions of which were used to send astronauts to the moon. Notably, the Space Act also emphasized that the U.S. approach to space would be "entirely for peaceful purposes for the benefit of mankind" and invited international cooperation through scientific knowledge and discoveries.[21] Research and development of satellites went hand in hand with advances in rocketry. In 1945, the U.S. Navy sponsored the first study of the concept of launching an artificial satellite into orbit to serve as a platform for future operations. From the beginning, satellites were seen to have potential military and civilian applications. A RAND study in May 1946 predicted that satellite innovations "would inflame the imagination of mankind, and would probably produce repercussions comparable to the explosion of the atomic bomb."[22] The National Reconnaissance Office (NRO) was created in 1960 to coordinate space research and remote sensing development, but its activities remain highly classified. In addition to satellite platforms themselves, the science behind orbital trajectories required substantial experimentation. Research helped define several different types of orbits, including low earth orbits (LEO) at altitudes of 500 to 2,000 kilometers above the earth's surface, medium earth orbits (MEO), and geostationary orbits (GSO), at around 36,000 kilometers above the equator.[23]

These advances allowed space to emerge as an important crossroads of both political/military and economic activity. The development of space launch capabilities came to be seen as both a prestigious national achievement that signals a country's technological prowess and power and a potential wealth generator for domestic and international contract launches. The number of countries engaged in (or very interested in) spacefaring has increased dramatically in recent decades. By 2007, a total of fifty-eight countries possessed dedicated civil space programs, forty-four had placed nationally owned satellites into orbit, and nine had achieved domestic space launches.[24] Sectors of these countries' economies also have grown dependent on satellites for productivity and growth, especially global communications and transportation, worth hundreds of billions of dollars.

The types of activities in space also have expanded dramatically. China celebrated its first spacewalk in 2008 and landed its first rover on the moon, the Jade Rabbit, in late 2013. The European Space Agency landed a probe on a comet in 2014 and plans to put a roving robot on the surface of Mars by 2018. India has launched multiple satellites into space on rockets (including a record ten satellites into space on a single rocket in 2008), and in 2014 successfully orbited a satellite around Mars. The Argentine government has been subsidizing growth in its satellite manufacturing sector and searching for foreign direct investment to build a market share in spacecraft subcomponents. Japan and China both have satellites circling the moon, and India and Russia are also working on lunar orbiters. The 17-nation European Space Agency and China are also cooperating on commercial ventures, including a rival to the U.S. space-based Global Positioning System. And plans are in the works for new satellites and spacecraft to carry European, Indian, Chinese, and Russian astronauts to the moon, to make Israel a center for launching "nanosatellites," and for Japan and the Europeans to explore the solar system and beyond with unmanned probes. South Korea, Taiwan, and Brazil have plans to quickly develop their space programs and offer lower-cost space launches.

Commercial activity in space has blossomed in recent decades. In 2014, more than two dozen private aerospace companies around the world focused primarily on launch and support of future human or robotic spaceflights.

Scores of companies and consortia also were developing satellites for launch on a variety of platforms. In 2013 alone there were more than eighty successful satellite launches from sites in locations as diverse as Baikonur, Kazakhstan (with the largest number of launches), Sriharikota, India, and Kourou, French Guiana.[25] Private corporations have not only taken over much of the heavy lifting for commercial and government space operations (such as SpaceX Corporation's contract deliveries of supplies to the International Space Station), they are responsible for the vast majority of technology innovations related to spacefaring today, including designing the infrastructure for future generations of space-based global communications and scientific platforms. U.S. companies such as ITT, Loral Skynet, Hughes Network Systems, and Teledesic have played important roles in developments of communications technology—with the emergence of spread-spectrum communications supported by satellites and high-bandwidth communications.[26] New microsatellites or nanosatellites use miniaturized electronics to serve often singular purposes such as monitoring specific atmospheric conditions or watching for forest fires. Commercial space vehicles are also becoming less expensive to produce and launch, suggesting we may be on the verge of yet another rush to space by high-technology private corporations.

Anti-Satellite and Missile Defense Systems

Another area of space technology—anti-satellite and missile defense systems—has had a profound impact on international political discourse. In fact, nearly as soon as the United States and Soviet Union devised satellite technologies they also began to develop offensive and defensive capabilities for space systems. Both superpowers experimented with satellite technologies that might carry nuclear warheads to be launched at targets from space, an unprecedented first-strike capability that could have destabilized the Cold War balance of power. Because U.S. and Soviet scientists also knew that satellites were fragile (indeed, any attack on a space system could easily damage or destroy it), they also began anti-satellite (ASAT) system research very early on.[27] The U.S. Army conducted an initial ASAT feasibility study in December 1957, just weeks after the launch of *Sputnik*. Research began by the Air Force in 1958 on several related projects, including a nuclear-tipped, air-launched ballistic missile that could be launched from a B-47 bomber to detonate in space to damage or destroy an enemy satellite. The United States also began a program for more serious anti-satellite technology research and development in its Project SAINT (Satellite Interceptor) in which the government explored the potential for locating and damaging other countries' satellites. In the early 1960s, the U.S. Army conducted research for an anti-satellite system using nuclear warheads placed on Nike-Zeuss ground-launched missiles. An Air Force system with a nuclear warhead based on a Thor rocket platform became operational in 1964, based on Johnston Island in the Pacific.

In the 1980s, the Reagan administration's proposed Strategic Defense Initiative, an anti-ballistic-missile shield, boosted interest in anti-satellite systems and other technologies that could be used to target missiles in space. The next generation of anti-satellite weapons would be designed for more accurate strikes against enemy systems and thus could carry a conventional warhead. The Soviet Union experimented with a hunter-killer satellite during the 1980s that was basically a satellite designed to track its target, maneuver close to it, and detonate. The United States developed a variant of this system, called the Miniature Homing Vehicle (MHV), which relied on high-speed direct impact between the interceptor and target. The MHV, a two-stage missile system, could be launched from a steeply climbing F-15 Eagle jet fighter instead of from a ground-based rocket.[28] The Air Force successfully tested the system on several occasions in the 1980s, including a strike on a dying satellite nearly 600 kilometers in orbit.[29] The Soviet Union and Russia also have developed several generations of co-orbital ASAT systems (meaning a satellite-like platform for kinetic killing of its neighbors in orbit).

Stage I: Technology Meets the Traditional Norm

Space technology and politics have always been intertwined. President Eisenhower adopted a dual-track strategy toward space. First, the United States would practice what expert Clay Moltz has called "cooperative restraint" in space endeavors.[30] U.S. officials promised that "future developments in outer space would be directed exclusively to peaceful purposes and scientific purposes" such as arms control, scientific research, and monitoring.[31] Advocacy of space openness was considered to have no real downside for the United States at the time. Expert Joanne Irene Gabrynowicz points out that because there was effectively a "legal void" related to normative constraints on activity in outer space in this era, early U.S. space laws represented small political and legal steps toward regime formation. While some countries followed suit, others such as France and Japan did not even develop and pass national space laws until the late 2000s.[32]

Technological achievements played into the broader narrative of openness and exploration. Neil Armstrong's first step on the moon in 1969 was purposefully framed as a "giant leap for mankind," even though it was primarily a success for the United States. Officials knew that their support for universal access to space and international norms provided the necessary foundations for a U.S. approach that would allow it to gain strategic advantages. A RAND study from the period actually coached the government to emphasize the scientific purpose of satellites and to establish a norm of free movement in space as a road to ensure U.S. security in the long run. The study argued, "Because of the political implications of the satellite instrument, it is of prime importance what we *say* about it, in addition to what we *do* with it."[33]

Indeed, U.S. leaders appeared determined to lay the cornerstones of a new normative architecture that would also serve national interests. The government secretly pursued a second-track strategy of research and development of space technology that might help it achieve dominance. In 1958, a classified National Security Council study of U.S. and Soviet space capabilities reached troubling conclusions: the United States was quickly falling behind the Soviet Union in nearly every category of space technology and programs, including developmental technologies for space stations and moon landings.[34] Cabinet officials and members of Congress pushed for new activities that would help ensure a position for the United States in space. The Department of Defense even tried to wrest control of space research and technologies away from NASA in the late 1950s, arguing that it had a proven track record of success with rockets and could more quickly advance strategic interests in space.

U.S. leaders maintained the dual-track approach to space in the 1960s, but President Kennedy famously upped the ante in the space race when he announced plans to send a manned mission to the moon by the end of the decade. The White House also championed the 1962 Commercial Communications Satellite Act (also known as the Comsat Act) to promote and develop space-based telecommunications programs. The Johnson administration helped negotiate the Outer Space Treaty of 1967, banning weapons of mass destruction and military installations in space. This did not end government consideration of other possibilities for gaining dominance in space, though. For example, the State Department's Policy Planning Council advised developing, but not deploying, ground-based anti-satellite systems to ensure that U.S. platforms could continue to operate effectively. Again, the goal was not to provoke strong responses from the Soviet Union and to stay within emerging normative boundaries.[35]

Stage II: Redefinition

The Outer Space Treaty (OST) characterized space as the "province of all"—an arena free for exploration. Space would not be "subject to national appropriation by claim of sovereignty, by means of use or occupation, or by any other means."[36] However, while the United States signed and ratified the OST, at least two presidents in recent history signaled a willingness to push existing normative boundaries and pursue outright dominance in space. Reagan's Strategic Defense Initiative (SDI) program in the 1980s effectively called for weaponization in space as a means to establish a defensive shield against incoming ballistic missiles. And, in the early 2000s, the George W. Bush administration took steps toward space dominance, including withdrawal from the 1972 Anti-Ballistic Missile Treaty (ABM Treaty) and increased funding for research and development of new ballistic missile defense systems. Many have characterized the actions of the Reagan and Bush administrations as shifting the U.S. emphasis toward weaponization and modernization of space assets designed to gain strategic advantage—devoting greater resources to the second track of the dual-track strategy toward space security.[37] Instead of deference to multilateral restrictions and exhibiting unilateral restraint, the Reagan and George W. Bush administrations seemed intent on focusing on space weapons and missile defense.

SDI and Norm Redefinition

On March 23, 1983, Reagan gave a nationally televised address in which he outlined his vision for the Strategic Defense Initiative, a new space-based defense shield against Soviet intercontinental ballistic missiles (ICBMs). The lofty goal of this new research and development program, Reagan claimed, was to make Soviet ICBMs "impotent and obsolete" by creating a shield that would employ cutting-edge technologies. The major themes of President Reagan's SDI speech reflected broader administration claims at the time that the United States could fight and win a nuclear war. The vision was to establish a tiered defensive network. A first layer of sensors would be deployed to detect incoming Soviet nuclear missile attacks. These would be based on the ground, in the air, and in space, and they would use radar, optical, and infrared threat-detection systems. The military would conduct additional research and development on new ultraviolet, laser, and radar sensor technologies. Once threats were detected, space- and earth-based battle stations could be employed to intercept Soviet ICBMs and independently targeted reentry vehicles with nuclear warheads. These stations might be equipped with kinetic-kill weapons or laser weapons.[38] A final layer of defense would involve kinetic-kill space-based platforms and ground-based defensive missiles clustered around high value U.S. targets. These systems would be designed to intercept missiles in one of three flight stages (boost, midcourse, and terminal).[39]

The plan for SDI clearly counted on advancements in enhanced/directed-energy weapons (lasers), including some that were still on the drawing board. Invented in the 1950s, lasers produce focused beams of electromagnetic radiation in the visible (light), ultraviolet, or X-ray regions of the spectrum. When an object is hit by a laser, its atoms or molecules may become excited by the energy and alter their form in a way that damages or destroys it. Scientists have found that the most effective lasers are strong beams that are concentrated on their targets, and some systems employ large mirrors to achieve maximum effect.[40] The U.S. military began experiments with rudimentary lasers in the 1960s.[41] As research continued in the 1990s, scientists found that beams of directed energy (such as microwaves or chemical lasers, or even columns of subatomic particles) might damage or kill enemy satellites. Advanced technology allows accurate tracking to help directed-energy lasers to strike, and lasers could burn through a satellite's circuits to kill it. Lasers offered speed and accuracy, as well as graduated levels of strike that could be used to temporarily disable systems or kill them altogether. Later the military developed the MIRACL system (Mid-Infrared Advanced Chemical Laser), a free-electron laser powered by a particle accelerator, which produces an extremely high-intensity beam of light.[42] The U.S. Air Force also conducted research on a next-generation ground-based jamming capability called the Counter Satellite Communication system.[43]

Reagan's SDI announcement implied that the United States was prepared to take actions that would challenge the integrity of the existing OST and the ABM treaties. The president and his advisors tried to deflect the issue at the time by claiming research plans would be "consistent with our obligations in the ABM Treaty," but SDI blueprints called for deployment of anti-ballistic missile systems on the ground and in space.[44] The Reagan administration also undertook significant efforts to try to build congressional support for SDI.

The president's vision was compelling to many: the creation of a defensive system that would protect the American people from harm, yet not offend other countries' sense of security. One analysis of Reagan's pitch described it as "skillfully structured to appeal first to fear and then to hope, to the wish for protection and invulnerability and the American feeling that technology is the nation's forte and space its destiny."[45] While the president enjoyed a burst of early support for the program on Capitol Hill, a number of factors conspired to limit Congress's support for SDI over time. Critics on the political left questioned the feasibility of the program as well as its potential unintended consequences in destabilizing the superpower balance. Eventually, the funding of key elements of SDI came under fire. For example, from 1985 to 1988, Congress statutorily prohibited the development of microsatellites or tests against other target satellites in space. Congress likewise barred the testing of the MIRACL laser against any object in space from 1991 to 1995. Critics charged there were really few differences, primarily limited to computer software and control algorithms, between ballistic missile defense systems and hit-to-kill ASAT capabilities.

George W. Bush and Ballistic Missile Defense

Officials in the George W. Bush administration were determined to change the tone and direction of space policy in the twenty-first century. A critical figure in this transformation was Secretary of Defense Donald Rumsfeld, who as a civilian had led the Commission to Assess U.S. National Security Space Management and Organization (hereafter referred to as the Rumsfeld Commission). The Rumsfeld Commission report recommended the government focus on coordination of all U.S. interests in space, be they commercial, civil, defense or intelligence. To avoid the possibility of a "space Pearl Harbor," the commission recommended a reinvigoration of U.S. programs to deploy both defensive and offensive weapons in space.[46] The goal of development of these systems, from ground stations to satellites, would be to deter and defend against hostile acts on U.S. interests in space. The report also identified Russia and China as the countries most likely to pose a threat to U.S. interests in space by developing microsatellites and space radio-frequency jamming capabilities that could be used to attack and disable U.S. command, control, and intelligence systems.

The Bush administration subsequently pursued several major, new space policy initiatives. First, President Bush announced the United States would

withdraw from the 1972 ABM Treaty. Administration officials saw that existing limits on its activity related to space might hinder its plan for innovative
new programs. Bush said, "The 1972 ABM Treaty was signed by the United
States and the Soviet Union at a much different time, in a vastly different
world." To address new challenges, he declared, "we must have the freedom
and the flexibility to develop effective defenses against those attacks. . . . I cannot and will not allow the United States to remain in a treaty that prevents us
from developing effective defenses."[47] Thus, the president sought to emphasize
the changing threat environment as justification for a redefined U.S. posture
toward this agreement. A new program of research and development would
build defenses against missile attacks from any adversary, be they great powers, rogue states, or terror groups. Any new theater or regional ballistic missile defense system would likely require sophisticated space-based technology
sensors for defense, monitoring, and command and control.

Next, the president announced the deployment of a national missile
defense (NMD) system by the end of 2004. Bush fast-tracked the program
by issuing an executive order that exempted the Missile Defense Agency
(MDA) from Department of Defense development, testing, and reporting
requirements. The government poured an estimated $15 billion into a "spiral
development" approach under which systems would be deployed long before
they were adequately flight tested. The result was profound: within several
years the United States had deployed five Ground-Based Midcourse (GMD)
national missile defense system interceptors (known as ground-based interceptors, or GBIs) in silos at Fort Greely, Alaska, with a plan to deploy up to
thirty systems in Alaska and California soon thereafter. These GBIs enabled
midcourse engagement of intermediate- and intercontinental-range ballistic missiles from launches in Eurasia. Notably, the Bush administration also
began planning for a missile defense program using a modified version of the
GMD interceptor to be deployed in Eastern Europe to intercept ballistic missiles launched from the Middle East.

The administration also proceeded apace with other recommendations
from the Rumsfeld Commission report. Bush administration Presidential
Directive NSC-49 set the tone for a greater commitment to space technology
and capabilities. It called for strengthening U.S. space leadership through
enhanced capabilities and "unhindered U.S. operations" in space as an
extension of national security and homeland security interests. Administration officials also issued rhetorical support for a more assertive posture that

included a drive for dominance in space. Officials at the Pentagon advocated pursuing a strategy of "space control" that includes war-fighting "in, from and through space."[48] General Lance Lord, commander of the U.S. Air Force Space Command, stated, "Space superiority is our imperative—it requires the same sense of urgency that we place on gaining and maintaining air superiority over enemy air space in times of conflict."[49] The Space Command's strategic master plan called for a strong position on space, arguing "we cannot fully exploit space until we control it."[50] In a 2004 U.S. Air Force Counterspace Operations document, officials asserted that "space superiority provides freedom to attack as well as freedom from attack."[51] Ultimately, the goal of space security—the "freedom *to* attack as well as freedom *from* attack"—provided a powerful lens for defining a more forward leaning, assertive space posture. Notably, the 2006 space policy explicitly rejected "the development of new legal regimes or other restrictions that seek to prohibit or limit US access to or use of space . . . to conduct research, development, testing, and operations or other activities in space for U.S. national interests."[52]

Finally, the Bush administration also pursued a redefinition of its stance on the normative architecture for space by working closely with Congress and commercial interests. In the early 2000s Congress appeared fairly amenable to some of the proposed changes in space policy in the wake of the 9/11 attacks. Concerns about a potential "space Pearl Harbor" resonated with members of Congress in a new way. What emerged were new debates about interpretation of standing normative commitments and foreign policy priorities. Indeed, administration officials and legislators viewed space as the intersection of numerous complementary interests, and seemed willing to devote resources to this potentially lucrative area. The government now had in place a bureaucratic structure dedicated to missile defense and space-based weapons, including the Missile Defense Agency (MDA), the Air Force Space Command, the Defense Advanced Research Projects Agency (DARPA), and the Army Space and Missile Defense Command. As expert Rex Wingerter put it, missile defense in the early twenty-first century had become "firmly embedded in the political economy of US defense policy and planning." He added, "Despite serious doubt about the effectiveness of missile defense and the technical feasibility of space-based weapons," the United States spent tens of billons of dollars on their research and development.[53]

Stage III: Constructive Norm Substitution

The Obama administration ushered in a sea change in U.S. support for multi-lateral steps to strengthen and modify the international space norm by creating a new international code of conduct for spacefaring nations. This section tells the story of a near reversal in U.S. policies and changes in the multilateral architecture as a function of both high-tech innovations (including the commercialization of satellites in the information age and new anti-satellite system testing) and low-tech challenges (the growing problem of space debris). The end result, a significant burst of diplomacy on more creative forms of multilateral cooperation on space, suggests a level of progress that would have been difficult to predict just a decade ago.

Commoditization and Commercialization of Space

As noted above, space emerged as an important crossroads of economic and political competition in the twenty-first century. Driven by the market imperative, political competition, and a desire for prestige, more countries have developed their own space operations. By 2014, fifteen states plus the European Space Agency consortium had launch capability and nearly sixty countries possessed dedicated civil space programs.[54] Two dozen private aerospace companies around the world also were focused on launch and support of future human or robotic spaceflights. Scores of companies and consortia have developed satellites for launch on a variety of platforms. In 2013 alone there were more than eighty successful satellite launches, from diverse locations around the world. Notably, private corporations have taken over much of the heavy lifting for commercial and government space operations as well as technology innovations related to spacefaring. These companies are designing the infrastructure for future generations of space-based activities, including global communications, scientific projects, spread-spectrum and high-bandwidth communications supported by satellites, and a new generation of nanosatellites for Earth observation.

Space Debris: High-Tech Advances Create a Low-Tech Crisis

Today, there are more than a thousand active satellites in orbit around Earth. Nearly half are in low earth orbit (LEO, orbiting between 200 and 2,000 kilometers in altitude); another four hundred active satellites are in geosynchronous earth orbit (GEO), approximately 36,000 kilometers above the Equator.[55] Only in recent years, though, has the challenge of space debris (also known as space junk) in orbit come to be recognized as a major challenge to commercial and national security interests. Space debris is primarily a man-made phenomenon. This includes thousands of dead satellites, along with spent rocket booster stages, solid rocket motor waste, and fragments of spacecraft and detritus related to human activity in space. In 2012, the U.S. Space Command reported tracking more than 20,000 pieces of human-generated debris in earth orbit that were larger than ten centimeters. Any of these pieces of debris could destroy a satellite in a collision. Experts estimate there are hundreds of thousands of additional objects between one and ten centimeters in diameter, and millions more smaller particles that could damage satellites or interfere with human exploration in space. These objects travel at an average speed of 18,000 miles per hour, giving even small pieces of debris incredible kinetic force. Furthermore, the vast majority (some 75 percent) of these debris fields reside in LEO, where there is the most activity in space.

Experts believe space debris represents "among the most underappreciated global commons challenges facing the world" today.[56] They are especially concerned about the potential for a catastrophic series of collisions that would spawn more and more debris, something known as the Kessler syndrome. A study by the National Research Council in 2011 estimated that portions of the space debris environment had already reached this tipping point, with enough material in orbit that it might set off a chain reaction of collisions that would damage or destroy private and government-owned satellites. A 2014 report for the Council on Foreign Relations argued that "the United States has strategic interests in preventing and mitigating dangerous space incidents, given its high reliance on satellites for a variety of national security missions and unparalleled global security commitments and responsibilities."[57] Intentional threats could be kinetic actions in space or more basic (and more achievable) ground-based jamming. Additionally, problems could emerge with direct ascent or co-orbiting anti-satellite tests, an electromagnetic pulse in space, or intentional or unintentional collisions that create a long-term problem of orbital space debris.

Actions and Reactions: ASAT Tests and Satellite Collisions

Several events heightened international concern and awareness of the debris threat. In January 2007, the Chinese military launched a missile from a ground installation near the Xichang Space Center that hit and destroyed one of its own aging weather satellites in orbit more than 500 miles above the earth. China proved it could use a kinetic-kill system in space to destroy a satellite at roughly the same altitude of U.S. spy satellites and missile defense systems.[58] Expert Victoria Samson called this "a 'wake up call' for the U.S. military posture." She added, "basically, the new technologies that China demonstrated and their lack of transparency meant that the U.S. military believed they had to look at the worst case scenario" in these circumstances.[59] Not only did the test show new capabilities, the destruction of the satellite caused a major debris field that threatened long-term security of orbital vehicles. It created 40,000 pieces of debris larger than one centimeter in diameter, and some 3,000 pieces were larger than ten centimeters in diameter. According to the U.S. military's Space Surveillance Network (SSN), this was the largest debris cloud ever generated by a single event in orbit—and in an area that was heavily trafficked by satellites used for mapping, meteorological, surveillance, remote sensing and communications.

Western reactions to the test were swift: critics charged that China's actions had broken a 25-year-old taboo on testing of anti-satellite (ASAT) weapons. Publicly, the White House issued a measured statement, saying that the Chinese development and testing of anti-satellite weapons was "inconsistent with the spirit of cooperation that both countries aspire to in the civil space area."[60] But privately, according to public documents and embassy cables published by WikiLeaks, the administration's response was much more forceful. Fearing the start of a secret space war, Secretary of State Condoleezza Rice sent a communiqué to her Chinese counterpart, warning, "Any purposeful interference with US space systems will be interpreted by the United States as an infringement of its rights and considered an escalation in a crisis or conflict. The United States reserves the right, consistent with the UN Charter and international law, to defend and protect its space systems with a wide range of options, from diplomatic to military."[61] In congressional testimony, Secretary of the Air Force Michael Wynne characterized the development as "seismic in nature." He said the Chinese test showed quite simply that "space is no longer a sanctuary."[62] Expert Michael Krepon concluded that "the Chinese were telling the Pentagon that they don't own space. We can play this game, too, and we can play it dirtier than you."[63]

In February 2008, the United States military launched Operation Burnt Frost to shoot down an NRO reconnaissance satellite known as *USA-193*. The Pentagon claimed the satellite was slowly falling out of orbit and should be destroyed so that it would present no threat to civilians on the ground.[64] An operation to destroy the satellite in orbit—at the lowest altitude possible to mitigate the debris cloud—was conceived by the Pentagon and carried out by the USS *Lake Erie*, an Aegis-class destroyer using an SM-3 missile.[65] Officials stressed that the action was taken in the interest of the environment and human safety, was conducted in low orbit to reduce the debris field, and would not violate international law. The U.S. government notified international bodies about the pending strike, including statements to the Conference on Disarmament (CD) and the COPUOS in February 2008.[66] Admiral Timothy J. Keating, commander of the U.S. Pacific Command, said that he believed the way the United States handled the shoot-down of the satellite would offer "a model of the transparency [which] encourages other countries more secretive about their military operations to adopt."[67]

A catastrophic episode in space in February 2009, just a month into the Obama presidency, also heightened concerns: two satellites, an American *Iridium 33* (a minimally operational platform) and a Russian *Cosmos 2251* (a dead satellite) collided in space, creating around two thousand pieces of new debris in a very congested region. As a result, the Obama administration ordered increased screening of active satellite orbits and an expanded warning program for the potential for collisions. U.S. Strategic Command also increased its information-sharing program to promote greater awareness and potentially avoid future collisions.[68] Ultimately, Krepon said that China's test had "a propulsive effect on norm building" and the 2009 collision could demonstrate that "a very low technology type of challenge might be the unifier that moves countries to change the rules."[69]

Space Policy and Multilateral Constructive Norm Substitution in the Obama Administration

The Obama administration appeared to engage in constructive norm substitution by attempting to modify the traditional architecture to address the challenges of space debris. In June 2010, the White House unveiled its new National Space Policy. Rather than focusing on military issues and national interests in space, as had been the case in the prior Bush-era NSP, the Obama administration statement emphasized international outreach and the need to develop common norms "to promote safe and responsible space operations."[70] Specifically, the new NSP emphasized the problem of space debris, noting that decades of space activity had "littered Earth's orbit with debris; and as the world's space-faring nations continue to increase activities in

space, the chance for a collision increases correspondingly." The policy statement declared that "all nations have the right to use and explore space, but
with this right also comes responsibility. The United States, therefore, calls
on all nations to work together to adopt approaches for responsible activity in
space to preserve this right for the benefit of future generations."[71] The Obama
administration thus embraced the potential for negotiation of new regime
components so long as they were "equitable, effectively verifiable, and would
enhance the national security of the United States."[72] It also pledged to expand
its work "in the United Nations and with other organizations to address the
growing problem of orbital debris and to promote 'best practices' for its sustainable use."[73]

After years of deadlock in the UN Conference on Disarmament, diplomats
attending the spring 2009 meetings were heartened by a new level of openness
to negotiations on the part of the Obama administration. The United States
withdrew its opposition to discussions of space security and found common
ground with China on matters of space security and nonproliferation. And
in the UN First Committee, the Obama administration changed policies for
the United States to vote "abstain" instead of oppose the resolution on the
Prevention of an Arms Race in Outer Space (PAROS) in the fall of 2009. U.S.
diplomats also engaged with Russia and China in 2009 on the question of the
Sino-Russian draft treaty on the Prevention of the Placement of Weapons in
Outer Space (PPWT). The two countries issued a formal response to clarify
the proposal's intended meaning, writing in response to the 2008 letter outlining Washington's objections to the treaty. While the United States, Russia, and China continued to disagree about the possibility of achieving such a
treaty, there were many reasons for optimism in negotiations.

The International Code of Conduct

The concept of a new international code of conduct for space began as
response by nongovernmental organizations and concerned nations to perceived challenges of U.S. policies in the George W. Bush years. NGOs, including the Stimson Center in Washington, were concerned by the implications
of the Bush administration's decision to withdraw from the Anti-Ballistic
Missile Treaty (ABM Treaty), as well as the unwillingness of the U.S. government to engage in any diplomatic negotiations in multilateral forums that
could reduce its freedom of action in space. Advocates believed a code of conduct could promote a new set of norms and standards for the modern era of

space technology. In the fall of 2007, the Portuguese EU presidency prepared the first version of a draft code of conduct, later updated by the Slovenian EU presidency into "Best Practice Guidelines for/Code of Conduct on Outer Space Activities." By the summer of 2008, the EU hosted a first round of informal consultations with key spacefaring nations, including the United States, China, and Russia. In December 2008 the EU released its first official draft code of conduct, and subsequently promoted the draft Space Code of Conduct through conferences in 2008, 2010, 2012, and 2013.[74] In each round of draft development, the EU invited a broader set of participants, ranging from Brazil and Indonesia to South Africa and Ukraine.

The United States' diplomatic position on the code appeared to shift from resistance to reluctance to a broad embrace in the same period. In January 2012, Secretary of State Clinton publicly announced U.S. readiness to engage in diplomacy and even promote the code. She stated, "The long-term sustainability of our space environment is at serious risk from space debris and irresponsible actors. Ensuring the stability, safety, and security of our space systems is of vital interest to the United States and the global community."[75] A more focused period of negotiations on a code began in June 2012 when EU diplomats introduced a significantly revised draft at the UN COPUOS in Vienna and with the establishment of a UN Group of Government Experts (GGE) on Outer Space Transparency and Confidence Building Measures in 2013. According to Deputy Assistant Secretary of State Frank Rose, the United States favored "expanding international cooperation and collaboration. Such opportunities include cooperation to mitigate orbital debris, share space situational awareness information, improve information sharing for collision avoidance, and develop transparency and confidence building measures." The United States also joined a UN COPUOS multiyear study of long-term sustainability in space, which Rose termed "a valuable opportunity for cooperation with established and emerging space actors and with the private sector to establish a set of 'best practice' guidelines that will enhance space flight safety."[76] In another forum, Rose called the development of a non-legally binding code of conduct "an effective, pragmatic, and timely way of strengthening the long-term sustainability, stability, safety and security of the space environment."[77] Critically, the United States also supported creation of a GGE on Outer Space Transparency and Confidence Building Measures, set up by UN General Assembly Resolution 65/68 and U.S. representatives participated actively in group deliberations. In 2013, the GGE released a report by consensus, calling for negotiations on a new round of confidence-building measures, debris mitigation, and initiatives to promote space situational awareness.[78] At this writing, experts predict that a new draft international code of conduct will likely emerge to define responses to contemporary challenges in space.

Outcome

This case presents highlights from nearly a century of historical advancement in humanity's reach for the stars and demonstrates how technological innovations have fostered legal and political debates over norms. Normative changes would not have occurred without technological advancements in this case given, of course, that space represented an entirely new region for cooperation and conflict. At the same time, activities in space—and the hazards they have come to present—fuel substantial political dialogues about regulations and codes of conduct.

Evidence suggests that U.S. attempts at norm substitution remain contested, though there appear to be evolving standards of legitimacy (such as the draft code of conduct) as well as bandwagoning behavior. Historically, two, contending perspectives seemed to dominate the discourse on space. One camp saw space as a region for cooperation and exploration that might benefit all. Proponents hailed the advent of telecommunications satellites and scientific advancements made as an offshoot of space exploration that could benefit all. Another group viewed space as a new littoral region for competition, where advances in missile and satellite technologies yield progress and advantage for some states rather than others. These different perspectives played out in decades of international negotiations on cooperation in outer space. But today the evidence suggests that the two camps of the past may be merging as the comparatively low-technology problem of space debris actually has brought great powers closer to cooperation on a new multilateral code. Those who view space as a region for universal access and appropriate behavior see benefits in the code as an outcome that would extend the principles of the existing regime in important ways. Those who propose seeking advantages in spacefaring would appear to be satisfied with a voluntary code that would help reduce (or at least attempt to manage) the threat of space debris. Cooperative measures for debris mitigation would, in other words, help clear the way for any future foray into new space-based ballistic missile defense systems or other innovations. These negotiations may yield cooperation on establishment of a new, legitimate international code that many states are likely to support.

8 Conclusion

Laws and institutions must go hand in hand with the progress of the human mind. As that becomes more developed, more enlightened, as new discoveries made, new truths discovered and manners and opinions change, with the change of circumstances, institutions must advance also to keep pace with the times.
—Thomas Jefferson[1]

It has been our willingness to work through multilateral channels that kept the world on our side. . . . You see, American influence is always stronger when we lead by example. We can't exempt ourselves from the rules that apply to everybody else. . . . [What] makes us exceptional is not our ability to flout international norms and the rule of law; it is our willingness to affirm them through our actions.
—Barack Obama[2]

THIS STUDY HAS EXAMINED THE EVOLUTION OF INTERnational norms in the face of technology innovations. From atomic fission and uranium enrichment to drones and space exploration, U.S. leaders often have seemed optimistic that new technologies can promote peace and prosperity. In many cases, though, they have also come to recognize heavy responsibilities associated with their development at home and abroad. This study has articulated a top-down pathway of norm change that infuses greater agency into the constructivist model. It has demonstrated that political debates over technological innovations have shaped the evolution of norms. Leaders sometimes practice norm redefinition and substitution through contestation to foster new cognitive frames and promote new ways of regulating state behavior in multilateral settings. Significant developments may occur beyond the final stage of the traditional norm life-cycle model.

Just how successful have agents been in their attempts to evolve standards of legitimacy and behavior in norm changes? This study suggests mixed results. Leaders do recognize technology innovations as having political implications. They often have sought to redefine U.S. commitments to traditional normative architectures and attempted to change international laws and agreements on the legitimacy of the use of new weapons systems. In some instances, such as the development of the discriminatory nonproliferation regime and targeted killing of foreign adversaries by unmanned aerial vehicles, U.S. leaders have successfully established new norm frames that have gained legitimacy and support from a critical mass of other states. However, in other cases, such as attempts to regulate sensitive nuclear technology exports or develop an international code of conduct for outer space, scientific innovations and policy changes have fostered contestation of the norm. At least one case study—the responsibility to protect—presents confounding results: major technological advances have allowed the world to "see and know" about mass violence, but they appear not to have fostered widespread legitimacy of intervention or bandwagoning behavior in humanitarian operations.

One goal of this study has been to address some of the most controversial new developments in military technologies and embed them in international relations theory—to analyze evolving social practice in norm contestation. Technological advancements have been particularly salient among the factors that may foster leaders' perceptions of gaps between general rules and state interests. This study also echoes Geoffrey Herrera's work on the relationship between technological advancements, political change, and system transformation, where institutions and social practices related to legitimacy remain critical.[3] Technological innovations and competitiveness may foster a much greater role for agency in norm discourse than allowed for by traditional constructivism.

Another goal of this study has been to use a critical constructivist lens to analyze the behavior of champions of international norms. Great powers like the United States may claim the mantel of norm leadership, but they also sometimes act as agents for norm change through contestation. Their stewardship has had a marked impact on norm evolution over time. For example, when President George W. Bush announced his intention to require nuclear client states to renounce uranium enrichment and reprocessing in exchange for trade in technology and materials, he sought to "strengthen" the norm in a way that his administration saw fit. Later, President Obama pledged moderation in space policy and supported negotiations on an international code of conduct for spacefaring. Taken together, the evidence of shifting winds in U.S. leadership suggests the need to revisit the dominant historical narrative. Far from exhibiting what first-wave constructivists would describe as a stabilized, internalized normative structure that is mutually constitutive—where norms become de facto and de jure constraints on state behavior—something very different appears to be occurring.

In sum, this study has demonstrated the fragility of international norms through circumstances of attempted norm change by great powers. It has explored how technology innovations can alter the political landscape by catalyzing norm change. Technology may highlight dissonant strands of norms (e.g., nuclear technology sharing versus preventing weapons proliferation) or dissonance between norms (e.g., absolute sovereignty versus prevention of ethnic cleansing and genocide). The result is a complex political process of contestation and norm evolution.

Empirical Results

Technological innovations appear to have caused leaders to consider changes in the international normative architecture and to pursue redefinition and constructive norm substitution in all five cases in this study. However, the evidence on outcomes is mixed. As illustrated in Table 8.1, there were at least two instances where norm change appeared successful, yielding shifts in both legitimacy and bandwagoning behavior. These cases show how technological advances magnified the potential for leaders to pursue new norms by changing dynamics for actors and circumstances.

Both the establishment of the discriminatory nuclear nonproliferation norm and the use of drones for targeted killings appear to be cases of successful norm substitution. In the post–World War II era, the United States led the international community in redefining what it meant to have this incredibly powerful new weapon. It successfully established legitimacy for its development and possession, and even managed to gain international endorsement of the value of nuclear deterrence. During the decades after World War II, U.S. leaders helped revise great-power approaches to the technology, establishing a nonproliferation regime with separate categories and rules for nuclear weapon

Table 8.1   Case Study Outcomes

Traditional norm	Technology innovation	Potential norm change	Outcome
Prohibition against weapons of mass destruction	Atomic fission, the atom bomb	Development of discriminatory nonproliferation norm (NPT)	Successful norm change
Peaceful uses of nuclear energy	Uranium enrichment and reprocessing technologies	Convention banning sensitive technology transfers	Contested norm development
Sovereignty and non-intervention	Satellite imagery, government and NGO monitoring	Humanitarian intervention and the responsibility to protect	Contested norm development
Norm against assassination of foreign adversaries	Unmanned aerial vehicles and drone strikes	Revising the doctrine of self-defense through preemption and counter-terrorism	Successful norm change
Prohibition on militarization of outer space	Lasers and kinetic-kill vehicles	Development of discriminatory norm against space-based missile defenses and ASAT technologies	Contested norm development

states and non-nuclear-weapon states. More recently, the development of an assassination/targeted-killing norm for use of advanced weaponry against foreign adversaries represents a successful change in international norms and is likely to have profound repercussions for global politics. This norm evolution challenges traditional foundations of sovereignty and the protection of noncombatants by shifting norm frames to focus on preemptive strikes for sovereign self-defense coupled with discretionary tactics and limits on the use of drones. Today, scores of countries are developing drone programs and experimentation is underway with next-generation technologies including stealth, jet-powered unmanned vehicles, and even autonomous hunter-killer robotic systems. In this case, the hegemonic leader in technology innovation appears to have successfully established an alternative frame that has legitimized targeted killing in some circumstances.

The three remaining case studies in this project illustrate contested outcomes. The United States achieved technological innovations and leaders perceived techno-normative dilemmas which they sought to address. They pushed for redefinition of U.S. commitments to norms and began to lobby the international community for shifting legal and political frameworks. However, the outcome in these cases reflects either a lack of established new legitimacy and the imprimatur of international institutions for implementation of the new technology or a lack of bandwagoning behavior. The United States may have changed its policies and pushed the international community to renegotiate norms, but many countries simply have not followed suit.

The case of U.S. attempts to ban new countries from developing uranium enrichment and reprocessing technology illustrates the dynamics of contestation. The foundations of this debate can clearly be seen in the development of the broader, discriminatory nonproliferation framework in the NPT and its associated agreements. When this normative framework failed to prevent the proliferation of sensitive nuclear technologies, the George W. Bush administration lobbied its fellow member states of the Nuclear Suppliers Group to demand a comprehensive ban on enrichment and reprocessing, but it failed to achieve a universal standard. The result has been a complicated diplomatic situation in which many recognize the legitimacy of restricting technology transfers, but limits have not been imposed in law nor manifested in bandwagoning behavior.

Discussion

Why Do States Violate Traditional Norm Frames?

If norms are truly regulative and constitutive, as most first-generation constructivists maintain, why would states ever consider violating them? This study has shown that leaders consider challenging normative standards in light of technology innovations on a regular basis. Technology advances raise dialectics that may allow great powers to transcend traditional normative boundaries. Leaders contemplate violating traditional norm frames with an eye toward changing international commitments to legitimize new behaviors. In other words, consistent with agentic constructivism, this study has identified circumstances in which great-power leaders have come to consider the redefinition of state commitments to norms and the search for the construction of a new norm frame. It is also notable that while endogenous technology advancement was underway, some of these innovations were undertaken (or sped up) in the face of exogenous challenges such as the spread of nuclear weapons or great-power rivalry.

Evidence from this study appears to confirm second-generation critical theory arguments that norms may not be as regulative and constitutive as traditional approaches suggest. Rather than unconditionally adhering to normative strictures, leaders consider potential state stances in light of new opportunities or constraints. Norm contestation, it seems, is alive and well, and hegemons sometimes seem to have advantages in pushing for new norm frames. As noted in Chapter 2, this challenges first-generation constructivist models of internalization in several ways. First and foremost, these results suggest leaders exhibit various levels of commitments to international norms or demonstrate variable internalization. For example, when faced with the opportunity to help define a new nonproliferation order upon the invention of nuclear weapons in the 1940s, 1950s, and 1960s, U.S. leaders determined that reinforcing past, universal prohibitionary frameworks would be unacceptable. Through discourses on norm redefinition, those who preferred the U.S. seek advantages by maintaining access to the weapons won out over those who did not.

Similar discourses have occurred in other issue areas, such as the emerging responsibility-to-protect norm frame. Here, the evidence suggests few constitutive or regulatory limits in relation to the traditional norms of sovereignty and nonintervention. Rather, from the Balkans crises of the 1990s to the present, U.S. officials have said they believe there is a new responsibility to protect civilian populations from mass violence, including ethnic cleansing and genocide. In recent years, the discourse has been further enlivened (or complicated, depending on one's perspective) by the presence of non-state actors who are also employing technology to aid them in their cause. Nongovernmental organizations like the Satellite Sentinel Project and Human Rights Watch have used evidence to argue forcefully that the United States government and its allies have the responsibility to intervene around the world to prevent human rights violations.

This study also has raised important questions about elite commitments to standing international agreements and has highlighted the potentially confounding variable of power. That is, when the United States experienced dramatic technology advances that appeared to provide it with significant power and leverage over others, even a monopoly in some cases, presidents appeared far less willing to consider potential normative constraints on the use or exhibition of this power. This dynamic arose often through the case studies. For example, when President Truman learned of the bomb and his advisors told him the United States would enjoy a nuclear monopoly for some time to come, he seemed in little hurry to limit or circumscribe its potential use. This pattern has been repeated in outer space in relation to anti-satellite technologies and the problem of debris: only when Obama administration officials seemed convinced of the real dangers and potential challenges to U.S. dominance in outer space did the government shift its position in an attempt to establish multilateral constraints on the behavior of spacefaring nations.

Another factor that appears to have influenced norm contestation is external shock. The constructivist literature is divided on the question of whether exogenous factors like shocks are more important catalysts for change than endogenous processes. Many works reference shocks as default explanations for events and outcomes in global politics. However, the results of this study suggest the need for a more balanced accounting of these influences relative to processes of norm change. While the case studies focus on the emergence of techno-normative dilemmas as a function of endogenous innovation, it is fair to say that such changes do not occur in a vacuum. Some research and development processes were either catalyzed by serious threats to international security or were significantly sped up and advanced by them. The exogenous threat of Germany's atomic bomb research helped fuel the drive to develop the U.S. bomb in the Manhattan Project. In some ways, the presence of the threat helped guarantee the flow of tremendous government resources to the secret project at a time when the Allies could have directed time, money, and scientific know-how to other programs. Likewise, in the twenty-first century, one must acknowledge that part of the motivation for the development of unmanned aerial vehicle technologies was the war on terrorism. In sum, as noted in Chapter 1, technological innovations may spur on system transformation, but critical to this process are institutions, social practices, and politics that help give it meaning.

How Do Great Powers Promote Norm Change?

This study has proposed a multistage model of norm change, flowing from technological innovation to redefinition to constructive norm substitution. Case evidence suggests it captures some of the factors involved in exchanges for norm change in recent decades and certainly characterizes the various diplomatic levels of engagement. The model assigns primary responsibility to leaders of great powers who recognize techno-normative dilemmas when facing new technologies, with the expectation they will engage in norm redefinition and constructive norm substitution efforts. The second and third stages of the norm change cycle proposed here do seem to capture some of the nature of those political deliberations on potential constraints and opportunities of new technologies. On the question of sensitive nuclear technology exports, for example, this study has highlighted long-running debates between key actors over the limits and legitimacy of actions in the international system with a special focus on export controls. Meanwhile, the third stage of the model—constructive norm substitution—focuses on competitive exchanges in multilateral settings. Here the United States has had less success in establishing legitimacy and consolidating support for some new international norm frames.

This study has also identified some limits of the three-stage model. First, while the linearity of the model offers a clear explanatory framework, and generally is supported by the story lines in these cases, the reality suggests a more challenging, complex political process at work. That techno-normative dilemmas were often the impetus for norm change is less in question than potential distinctions between the second and third stages. In many cases, the process of norm redefinition at home was echoed by the beginnings of attempts at constructive norm substitution through contestation abroad. There were often multiple dialogues underway simultaneously at several levels, reflecting dynamics akin to those in nested game theory or two-level game theory. Case evidence shows that in some instances these processes may have occurred simultaneously in select circumstances and not in a divided, linear fashion. In several instances there were critical dialectical processes at work in the second and third stages of change, including debates over the new international code of conduct for outer space and restraints on uranium enrichment and reprocessing technologies. In the case of space, the Bush and Obama administrations were indeed engaged in nested games by pursuing multiple tracks at the same time: they were secretly authorizing advances in research on anti-satellite technologies at the same time they were publicly coming to terms with challenges from advances by other countries coupled with the low-tech debris challenge to their high-technology advances. The White House was thus engaged with multiple lobbies and congressional offices on questions of advancement of ballistic missile defense and ASAT technologies while at the same time it was supportive of a new National Space Policy program and international code of conduct for outer space that might effectively ban such systems. Figure 8.1 suggests an amended recursive model of norm change.

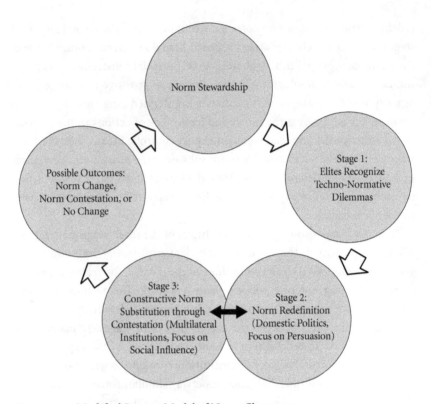

Figure 8.1   Modified Process Model of Norm Change

A second complicating factor for the model is defining the dependent variable of "success," especially in the second and third stages. If there is a simultaneous process of exchange going on in both stages of the model, there appear to be open questions about what constitutes legitimacy and bandwagoning behavior. "Legitimacy" is an especially challenging precept. When approaching the question of whether legitimacy can be established through the second and third stages, it is important to frame this in terms of propriety and acceptability. If the executive branch receives the blessing of domestic political actors in the second stage, this may boost its ability to find legitimacy in acceptable, new international standards. But so long as there are substantial challenges to legitimacy in the domestic level, questions remain as to whether endorsement by the international community can provide a sufficient foundation for new modes of state behavior.

Do Technology Innovations Always
Yield Successful Norm Shifts?

The presumption at the start of this study is that the model would illustrate the process by which the United States has successfully pursued normative change in all five issue areas. Empowered by technology innovations, U.S. leaders should be highly effective at convincing others of the legitimacy and utility of new systems. However, on this question, the results of the study are mixed. Leaders appeared to recognize techno-normative dilemmas and pursue norm change through stages of attempted norm redefinition and substitution through contestation. But the outcomes were less clear since a number of cases produced substantial contestation but not definitive success in norm substitution. In these cases, either legitimacy of the new norm remained contested or states were not following suit by bandwagoning in support of new norm frames.

This study suggests several scope conditions associated with great-power-driven norm shifts. First, great powers may be more successful in leading norm changes when they have the monopoly of the technology and the international balance of power appears favorable. When the United States enjoyed a monopoly or near-monopoly of the technology, its openness to any international agreement that would limit its potential freedom of action tended to be supported by the international community. But when the United States faced rival great powers that had achieved similar capabilities, it appeared to make only limited progress in achieving new legitimate and power-balanced norm frames. This outcome seems to address both rationalist and constructivist dimensions of the study. That is, the ideational dimension is manifest in great-power efforts to find negotiated settlements on agreements that may curtail behavior in select issue areas. Material considerations of relative power and influence allow certain players to advance and sometimes succeed with constructive norm substitution even when others have not. This echoes an argument by Renée de Nevers from an insightful recent study of this dynamic: "In norm promotion, great powers appear to 'speak softly' to those they regard as their peers, but they 'carry a big stick' to force others into line."[4] Great powers who take the lead in advocating norm change for instrumental or principled reasons can employ significant resources to try to achieve their goals. The case of changing the norm regarding assassination and targeted killing appears to illustrate these dynamics well. The United States seemed successful in reshaping modern understandings of the sovereignty norm and the legitimacy of this type of use of force. President Bush articulated a strong new posture on the question in the aftermath of September 11, arguing, "We must use the full influence of the United States to delegitimize terrorism and make clear that all acts of terrorism will be viewed in the same light as slavery, piracy, or genocide: behavior that no respectable government can condone or support and all must oppose."[5] The government then set about persuading the international community that a more proactive posture of preemption was a legitimate extension of its sovereign right to self-defense. To the extent possible, the Bush administration argued, it also would pursue the discriminate use of force for the protection of noncombatants. This suggests that there is a process of norm substitution underway, and the United States is greatly aided in this by relative balances of power.[6]

The contested R2P norm also illustrates these variable dynamics at work, but in the opposite causal direction. That is, this study has shown that the United States and other great powers have made tremendous progress in satellite reconnaissance and information communication technologies that have changed what the world knows and when. At the same time, the world has borne witness to critical challenges to human security over the last two decades, including ethnic cleansing, genocide, and politicide. To the casual observer the combination of these circumstances—the rise in connectivity and worldwide awareness of desperate circumstances (not to mention the end of Cold War political divisions)—should lead automatically to action. Unfortunately, a mix of power-based considerations appears to have intervened in the relationship between awareness and action. Debates over the meaning of the emerging responsibility-to-protect norm as well as we how it should be applied have led to stagnation in international forums. Despite vast amounts of evidence gathered through technical means, the world has seemed to stand idly by in the face of major humanitarian challenges such as the civil war in the Sudan and genocide in Darfur, sectarian violence in the Central African Republic, Iraq, and Afghanistan, and the use of chemical weapons by the Syrian government in 2013. The rhetoric of human rights belies the reality: the United States and other great powers do not agree on standards of international behavior in a new era of the "responsibility to protect," prompting some to question whether we are witnessing a failed norm evolution.

In sum, recognizing favorable balances of power as a scope condition does not negate the power of ideational struggles over norms. Norms are not merely epiphenomenal to interests. Rather, this demonstrates that leaders may perceive more favorable settings for engagement with the international community on regulative and constitutive constructs. Great powers are still acting in a sense beyond their deeper security interests by changing international understandings of new technologies and attempting to regulate state behavior in accordance with new standards.

Scope conditions associated with less successful outcomes include the timing of the initiation of norm change, the level of contestedness in the redefinition stage, and the pursuit of particular formats for outcomes, such as international treaties. First, the United States may not succeed in achieving legitimacy for new norm constructs because it is only one of several actors pushing for change and *not* the original initiator of the effort. In at least three cases—the debates over the responsibility to protect and outer space—the United States appears to have come somewhat late to the game of international negotiations on norm change. Regarding R2P, U.S. activism lagged that of other players, especially middle powers like Canada and Australia, in endorsing the need for humanitarian intervention in the face of mass violence. For a time, the United States opposed some of these changes as a function of principled commitments to sovereignty. To some extent, U.S. leaders might have been reluctant to endorse R2P given the practical implications of endorsement: the expectation that the country with the greatest power projection capabilities in the world would commit substantial resources to such operations around the world. The White House knew that the government could not sustain domestic political support for such a new and proactive stance, nor would all operations necessarily fit with U.S. national interests.

The United States also was surprisingly slow to embrace norm changes for outer space. It was clearly a technology leader and architect of the Outer Space Treaty in the 1960s. But when other great powers began in the 1990s to push for initiatives that would limit certain types of activities in Earth's orbit, the United States seemed to drag its feet. Both Russia and China had initiated international agreements in forums, including the Conference on Disarmament and the UN Committee on Peaceful Uses of Outer Space, that were designed to regulate international standards and provide greater security. But in the 2000s these proposals were interpreted by the George W. Bush administration as direct challenges to potential U.S. technological advantages. The Obama administration's pronouncements on international space policy changes have come only since 2010.

Second, the slower pace of the United States in addressing issues served to magnify concerns on the part of other countries that U.S. intentions might not be all that resolute. That is, shifts in U.S. policies raised suspicions of a utilitarian approach to the issue and a lack of resolve to lead international negotiations toward a defined outcome. Here we see a difference in external perceptions of the status of executive efforts to redefine U.S. foreign policy commitments (e.g., would members of Congress really approve of this newly defined posture from the executive?) and U.S. intentions rather than capabilities (e.g., how to interpret differences between the rhetoric on issues like anti-satellite technologies and the reality of U.S. advances?). So long as other great powers had reason to question the true depth of the U.S. commitment to change policies, such as in the case of cyber-norms, the possibility of achieving successful norm substitution seemed limited.

A third potential constraint on norm substitution may be linked to the institutional structure of the final outcome. A number of experts and policy-makers interviewed for this study suggested that the U.S. government might be moving away from developing international treaties to formalize or legitimize new normative architectures. They argued that the effort involved in negotiating a treaty that could be signed and ratified by the majority of governments around the world might not be commensurate with the benefits. As an alternative, experts and policy-makers contend, more and more governments around the world have come to favor voluntary international codes of conduct, or promises of certain behaviors that fall short of formal treaty status or even legal limitations on state behavior. The product of such an effort would be de facto, not de jure, limits on state actions, but the perceived outcome for many players would be the same. At this writing, diplomats have made substantial progress on the development of codes of conduct regarding outer space and cyber-security, even though divisions remain throughout the world (and within key governments, like the United States) on the potential for development of an international treaty.

Theoretical Implications

What are the implications of a model of norm change for policy-makers and theories of international cooperation? This study has yielded substantial evidence of leaders as a different kind of norm entrepreneur. Leaders' actions defied predictions of constructivist theories regarding the power of norms as well as challenged dominant historical narratives regarding U.S. engagement in global politics. First-generation (or what Andrew Cortell and James Davis term "first wave")[7] constructivist international relations theory describes these developments as products of predictable "life cycles"; ideas for standards of behavior cascade through political systems and take on constitutive and regulatory qualities. Government leaders would be expected to internalize new norms, thus constraining the behaviors or norm modifications that leaders might even consider in relation to international cooperation and conflict.

First-generation norm theory does not fully capture how determined leaders may develop strategies intended to change or manipulate normative security architectures for their own utilitarian purposes. Endogenous technology advances prompt fascinating dialectics, which have in turn altered the political landscape by catalyzing norm change processes. Technology can highlight dissonant strands of norms and dissonance between norms, increasing the chances norms will be subject to contestation. Techno-normative dilemmas recast leaders' considerations of state interests versus international commitments and generate processes of norm change through redefinition and constructive norm substitution. While popular accounts of challenges to the global order focus on the behaviors of "rogue states" or dramatic events, this book has shown how some of the most profound norm changes are a function of quiet, persistent campaigns by great powers to adapt international standards to emerging realities.

In the process, this study has underscored the value of constructivist accounts of international cooperation. Constructivists identify international norms as "shared understandings that constitute actors' identities and interests"—as well as their potential role in international cooperation by effectively binding state policy latitude.[8] The norm life-cycle model stands as a valuable contribution to the evolution of international norms—and it has influenced scores of works studying the stages of norm "life": emergence, broad acceptance (also referred to as a "norm cascade"), and internalization. Critical players in norm development have helped establish dense normative webs but also spurred on auxiliary norm development, life, and contestation dynamics. First-generation models focused on bottom-up processes in the development of international standards, but have launched newer investigations of efforts by traditional norm stewards to change the meaning of a norm or rule within multilateral frameworks.

Second-generation work has advanced the field significantly. It has begun to meet the challenge first raised by Robert Axelrod in the 1980s that any viable norm theory should explain three things: "how norms arise, how norms are maintained, and how one norm displaces another." This should "account not only for the norms existing at any point in time, but also for how norms change over time."[9] A more balanced accounting of the agent-structure relationship may provide more comprehensive explanations of international politics. It is here that second-generation contributions are felt most acutely— early work on the development of normative architectures devoted surprisingly little attention to the variety of actors that might have vested interests in norm development and contestation. Subsequently, scholars have begun to revisit the traditional norm life-cycle model to incorporate stages in which leaders may seek to reinterpret the meaning of norms to accommodate exceptions to international standards related to security.

This study also has yielded insights on the microprocesses of norm change. Drawing on the social psychology literature, it has demonstrated the power of persuasion in redefinition in domestic political settings. This typically involves elite-driven political engagement and persuasion, where the executive branch initiates contact with the legislature with persuasive messages designed to change preferences and create new meanings. While leaders attempt to use leverage to influence others, scholar Rodger Payne argues that inducing change also plays on the "instrumentality and social functions of alternative frames."[10] With government resolve, leaders then turn their attention to engagement in multilateral forums using social influence to generate legitimacy and bandwagoning behavior. Great powers may convince others of the pro-social value of conformity and find areas of agreement that can help produce new normative architectures. These dynamics do not occur in ideational vacuums, of course, but rather in contested environments where maneuvering is critical.[11]

Lessons for SCOT Theory and Norm Change

This study has demonstrated that technology innovations are among the factors that may foster leaders' perceptions of gaps between general rules and state interests. In all the cases there were links between technological innovations and deliberations on revisiting critical normative structures of the past and adapting them to new material and ideational boundaries. Where leaders perceived limits, they developed plans to justify actions through changes in the rules or reinterpretations of normative strains that effectively modified international standards. Technological competitiveness fostered a greater role for agency in norm discourse than allowed for by traditional constructivism. And while this connection may be age old, we are clearly witnessing an important period of transformation in the post–September 11 international security environment as dramatic new technological innovations help catalyze debates about the limits of power.

Evidence from this study supports assertions of technological endogeneity. This study has shown that far from being an exogenous factor that dictates state behavior (the "technological imperative" hypothesis), the relationship between political decisions and technological opportunities is dialectical. Consistent with the social construction of technology theory, innovations have been the impetus for important social trends and transformations, but their development also has been mediated through stabilization processes and domestic and multilateral political decisions. An emphasis on subjective interpretations of the meaning of scientific advancements and knowledge is one of the strongest areas of intersection between SCOT theory and constructivist international relations theory—a synergistic relationship between technological advances and political developments.

The story of the development and use of armed UAVs illustrates the dialectical process often at work with innovations and policy decisions. For example, the development of UAVs by the Clinton and George W. Bush administrations represented major advances in technology. At the time of their origin, though, these were seen to have their most value in reconnaissance operations. Only with the identification of the threat from Osama bin Laden and al Qaeda did the leadership determine that what it needed was a modified capability to both see and strike potential targets instantly from drone platforms. In other words, the innovations undertaken to arm drones were both military/strategic and political—developing with nearly simultaneous pressures to expand capabilities for specific purposes. The Bush administration dramatically ramped up UAV research and development as well as targeted-killing operations. Critically, though, all this occurred against a backdrop of considerations about international law and justification and the legality and ethics of operations. The executive branch of the U.S. government determined these operations were lawful, and officials proclaimed to the world they were lawful. While the Obama administration appeared to pull back rhetorically from some of the bolder pronouncements of the Bush-era war on terror, the

U.S. government clearly made the political determination that it was legal and even ethical to assassinate foreign adversaries without due process. Other advanced industrialized countries have quickly (yet quietly) followed suit. Today, we are witnessing a period of intense research and development—and the dramatic proliferation—of UAV technologies.

These developments support a historical sociological approach that explains the role of technology in a broader social context, exploring how interests are shaped and, critically, the key players involved in the policy process. Orlikowski's model of the instantiation in practice of technology and political rules and resources can be seen at work in several case studies.[12] For example, the rules and practices of satellite surveillance have been very dependent in their development on each other, along with the role of political pressures to shape social development. Innovations thus influence the path of what are recurrent social practices, where government knowledge of new technologies enlightens perspectives on traditional practice. Satellite reconnaissance began as a platform to enhance strategic advantages for both the United States and the Soviet Union. But with the expansion of space technologies and the modern-day commercialization and commoditization of space, the political dynamics associated with space-based reconnaissance operations have changed dramatically. Today, scores of states, non-state actors, and international governmental organizations are involved in monitoring challenges around the world and calling attention to their limitations and problems. The political discourse associated with the responsibility to protect has thus evolved in complicated and convoluted ways. As Herrera argues, technological innovations may indeed spur on system transformation, but critical to this are "institutions, social practices and politics surrounding it and giving it political (and military) meaning."[13] Technology thus becomes part of the structure of international politics; international politics is one of the factors governing technological change.

In sum, SCOT theorists argue that certain technologies—especially large technical systems—will have direct consequences for the international system. Yet, since these are also products of the international system, this relationship is clearly a two-way street. Building on the social construction of technology literature, this study has shown that normative change may not have occurred, or at least would have been different, absent the technological changes identified here. In this sense, this study builds on this literature to develop an even stronger model of causality through a structured, focused comparison of the case studies and outcomes, with the goal of comparing the cases where technological innovation produced normative change to cases of important technological innovation that have not shifted prevailing normative understandings. This helps to identify important institutional features of the cases that have made agency possible.

Second-Generation Theories of Contestation and Norm Change

If one accepts that continuous norm change is underway as a function of technology innovations that encourage policy-makers to push the envelope of acceptable behaviors, what are the implications of these changes for international politics? Do norm changes strengthen or weaken international cooperation? And what is the process by which this occurs?

Norm change has been defined for this study as the substantive alteration of "acceptable" or "unacceptable" behavior as articulated by a critical mass of players.[14] This study has focused primarily on normative standards that were fairly well organized and specified through multilateral institutions, treaties, and agreements, yet underwent challenges and debate in multilateral institutions. Changes were framed as the creation of alternative, legitimate international agreements for behavior plus bandwagoning behavior. Ann Florini characterizes the legitimacy of a new norm frame as within a "rule community when it is itself a reasonable behavior response to the environmental conditions facing the members of the community and when it 'fits' coherently with other prevailing norms."[15] At the same time, successful norm change should be manifest in bandwagoning behavior, in official discourse and policy actions toward prevailing norms. The expectation is that states follow suit in policies and behaviors in support of the new norm frame.

Another possible outcome, contested norm change, may occur when great powers attempt to change standards through international organizations, but the critical elements of legitimacy or bandwagoning behavior are limited or absent.[16] Such an arrangement leaves open the possibility that norms may evolve beyond the outcome championed by the norm steward advocating change, or that the international community will revert to traditional interpretations of the norm. Three of the five case studies examined in this study reveal that contestation was underway—an ongoing dispute about the legitimacy and feasibility of new norm frames. But should these outcomes actually be characterized as "unsuccessful" cases relative to the research design, or something qualitatively different? Existing scholarship is divided on the question. For example, some scholars suggest that successful norm development is necessarily progressive, often reflecting liberalism and Western trends of thought, and that the process of exchange involved in achieving norm change promotes higher levels of cooperation. Critical constructivism, a subset of second-general literature that conceptualizes norms as contingent, inherently contested, and ambiguous, develops the theme of ongoing contestation and ambiguity in norm development. For example, Richard Price confronts the critique of a "progressive" bias inherent to norm research by demanding his fellow constructivists be explicit about their normative stance toward the phenomena they study and not shy away from facing difficult moral dilemmas that may arise as side effects of moral progress. Adopting an explicit normative stance, according to Price, would enable constructivists "to identify some of the morally undesirable implications of erstwhile progressive developments. This includes identification of complicity of the progressive with the oppressive."[17] In sum, this suggests that norm change may be highly contested; it is what actors make of it, rather than definitively progressive or retrogressive.

Another research question is whether there is value in contestation itself—whether debates over norm parameters are inherently healthy, serving to strengthen and stabilize international agreements. Once again, scholars are divided. Traditional approaches suggest any contestation may weaken the regime or present problems for the norm, that is, any challenge may create a legitimacy crisis for international norms. More recent research suggests that in the face of contradictions and noncompliance, norms may erode or even die. For example, Diana Panke and Ulrich Petersohn and others question whether developments in the war on terrorism represent the decay of the anti-torture norm and wonder if other norms, such as the emerging responsibility to protect, are in danger of premature demise.[18]

In contrast, Antje Wiener's work on critical constructivist theory provides perhaps the strongest guidance for consideration of the value of contestation of norms. For Wiener contestation is a positive phenomenon as it is the condition for a deliberation over meanings of norms necessary to produce norm legitimacy. She argues, "It is through this transfer between contexts, that the meaning of norms becomes contested, as differently socialized actors such as politicians, civil servants, parliamentarians or lawyers trained in different legal traditions seek to interpret them."[19] Given that the "legitimacy of international law may actually depend on sorting out the normative baggage brought to bear in international encounters," the process itself can be framed as a healthy exchange destined to promote positive outcomes.[20] While there is always a danger of "too much" contestation—a level that Wiener contends involves such conflict that adherents no longer consider something a shared norm—empirical research suggests the potential for normative discourse to strengthen and stabilize international cooperation.

Other recent work suggests the type of contestation matters more than the level in relation to expansion or diminishment of the norm. For example, Amitav Acharya suggests that internalization processes at local levels involve change or reinterpretation, but that the net effect of the transmission of norms from international organizations to supporting states strengthens the normative understanding.[21] Nicole Deitelhoff and Lisbeth Zimmermann argue there are at least two types of norm challenges: applicatory contestation and justificatory/validity contestation. Contestation over norm application may not undermine the strength of norms, and they may relate well to a study of changing interpretations of a norm following technological inventions or general normative change in societies. In contrast, they expect contestation of the validity of a norm to lead to its weakening. As the validity of a norm is increasingly questioned, noncompliance becomes more widespread and will no longer be denounced by norm addressees, leading to norm decay.[22]

The results of this study suggest that norm contestation may have a strengthening effect. In all five case studies, the debates that flowed from technological change prompted leaders to consider changes or modifications of traditional norm frames in a way that filled gaps or closed loopholes in interpretation. Norm discourse focused primarily on norm strengthening—working to effect changes in the international system that would provide answers to open questions. For example, U.S. support of a new international code of conduct for outer space has been geared toward defining the boundaries of acceptable behaviors in this new region. The code, though heavily contested through years of negotiation, suggests a move toward a progressive outcome. One could argue that even the standards of conduct promoted by President Obama regarding the use of armed drones—which critics term the evolution of an illiberal norm—represent efforts to define standards nonetheless, and that the United States is attempting to provide boundaries and further define new norms in both liberal, progressive ways, and through liberal boundaries on illiberal behavior.

Finally, this raises implications for the study of the role of hegemons and non-hegemons in norm change. Critical questions have been raised about whether the effects of technological changes are homogenous or heterogeneous across the international system. This study has clearly focused on the United States as a hegemonic player in norm development, but it also reveals important limits regarding the scope of its influence. As noted above, hegemonic drives to change international norms appear to be more successful during times of war or international crisis. But there is also a role for non-hegemons in norm contestation. This model also does not preclude the possibility that other countries might advance technologies that challenge norms. Carmen Wunderlich's exploration of alternative norm entrepreneurs, including rogue states, suggests an exciting research avenue in this spirit.[23]

Summary

This study has examined the relationship between a select set of technology innovations and the evolution of international norms through contestation. It has demonstrated the often double-edged nature of technology innovations: U.S. leaders have expressed optimism that new technologies could promote global peace and security, while at the same time they have authorized exploration of potential strategic advantages afforded by innovations. Advances in space technology led to calls by the United States for an Outer Space Treaty but also fueled a Cold War space race. Contemporary challenges of space debris and the refinement of anti-satellite technologies produced yet another push by the United States and its allies for an international code of conduct for space. Atomic fission and uranium enrichment contributed to advances in peaceful nuclear energy development and behaviors were codified in the NPT, but they also produced challenges for countries seeking to develop clandestine weapons of mass destruction. In the process of investigation, this study also has identified a number of avenues for future research.

Drawing technology into existing theories of international relations adds a valuable perspective on prospects for international cooperation. Innovations can be an endogenous cause of foreign policy development, as leaders recognize that advancements matter not only for their own policies but also for their state's behavior relative to international agreements. For example, the development of the atomic bomb, as well as technologies that could be used for peaceful nuclear energy, served to move the U.S. foreign policy needle substantially over time. Advances in space technologies and anti-satellite capabilities heightened awareness of both strategic high-technology threats (in China's development of missiles that could kill American satellites) and low-technology threats (in space debris). These advancements have created pressures for great powers to embrace development of an international code of conduct for space.

This study has begun to trace how states revisit normative commitments as a function of technology advancements, but it also raises interesting theoretical questions for further research. For example, it has identified different avenues for normative discourse and potential influence. Empowered leaders may revisit state commitments to international norms when they recognize new opportunities or challenges. At the same time, non-state actors that acquire new abilities, such as to "see and know" more about ongoing humanitarian tragedies, may become much more active in forming transnational advocacy networks for change. Early forays into satellite activism, such as those conducted by the Satellite Sentinel Project and Human Rights Watch, have been limited and subject to criticism. But these efforts are in their nascent stages and there is every indication that reconnaissance from drones and satellites may become much more "democratic" and scientific in the twenty-first century. Nongovernmental organizations may be able to better use satellite and drone imagery to capture needs in the aftermath of a natural disaster or uncover abuses around the world. This suggests the potential for greatly empowered epistemic communities to influence future international policy processes.

This study also has highlighted the importance of what Harald Müller and Carmen Wunderlich call "norm dynamics," or "the process of how norms—and thus regimes—develop, that is, how they emerge, diffuse, become internalized, and once established, become subject to change." This and related second-generation scholarship on norms highlights the "fundamental contestedness and ambiguity of norms"[24] This study suggests that an important intersection of these approaches is somewhere between the cognitive approaches advocated by some constructivists and the rational approaches that treat norms as emerging from actors rational preference-based calculations. A critical dimension of the study of norm dynamics focuses on how to theorize the conditions under which the breaking of a norm is likely to strengthen rather than undermine it. Maria Rost Rublee points out that "charting out the major mechanisms through which norms exert influence, specifying the conditions under which the mechanisms are most likely to work, and identifying possible intervening and mediating variables would take us further in this quest."[25] For example, the localization and adaptation of norms to different regional contexts or strategic cultures may be dynamics that serve to strengthen or weaken normative structures.

Finally, scholars should continue to explore how modern technologies foster techno-normative dilemmas. Ongoing norm reconsideration was illustrated in 2013 when Syria's President Assad ordered the use of chemical weapons against rebels challenging his government. The results of the attack were shared on line through heart-wrenching videos of the victims taken with cellphones, live tweeting of the attacks and casualty figures, and televised news coverage of events. What followed in international diplomacy, though, suggests the limits of modern norms: policy-makers and scholars debated whether the West should carry out military strikes against Syria in retaliation for "violating the norm" against the use of chemical weapons in modern war. Many championed the need to send a strong signal to Assad through a missile strike; others cautioned that the punishment, too, would violate international normative commitments. In the end, permanent members of the UN Security Council threatened to veto any resolution authorizing the strike, and President Obama backed down from earlier threats and warnings. A similar dynamic arose in 2015 when the United States accused China of a serious cyber attack against the federal Office of Personnel Management and the theft of millions of records of government employees and diplomats, and officials began to debate the scope and nature of a "proper" response within the emerging normative boundaries of the information age. These, and other events continue to highlight the importance of studying norm contestation in twenty-first-century global politics.

Reference Matter

Notes

Chapter 1

1. Barack Obama, "Address on NSA Surveillance Policies," U.S. Department of Justice, January 17, 2014, qtd. in Mark Landler and Charlie Savage, "Keeping Wide Net, Obama Sets Limits on Phone Spying," *New York Times*, January 18, 2014, p. A1.

2. Reinhold Niebuhr, *Moral Man and Immoral Society: A Study in Ethics and Politics* (New York: Charles Scribner & Sons, 1932), p. 4.

3. Harry Truman, Statement by the President of the United States, White House Press Release, August 6, 1945, Harry S. Truman Library, http://www.trumanlibrary. org/whistlestop/study_collections/bomb/large/documents/index.php?pagenumber=1 &documentdate=1945-08-06&documentid=59&studycollectionid=abomb (accessed May 4, 2013).

4. See Eric Schlosser, *Command and Control: Nuclear Weapons, the Damascus Accident, and the Illusion of Safety* (New York: Penguin, 2013), pp. 75–77.

5. White House, "Presidential Studies Directive on Mass Atrocities," PSD-10, August 4, 2011, https://www.whitehouse.gov/the-press-office/2011/08/04/presidential-study-directive-mass-atrocities (accessed January 10, 2016).

6. Confidential interview, former National Security Council staff member, Washington, DC, February 24, 2014.

7. See Andrew P. Cortell and James W. Davis, Jr., "Understanding the Domestic Impact of International Norms: A Research Agenda," *International Studies Review* 2:1 (2000), pp. 65–87.

8. Ryan Goodman and Derek Jinks, "How to Influence States: Socialization and International Human Rights Law," *Duke Law Journal* 54:3 (2004), p. 640.

9. This book builds significantly on and expands themes mentioned in Jeffrey S. Lantis, "Nuclear Technology and Norm Stewardship: U.S. Nonproliferation Policies Revisited," *International Studies Perspectives* 16:4 (2015).

10. Martha Finnemore, "Constructing Norms of Humanitarian Intervention," in Peter J. Katzenstein, ed. *The Culture of National Security: Norms and Identity in World Politics* (New York: Columbia University Press, 1996), pp. 153–185; Martha Finnemore and Kathryn Sikkink, "International Norm Dynamics and Political Change," *International Organization* 52:4 (1998), pp. 887–917; Thomas Risse, Stephen C. Ropp, and Kathryn Sikkink, eds., *The Power of Human Rights: International Norms and Domestic Change* (Cambridge: Cambridge University Press, 1999).

11. Finnemore and Sikkink, "International Norm Dynamics and Political Change," p. 895. See also Risse, Ropp, and Sikkink, eds., *The Power of Human Rights.*

12. Finnemore and Sikkink, "International Norm Dynamics and Political Change," p. 901.

13. For more critique of the limits of first-generation constructivism, see Harald Müller and Carmen Wunderlich, eds., *Norm Dynamics in Multilateral Arms Control: Interests, Conflicts, and Justice* (Athens: University of Georgia Press, 2013).

14. Mona Lena Krook and Jacqui True, "Rethinking the Life Cycles of International Norms: The United Nations and the Global Promotion of Gender Equality," *European Journal of International Relations* 18:1 (2010), pp. 103–127.

15. Robert Axelrod, "An Evolutionary Approach to Norms," *American Political Science Review* 80:4 (1986), p. 1096.

16. Kathryn Sikkink, "Beyond the Justice Cascade: How Agentic Constructivism Could Help Explain Change in International Politics," revised paper from the Millennium Annual Conference, October 22, 2011, p. 2, http://www.princeton.edu/politics/about/file-repository/public/Agentic-Constructivism-paper-sent-to-the-Princeton-IR-Colloquium.pdf (accessed January 4, 2013).

17. Alec Stone Sweet, "Judicialization and the Construction of Governance," *Comparative Political Studies* 32:2 (1999), pp. 147–184.

18. This also contrasts with generalized exogenous shock arguments; see Daniel H. Deudney, "Dividing Realism: Structural Realism Versus Security Materialism on Nuclear Security and Proliferation," *Security Studies* 2:3 (1993), pp. 7–36; Donald Mackenzie and Judy Wajcman, *The Social Shaping of Technology* (Philadelphia: Open University Press, 1999). For examples of realist interpretations of the technological imperative, see Barry Buzan, *An Introduction to Strategic Studies: Military Technology and International Relations* (London: Macmillan, 1987).

19. Merritt Roe Smith and Leo Marx, eds., *Does Technology Drive History? The Dilemma of Technological Determinism* (Cambridge, MA: MIT Press, 1994).

20. Trevor J. Pinch and Wiebe E. Bijker, "The Social Construction of Facts and Artefacts: Or How the Sociology of Science and the Sociology of Technology Might Benefit Each Other," *Social Studies of Science* 14:3 (1984), pp. 399–441.

21. Wayne Sandholtz and Kendall Stiles, *International Norms and Cycles of Change* (Oxford: Oxford University Press, 2008), p. 328.

22. Saskia Sassen, "Towards a Sociology of Information Technology," *Current Sociology* 50:3 (2002), pp. 365–388; Wanda J. Orlikowski, "Using Technology and Constituting Structures: A Practice Lens for Studying Technology in Organizations," *Organization Science* 11:4 (2000), pp. 404–428.

23. Ronald Kline and Trevor Pinch, "Users as Agents of Technological Change: The Social Construction of the Automobile in the Rural United States," *Technology and Culture* 37:4 (1996), p. 766.

24. Geoffrey L. Herrera, *Technology and International Transformation: The Railroad, the Atom Bomb, and the Politics of Technological Change* (Albany: State University of New York Press, 2006), p. 2.

25. Ibid., pp. 2–3; Ronald J. Deibert, *Parchment, Printing, and Hypermedia: Communication in World Order Transformation* (New York: Columbia University Press, 1997).

26. Kline and Pinch, "Users as Agents of Technological Change," pp. 764–768.

27. Carroll W. Pursell, Jr., *Readings in Technology and American Life* (New York: Oxford University Press, 1969), p. 3.

28. Robert E. Baldwin and Anne O. Krueger, *The Structure and Evolution of Recent U.S. Trade Policy* (Chicago: University of Chicago Press, 1984); Paul Krugman, ed., *Strategic Trade Policy and the New International Economics* (Cambridge, MA: MIT Press, 1986).

29. Russell F. Weigley, *The American Way of War: A History of United States Military Strategy and Policy* (New York: Macmillan, 1973), p. xxii.

30. F. G. Hoffman, *Decisive Force: The New American Way of War* (Westport, CT: Praeger, 1996), p. 9.

31. Max Boot, "The New American Way of War," *Foreign Affairs* 82:4 (July/August 2003), p. 42.

32. United States Department of State, *National Strategy for Combating Terrorism*, 2003, pp. 23–24 (emphasis added), http://www.state.gov/documents/organization/60172.pdf (accessed July 19, 2014); Renée de Nevers, "Imposing International Norms: Great Powers and Norm Enforcement," *International Studies Review* 9:1 (2007), p. 53.

33. Confidential interview, senior government official, Washington, DC, February 26, 2014.

34. As Panke and Petersohn argue, "the literature has rich explanations for norm creation, diffusion and socialization, yet there is a theoretical and empirical gap on both the dynamics and scope conditions" for change." Their specific focus on the "degeneration of international norms" departs from this study. Diana Panke and Ulrich Petersohn, "Why International Norms Disappear Sometimes," *European Journal of International Relations* 18:4 (2012), pp. 719–742.

Chapter 2

1. Jeffrey W. Legro, *Rethinking the World: Great Power Strategies and International Order* (Ithaca, NY: Cornell University Press, 2005), pp. 1–2.

2. Andy Warhol (1928–1987), *The Philosophy of Andy Warhol*, selected quotes, http://www.quotationspage.com/quote/25824.html.

3. Andrew P. Cortell and James W. Davis, Jr., "How Do International Institutions Matter? The Domestic Impact of International Rules and Norms," *International Studies Quarterly* 40:4 (1996), pp. 451–478.

4. Alexander Wendt, "Anarchy Is What States Make of It: The Social Construction of Power Politics," *International Organization* 46:2 (1992), p. 392; Peter J. Katzenstein, ed., *The Culture of National Security: Norms and Identity in World Politics* (New York: Columbia University Press, 1996).

5. John Gerard Ruggie, "What Makes the World Hang Together? Neo-Utilitarianism and the Social Constructivist Challenge," *International Organization* 52:1 (1998), p. 856.

6. Alexander Wendt, "Constructing International Politics," *International Security* 20:1 (1995), pp. 73–74.

7. Martha Finnemore, *National Interests in International Society* (Ithaca, NY: Cornell University Press, 1996), p. 22.

8. Thomas Risse, Stephen C. Ropp, and Kathryn Sikkink, eds., *The Power of Human Rights: International Norms and Domestic Change* (Cambridge: Cambridge University Press, 1999), p. 5.

9. Theo Farrell, "Constructivist Security Studies: Portrait of a Research Program," *International Studies Review* 4:1 (2002), pp. 49–72. Conceptually, Scott Feld characterizes norms as "regularities of behavior" containing "sanctions for failing to follow them"; Feld, "On the Emergence of Social Norms," *Contemporary Sociology* 31:6 (2002), p. 638.

10. Harold H. Koh, "Why Do Nations Obey International Law?" *Yale Law Journal* 106:8 (1997), p. 2628; see also Jack A. Goldsmith and Eric A. Posner, *The Limits of International Law* (Oxford University Press, 2005); Judith Goldstein, Miles Kahler, Robert O. Keohane, and Anne-Marie Slaughter, "Legalization and World Politics," *International Organization* 54:3 (2000), pp. 385–399.

11. Martha Finnemore and Kathryn Sikkink, "International Norm Dynamics and Political Change," *International Organization* 52:4 (1998), p. 895.

12. Ibid.

13. Ronald Jepperson, Alexander Wendt, and Peter J. Katzenstein, "Norms, Identity, and Culture in National Security," in Peter J. Katzenstein, ed. *The Culture of National Security: Norms and Identity in World Politics* (New York: Columbia University Press, 1996), p. 54.

14. Finnemore and Sikkink, "International Norm Dynamics and Political Change," p. 895.

15. Ibid., p. 893.

16. Risse, Ropp, and Sikkink, *The Power of Human Rights*, p. 5.

17. Finnemore and Sikkink, "International Norm Dynamics and Political Change," p. 896.

18. James G. March and Johan P. Olsen, *Rediscovering Institutions: The Organizational Basis of Politics* (New York: Free Press, 1989).

19. Risse, Ropp, and Sikkink, *The Power of Human Rights*.

20. Christine Ingebritsen, "Norm Entrepreneurs: Scandinavia's Role in World Politics," *International Studies Perspectives* 37:1 (2002), pp. 11–23; Mona Lee Krook and Jacqui True, "Rethinking the Life Cycles of International Norms: The United Nations and the Global Promotion of Gender Equality," *European Journal of International Relations* 18:1 (2012), pp. 103–127.

21. Matthew J. Hoffmann. "Norms and Social Constructivism in International Relations," in Robert A. Denemark, ed., *The International Studies Encyclopedia*, vol. 9, pp. 5410–5426 (London: Wiley-Blackwell, 2010), p. 5413.

22. Ibid.; Thierry Balzacq, "The Three Faces of Securitization: Political Agency, Audience, and Context," *European Journal of International Relations* 11:2 (2005), pp. 171–201.

23. Wayne Sandholtz, *Prohibiting Plunder: How Norms Change* (Oxford: Oxford University Press, 2007), p. 3.

24. Legro, *Rethinking the World*, p. 11.

25. On the concept of decay, see Harald Müller and Carmen Wunderlich, eds., *Norm Dynamics in Multilateral Arms Control: Interests, Conflicts, and Justice* (Athens: University of Georgia Press, 2013); Elvira Rosert, Una Becker-Jakob, Giorgio Franceschini, and Annette Schaper, "Arms Control Norms and Technology," in ibid., pp. 109–140; Antje Wiener, *The Invisible Constitution of Politics: Contested Norms and International Encounters* (Cambridge: Cambridge University Press, 2008); Clifford Bob, *The Global Right Wing and the Clash of World Politics* (New York: Cambridge University Press, 2012).

26. Some of these limitations are discussed in Jeffrey S. Lantis, "Nuclear Technology and Norm Stewardship: U.S. Nonproliferation Policies Revisited," *International Studies Perspectives* 16:4 (2015). DOI: 10.1111/insp.12070.

27. Legro, *Rethinking the World*, pp. 1–2.

28. Earlier iterations of these ideas appear in Jeffrey S. Lantis, "Irrational Exuberance? The 2010 NPT Review, Nuclear Assistance, and Norm Deconstruction," *Nonproliferation Review* 18:2 (July 2011), pp. 389–409.

29. John G. March and Johan P. Olsen, "The New Institutionalism: Organizational Factors in Political Life," *American Political Science Review* 78:4 (1984), pp. 734–749.

30. Thomas Risse, "'Let's Argue!': Communicative Action in World Politics," *International Organization* 54:1 (2000), p. 6.

31. Sandholtz, *Prohibiting Plunder*, p. 3.

32. Indeed, other domestic actors and institutions may contribute to norm development and decline.

33. The role of elites is highlighted among relevant domestic political actors involved in policy-making. This is not to argue that other factors—such as the nature of security threats, economic interdependence, culture, history, and public opinion—are unimportant in explaining state decisions vis-à-vis norms. Rather, consistent with

foreign policy decision-making studies, I suggest that these factors are taken into consideration and affect foreign policy decisions by how they are filtered through norm stewardship.

34. Sandholtz, *Prohibiting Plunder*, p. 3; Walton L. Brown, "Presidential Leadership and U.S. Nonproliferation Policy," *Presidential Studies Quarterly* 24:3 (1994), p. 563.

35. Ryan Goodman and Derek Jinks, "How to Influence States: Socialization and International Human Rights Law," *Duke Law Journal* 54:3 (2004); Vaughn P. Shannon, "Norms Are What States Make of Them: The Political Psychology of Norm Violation," *International Studies Quarterly* 41:1 (2000), pp. 293–316; Jacques E. C. Hymans, *The Psychology of Nuclear Proliferation: Identity, Emotions, and Foreign Policy* (Cambridge: Cambridge University Press, 2006).

36. Paul Kowert and Jeffrey Legro, "Norms, Identity, and Their Limits: A Theoretical Reprise," in Peter J. Katzenstein, ed. *The Culture of National Security: Norms and Identity in World Politics* (New York: Columbia University Press, 1996), p. 489; and John G. Ruggie, "Continuity and Transformation in the World Polity: Toward a Neorealist Synthesis," *World Politics* 35:2 (1983), pp. 261–285.

37. Thus, this argument is partially consistent with Jeffrey Checkel's description of internalization occurring in two stages—the first being acceptance of legitimacy of central norms where leaders "act" in accord with normative expectations; see Checkel, "International Institutions and Socialization in Europe," *International Organization* 59:3 (Fall 2005), pp. 801–826.

38. Michael Barnett, "Culture, Strategy, and Foreign Policy Change: Israel's Road to Oslo," *European Journal of International Relations* 5:1 (1999), pp. 5–36.

39. See Liesbet Hooghe, "Several Roads Lead to International Norms, But Few via International Socialization: A Case Study of the European Commission," *International Organization* 59:3 (2005), pp. 861–898.

40. Amitav Acharya, "How Ideas Spread: Whose Norms Matter? Norm Localization and Institutional Change in Asian Regionalism," *International Organization* 58:2 (2004), pp. 239–275.

41. Antje Wiener and Uwe Puetter, "The Quality of Norms Is What Actors Make of It: Critical Constructivist Research on Norms," *Journal of International Law and International Relations* 5:1 (2009), pp. 1–2.

42. Antje Wiener, *A Theory of Contestation* (Berlin: Springer Verlag, 2014).

43. Goodman and Jinks, "How to Influence States," p. 640.

44. Anthony Giddens, *Central Problems in Social Theory: Action, Structure, and Contradictions in Social Analysis* (London: Macmillan, 1979), p. 69.

45. Ibid., p. 65; see also Giddens, *The Constitution of Society* (Berkeley: University of California Press, 1984).

46. For more on norm "degeneration," see Diana Panke and Ulrich Petersohn, "Why International Norms Disappear Sometimes," *European Journal of International Relations* 18:4 (2012), pp. 719–742.

47. Jeffrey Checkel and Andrew Moravcsik, "A Constructivist Research Program in EU Studies?" *European Union Politics* 2 (2001), p. 221.

48. Ethan A. Nadelmann, "Global Prohibition Regimes: The Evolution of Norms in International Society," *International Organization* 44:4 (1990), pp. 479–526.

49. Risse, "'Let's Argue!'" p. 6; see also Lantis, "Irrational Exuberance."

50. William A. Gamson and Andre Modigliani, "The Changing Culture of Affirmative Action," in Richard D. Braungart, ed., *Research in Political Sociology*, vol. 3 (Greenwich, UK: JAI Press, 1987), p. 243.

51. Robert M. Entman, "Framing: Toward Clarification of a Fractured Paradigm," *Journal of Communication* 43:3 (1993), pp. 51–58.

52. Barnett, "Culture, Strategy, and Foreign Policy Change," p. 11; See also Sidney Tarrow, *Power in Movements: Collective Action and Politics* (New York: Cambridge University Press, 1994).

53. Entman, "Framing," p. 58.

54. Amitai Etzioni, "Social Norms: Internalization, Persuasion, and History," *Law and Society Review* 34:1 (2000), pp. 41–59.

55. Lawrence Lessig, "The Regulation of Social Meeting," *University of Chicago Law Review* 62:943 (1995), p. 1044.

56. Cass Sunstein, "Social Norms and Social Roles," *Columbia Law Review* 96:903 (1996), p. 939.

57. Goodman and Jinks, "How to Influence States."

58. Amitav Acharya, *Whose Ideas Matter? Agency and Power in Asian Regionalism* (Ithaca, NY: Cornell University Press, 2009); Amitav Acharya, *Constructing a Security Community in Southeast Asia* (London: Routledge, 2009).

59. Rodger A. Payne, "Persuasion, Frames, and Norm Construction," *European Journal of International Relations* 7:1 (2001), p. 38.

60. Thomas Risse-Kappen, "Ideas Do Not Float Freely: Transitional Coalitions, Domestic Structures, and the End of the Cold War," *International Organization* 48:3 (1994), pp. 185–214.

61. Nadelmann, "Global Prohibition Regimes," p. 482.

62. Payne, "Persuasion, Frames, and Norm Construction," p. 41; Marc Lynch, *State Interests and Public Spheres: The International Politics of Jordan's Identity* (New York: Columbia University Press, 1999).

63. Sandholtz, *Prohibiting Plunder*, p. 10.

64. Matthew J. Hoffmann, "My Norm Is Better Than Your Norm: Contestation and Norm Dynamics," paper presented at the Annual Meeting of the International Studies Association, Chicago, March 2, 2007, p. 2.

65. Kathryn Sikkink, "Beyond the Justice Cascade: How Agentic Constructivism Could Help Explain Change in International Politics," revised paper from the Millennium Annual Conference, October 22, 2011, http://www.princeton.edu/politics/about/file-repository/public/Agentic-Constructivism-paper-sent-to-the-Princeton-IR-Colloquium.pdf (accessed January 4, 2013), p. 2.

66. Alastair Iain Johnston, "Treating International Institutions as Social Environments," *International Studies Quarterly* 45:5 (2001), p. 495.

67. Antje Wiener, "The Dual Quality of Norms and Governance Beyond the State: Sociological and Normative Approaches to 'Interaction,'" *Critical Review of International Social and Political Philosophy* 10:1 (2007), p. 43.

68. Ibid., p. 53.

69. Wiener, *Invisible Constitution*, p. 53.

70. Wiener, "Contested Compliance: Interventions on the Normative Structure of World Politics," *European Journal of International Relations* 10:2 (2004), p. 190.

71. Gerry Simpson, *Great Powers and Outlaw States: Unequal Sovereigns in the International Legal Order* (Cambridge, Cambridge University Press, 2004), p. x.

72. Barnett, "Culture, Strategy, and Foreign Policy Change," p. 5.

73. Jennifer Bailey, "Coalitions and Norm Stability: The Case of Whaling," paper presented to the Annual Meeting of the International Studies Association, New York, February 17, 2009, p. 3.

74. Mlada Bukovansky, *Legitimacy and Power Politics: The American and French Revolutions in International Political Culture* (Princeton, NJ: Princeton University Press, 2001), p. 1.

75. Maria Rost Rublee, "Taking Stock of the Nuclear Nonproliferation Regime: Using Social Psychology to Understand Regime Effectiveness," *International Studies Review* 10 (2008), p. 421.

76. Antje Wiener, *A Theory of Contestation* (Berlin: Springer Verlag, 2014), p. 2.

77. Wiener, "The Dual Quality of Norms," p. 43.

78. Ibid., p. 53.

79. Mark C. Suchman, "Managing Legitimacy: Strategic and Institutional Approaches," *Academy of Management Review* 20:4 (1995), p. 574.

80. Ryder McKeown, "Norm Regress: U.S. Revisionism and the Slow Death of the Torture Norm," *International Relations* 23:1 (2009), pp. 5–25.

81. Simpson, *Great Powers and Outlaw States*, p. x.

82. McKeown, "Norm Regress."

83. See Alexander L. George, "Case Studies and Theory Development: The Method of Structured, Focused Comparison," in Paul Gordon Lauren, ed., *Diplomacy: New Approaches in History, Theory, and Policy* (New York: Free Press, 1979); Harry Eckstein, "Case Studies and Theory in Political Science," in Fred Greenstein and Nelson Polsby, eds., *Handbook of Political Science*, vol. 7 (Reading, MA: Addison-Wesley, 1975), pp. 79–138; Arend Lijphart, "Comparative Politics and the Comparative Method," *American Political Science Review* 65:3 (September 1971), pp. 682–693; Alexander L. George and Andrew Bennett, *Case Studies and Theory Development in the Social Sciences* (Cambridge, MA: MIT Press, 2004).

Chapter 3

1. Qtd. in Richard Polenberg, ed., *In the Matter of J. Robert Oppenheimer: The Security Clearance Hearing* (Ithaca, NY: Cornell University Press, 2002), p. 41.

2. "Treaty on the Non-Proliferation of Nuclear Weapons," United Nations, 1970, http://www.un.org/en/conf/npt/2005/npttreaty.html (accessed February 2, 2012).

3. Franklin D'Olier et al., "The United States Strategic Bombing Survey: The Effects of the Atomic Bombings of Hiroshima and Nagasaki," June 30, 1946, Harry S. Truman Presidential Library, Independence, MO, http://www.trumanlibrary.org/whistlestop/study_collections/bomb/large/documents/index.php?documentdate=1946-06-30&documentid=7-1&studycollectionid=&pagenumber=1 (accessed July 19, 2013).

4. "White House Press Release, 6 August 1945," qtd. in Robert C. Williams and Philip L. Cantelton, eds. *The American Atom: A Documentary History of Nuclear Policies from the Discussion of Fission to the Present, 1939–1984* (Philadelphia: University of Pennsylvania Press, 1984), p. 69.

5. See Dietrich Schindler and Jiri Toman, eds., *The Laws of Armed Conflicts: A Collection of Conventions, Resolutions, and Other Documents*, 3rd ed. (Dordrecht: Martinus Nijhoff, 1988).

6. Matthew Evangelista, *Law, Ethics, and the War on Terror* (Cambridge: Polity Press, 2008), p. 7.

7. Convention (II) with Respect to the Laws and Customs of War on Land and its annex: Regulations Concerning the Laws and Customs of War on Land, The Hague, July 29, 1899, http://www.icrc.org/ihl.nsf/FULL/150 (accessed May 4, 2013).

8. Michael Walzer, *Just and Unjust Wars: A Moral Argument with Historical Illustrations* (New York: Basic Books, 2006), p. 36.

9. Louis Henkin, *How Nations Behave: Law and Foreign Policy* (New York: Columbia University Press, 1979); Anne-Marie Slaughter Burley, "International Law and International Relations Theory: A Dual Agenda," *American Journal of International Law* 205:2 (1993), pp. 205–239.

10. Adrian S. Fisher, "Arms Control and Disarmament in International Law," *Virginia Law Review* 50:7 (1964), pp. 1200–1219.

11. Edward Condon, qtd. in Richard Rhodes, *The Making of the Atomic Bomb* (New York: Simon & Schuster, 2012), p. 460. The larger story of the development of the atomic bomb has been told in multiple, rich historical accounts, and is beyond the scope of this book. See, for example, Ray Monk, *Robert Oppenheimer: A Life Inside the Center* (New York: Doubleday, 2013); and Cynthia Kelly, ed., *The Manhattan Project: The Birth of the Atomic Bomb in the Words of Its Creators, Eyewitnesses, and Historians* (London: Black Dog & Leventhal, 2009).

12. Rhodes, *The Making of the Atomic Bomb*, p. 4; see also Tom Zoellner, *Uranium: War, Energy, and the Rock That Shaped the World* (New York: Viking 2009).

13. Philip L. Cantelon, Richard G. Hewlett, and Robert C. Williams, eds., *The American Atom: A Documentary History of Nuclear Policies from the Discovery of Fission to the Present* (Philadelphia: University of Pennsylvania Press, 1992).

14. Williams and Cantelon, eds., *The American Atom: A Documentary History of Nuclear Policies from the Discovery of Fission to the Present, 1939–1984*.

15. Lise Meitner and Otto R. Frisch, "Letter to the Editor: Disintegration of Uranium by Neutrons: A New Type of Nuclear Reaction, *Nature* 143, February 11, 1939, pp. 239–240, http://www.atomicarchive.com/Docs/Begin/Nature_Meitner.shtml (accessed June 26, 2013).

16. Kai Bird and Martin J. Sherwin, *American Prometheus: The Triumph and Tragedy of J. Robert Oppenheimer* (New York: Vintage Books, 2006).

17. See Martin J. Sherwin, *A World Destroyed: The Atomic Bomb and the Grand Alliance* (New York: Knopf, 1975); Lillian Hoddeson et al., *Critical Assembly: A Technical History of Los Alamos during the Oppenheimer Years, 1943–1945* (New York: Cambridge University Press, 1993).

18. Henry DeWolf Smyth, *Atomic Energy for Military Purposes: The Official Report on the Development of the Atomic Bomb under the Auspices of the United States Government, 1940–1945* (Princeton, NJ: Princeton University Press, 1945).

19. Arthur Holly Compton, *Atomic Quest* (Oxford: Oxford University Press, 1956).

20. Eric Schlosser, *Command and Control: Nuclear Weapons, the Damascus Accident, and the Illusion of Safety* (New York: Penguin, 2013).

21. Ibid., pp. 40–41; see also Hoddeson et al., *Critical Assembly.*

22. National Security Archives project website: http://www.gwu.edu/~nsarchiv/NSAEBB/NSAEBB162/index.htm (accessed February 2, 2013).

23. Excerpt from Harry S. Truman's diary, "American Experience Series," http://www.pbs.org/wgbh/americanexperience/features/primary-resources/truman-diary/ (accessed January 29, 2013).

24. Bird and Sherwin, *American Prometheus*, pp. 272–273.

25. Zoellner, *Uranium*, p. 76.

26. Qtd. in "August 6, 1945: A-Bomb Dropped on Hiroshima," *CNN*, http://www.cnn.com/2003/US/03/10/sprj.80.1945.hiroshima/ (accessed January 24, 2013).

27. "Foreign Affairs 1945–1946: Acheson-Lilienthal Report," *U.S. History. com*, http://www.u-s-history.com/pages/h1839.html (accessed June 3, 2011); Schlosser, *Command and Control*, pp. 74–77.

28. See George C. Holt, "The Conference on World Government," *Journal of Higher Education* 17:5 (May 1946), pp. 227–235.

29. Qtd. in Bird and Sherwin, *American Prometheus*, p. 319.

30. "Acheson-Lilienthal Report," Council on Foreign Relations, http://www.cfr.org/proliferation/acheson-lilienthal-report/p19028 (accessed June 4, 2011).

31. Henry D. Sokolski, *Best of Intentions: America's Campaign against Strategic Weapons Proliferation* (Westport, CT: Praeger, 2001), p. 15.

32. Zoellner, *Uranium*, p. 68.

33. Sokolski, *Best of Intentions*, p. 96.

34. Ibid., p. 15.

35. Ibid.

36. Ibid.

37. Ibid., p. 19.

38. Qtd. in ibid., p. 96.

39. Dwight D. Eisenhower, *Mandate for Change, 1953–1956: The White House Years* (New York: Doubleday, 1963), p. 181.

40. Nina Tannenwald, *The Nuclear Taboo: The United States and the Non-Use of Nuclear Weapons since 1945* (Cambridge: Cambridge University Press, 2007), p. 142.

41. John Foster Dulles, "The Evolution of Foreign Policy," January 12, 1954, *U.S. Department of State Bulletin* 30:761 (January 25, 1954), pp. 107–110.

42. John Baylis, "Exchanging Nuclear Secrets: Laying the Foundations of the Anglo-American Nuclear Relationship," *Diplomatic History* 25:1 (2001), p. 36.

43. *Atomic Energy Act*, U.S. Department of Energy. http://www.etec.energy.gov/regulation/atomic-energy-act.html (accessed June 3, 2011).

44. "Summary of the Atomic Energy Act," United States Environmental Protection Agency, March 2, 2001, http://www.epa.gov/regulations/laws/aea.html (accessed June 3, 2011).

45. Qtd. in Richard G. Hewlett and Jack M. Holl, *Atoms for Peace and War, 1953–1961* (Berkeley: University of California Press, 1989), p. 194.

46. U.S. Department of State, Draft Position Paper, "Non-Proliferation of Nuclear Weapons," August 14, 1968, *Foreign Relations of the United States, 1964–1968, Vol. XI, Arms Control and Disarmament*, Document 44 (Washington, DC: U.S. Government Printing Office, 1997).

47. U.S. Department of State, Report by the Committee on Nuclear Proliferation, January 21, 1965, *Foreign Relations of the United States, 1964–1968, Vol. XI, Arms Control and Disarmament*, Document 64 (Washington, DC: U.S. Government Printing Office, 1997), pp. 1–3.

48. Jacques E. C. Hymans, "Proliferation Implications of Civil Nuclear Cooperation: Theory and a Case Study of Tito's Yugoslavia," *Security Studies* 20:1 (2011), p. 74.

49. Leonard Beaton, *Must the Bomb Spread?* (Baltimore, MD: Penguin, 1966), pp. 88–89.

50. Thomas C. Reed and Danny B. Stillman, *The Nuclear Express: A Political History of the Bomb and Its Proliferation* (Minneapolis: Zenith, 2009), p. 56.

51. John F. Kennedy, "News Conference Transcript," March 21, 1963, *American Presidency Project*, http://www.presidency.ucsb.edu/ws/?pid=9124 (accessed June 3, 2013).

52. Mohamed I. Shaker, *The Nuclear Non-Proliferation Treaty: Origin and Implementation, 1959–1979* (London: Oceana Publications, 1980), p. 4.

53. Jack A. Homer, "ENDC at the General Assembly," report for the *Bulletin of the Atomic Scientists* (February 1967), pp. 30–33.

54. Johnson, qtd. in Mark Hibbs, "LBJ's Safeguards Legacy," *Arms Control Wonk*, June 25, 2013, carnegieendowment.org/2013/06/25/lbj-s-safeguards-legacy/gc7r (accessed November 17, 2013).

55. Daniel H. Joyner, *International Law and the Proliferation of Weapons of Mass Destruction* (Oxford: Oxford University Press, 2009).

56. "'The Impulse Toward a Safer World': 40th Anniversary of the Nuclear Nonproliferation Treaty," *The Nuclear Vault*, National Security Archives, p. 3, www2.gwu.edu/nsarchiv/nukevault/ebb253/index.htm.

57 Ibid.

58. U.S. Department of State, "Memorandum from the Director of the Arms Control and Disarmament Agency (Foster) to President Johnson," April 6, 1967, *Foreign Relations of the United States, 1964–1968, Vol. XI, Arms Control and Disarmament,* Document 193, http://history.state.gov/historicaldocuments/frus1964-68v11/d193 (accessed January 28, 2014).

59. "'The Impulse Toward a Safer World,'" p. 3.

60. United States Delegation to the 2010 Nuclear Non-Proliferation Treaty Review Conference, "Treaty on the Non-Proliferation of Nuclear Weapons," U.S. State Department, April 8, 2010, www.state.gov/documents/organization/141503.pdf (accessed May 18, 2011).

Chapter 4

1. "Treaty on the Non-Proliferation of Nuclear Weapons," United Nations, 1970, http://www.un.org/en/conf/npt/2005/npttreaty.html (accessed February 2, 2012).

2. George W. Bush, "Speech at the National Defense University on February 10, 2004," *New York Times,* February 11, 2004, nytimes.com/2004/02/11/politics/10WEB-PTEX.html (accessed January 14, 2012).

3. International Atomic Energy Agency, *Nuclear Power Reactors in the World,* 2012 edition, Reference Data Series no. 2, IAEA-RDS-2/32, http://pub.iaea.org/MTCD/Publications/PDF/FDS2032_web.pdf.

4. David Fischer, *History of the International Atomic Energy Agency: The First Forty Years* (Vienna: IAEA Division of Publications, 1997), pp. 15–28.

5. International Atomic Energy Agency, Statute of the International Atomic Energy Agency, Art. III, 5, http://www.iaea.org/About/statute.html (accessed April 11, 2013).

6. Author's interview with Dean Rust, Washington, DC, October 6, 2010.

7. Robert Chadwell Williams and Philip L. Cantelon, eds., *The American Atom: A Documentary History of Nuclear Policies from the Discovery of Fission to the Present, 1939–1984* (Philadelphia: University of Pennsylvania Press, 1984); United States Department of State, Office of the Historian, *Foreign Relations of the United States, 1961–1963,* vol. 15 (Washington, DC: Government Printing Office, 1995).

8. International Atomic Energy Agency, "The Safeguards System of the International Atomic Energy Agency," http://www.iaea.org/OurWork/SV/Safeguards/documents/safeg_system.pdf (accessed January 20, 2013).

9. For more on the history and science of the atomic bomb program, see Niels Bohr, *Atomic Physics and Human Knowledge* (New York: John Wiley, 1958).

10. "Gaseous Diffusion Uranium Enrichment," *GlobalSecurity.org,* April 27, 2005 (accessed January 4, 2014).

11. Virginius Dabney, *Mr. Jefferson's University: A History* (Charlottesville: University of Virginia Press, 1981), p. 463.

12. R. B. Kehoe, *The Enriching Troika: A History of Urenco to the Year 2000* (Marlow, UK: Urenco Limited, 2002).

13. Ibid.

14. Kurt M. Campbell, Robert J. Einhorn, and Mitchell B. Reiss, *The Nuclear Tipping Point: Why States Reconsider Their Nuclear Choices* (Washington, DC: Brookings Institution Press, 2004).

15. Scott Kemp, "Centrifuges: A New Era for Nuclear Proliferation," report for the Nonproliferation Policy Education Center, June 5, 2012, http://www.npolicy.org/article_file/Centrifuges-_A_new_era_for_nuclear_proliferation.pdf (accessed November 29, 2012).

16. Author's interview with Matthew Kroenig, Washington, DC, October 4, 2010; Author's interview with Deepti Choubey, Washington, DC, October 5, 2010; Confidential interview, Washington, DC, October 10, 2010.

17. "Early Atomic Energy Commission Studies Show Concern over Gas Centrifuge Proliferation Risk," *National Security Archive Electronic Briefing Book* No. 385, July 23, 2012, www.gwu.edu/-nsarchiv/nukevault/ebb385/ (accessed February 8, 2014).

18. See A. A. Wells, "Control of and Cooperation in Gas Centrifuge Research and Development Technology," memorandum to Philip J. Farley, United States Atomic Energy Commission, February 19, 1960, pp. 44–48, www.documentcloud.org/documents/399992-doc-3-wells-report.html (accessed February 8, 2014).

19. Sheena Chestnut, "Illicit Activity and Proliferation: North Korean Smuggling Networks," *International Security* 32:1 (2007), pp. 80–111.

20. Reprocessing was a popular technology in the early Cold War because it was believed that natural supplies of uranium were very limited. For more on the history of these technologies, see Richard G. Hewlett and Jack M. Holl, *Atoms for Peace and War, 1953–1961* (Berkeley: University of California Press, 1989).

21. Steve Fetter and Frank von Hippel, "Is U.S. Reprocessing Worth the Risk?" *Arms Control Today* (September 2005), http://www.armscontrol.org/act/2005_09/Fetter-VonHippel (accessed February 1, 2012).

22. Author's interview with Deepti Choubey, Washington, DC, October 5, 2010.

23. Frank von Hippel, *Managing Spent Fuel in the United States: The Illogic of Reprocessing*, Research report no. 3, International Panel on Fissile Materials (January 2007), http://www.npolicy.org/article_file/Managing_Spent_Fuel_in_the_United_States-The_Illogic_of_Reprocessing.pdf (accessed February 19, 2012).

24. David Albright and Kevin O'Neill, eds., *Solving the North Korean Nuclear Puzzle* (Washington, DC: Institute for Science and National Security, 2000).

25. Victor Gilinsky, Marvin Miller, and Harmon Hubbard, *A Fresh Examination of the Proliferation Dangers of Light Water Reactors* (Washington, DC: Nonproliferation Policy Education Center, 2004).

26. William Bundy, *A Tangled Web: The Making of Foreign Policy in the Nixon Presidency* (New York: Hill and Wang, 1998), p. 87.

27. Minutes of National Security Council Meeting, 29 January 1969, in *Foreign Relations of the United States, 1969–1976* (Washington, DC: Department of State, 1998), p. E-2:6.

28. Qtd in F. J. Gavin, "Nuclear Nixon: Ironies, Puzzles, and the Triumph of Realpolitik," in Fredrik Logevall and Andrew Preston, eds., *Nixon in the World: American Foreign Relations, 1969–1977* (New York: Oxford University Press, 2008), pp. 139–140.

29. Organization for Economic Cooperation and Development, *The Security of Energy Supply and the Contribution of Nuclear Energy* (Paris: OECD Publications, 2010), http://www.oecd-nea.org/pub/security-energy-exec-summary.pdf (accessed May 19, 2013).

30. Walton L. Brown, "Presidential Leadership and U.S. Nonproliferation Policy," *Presidential Studies Quarterly* 24:3 (1994), p. 565.

31. See Walton L. Brown, "Assessing the Impact of American Nonproliferation Policy: 1970–1980," Ph.D. diss. (Ann Arbor, MI: University Microfilms, 1982), p. 49.

32. "Secret: Discussion Paper on U.S. Non-Proliferation Policy," Department of State Briefing Memorandum to Secretary Kissinger from Winston Lord, July 11, 1974, Declassified record number 115198: Nuclear Nonproliferation 2, July 11, 1974 (paper copy at National Security Archive, viewed February 21, 2014).

33. United States Arms Control and Disarmament Agency and U.S. Department of State Policy Planning Staff, Analytic Staff meeting on non-proliferation strategy, July 31, 1974, Record number 117436: Nuclear Nonproliferation 2 (paper copy at National Security Archive, viewed February 21, 2014).

34. Ibid.

35. Daniel H. Joyner, "The Nuclear Suppliers Group: History and Functioning," *International Trade Law and Regulation* 11:2 (2005), pp. 84–96.

36. National Security Council Undersecretaries Committee, "Memorandum for the President, Subject: U.S. Nuclear Nonproliferation Policy," Record Number 117590, August 25, 1974, secret document of the State Department Policy Planning Staff (paper copy at National Security Archive, viewed February 21, 2014). Additional background information was provided by author's interview with Dean Rust, Washington, DC, October 6, 2010.

37. "Nuclear Suppliers Guidelines: Memorandum for Mr. Brent Scowcroft, the White House," December 31, 1975, Record no. 117001, Nuclear Nonproliferation 2 (paper copy viewed at National Security Archive, viewed February 21, 2014).

38. The establishment of an export program demanding full-scope safeguards—as well as related ideas like a fuel bank, multinational enrichment facilities, and spent fuel repositories—is still a contemporary issue of debate.

39. Gerard Smith and Helena Cobban, "A Blind Eye to Nuclear Proliferation, *Foreign Affairs* 68:3 (1989), pp. 53–70. See also Ronald Reagan, "Statement on United States Nuclear Nonproliferation Policy," July 16, 1981, reprinted in *Public Papers of Ronald Reagan*, University of Texas Library, http://www.reagan.utexas.edu/archives/speeches/1981/71681a.htm (accessed April 14, 2012).

40. Joseph F. Pilat and Warren H. Donnelly, "The Nuclear Export Policy of the Reagan Administration," *Energy Policy* (June 1983), pp. 168–171.

41. United States Senate, Committee on Foreign Relations, Nuclear Proliferation: Learning from the Iraq Experience, hearing before the Committee on Foreign Relations, 102 Cong. 1st Sess., October 17, 1991, p. 20.

42. See Matthew Kroenig, "Exporting the Bomb: Why States Provide Sensitive Nuclear Assistance," *American Political Science Review* 103:1 (2009), pp. 113–133.

43. See Mark Hibbs, *The Future of the Nuclear Suppliers Group* (Washington, DC: Carnegie Endowment for International Peace, 2011).

44. Nuclear Threat Initiative, "Russia: Nuclear Exports to India," Center for Nonproliferation Studies, 2010, www.nti.org/db/nisprofs/russia/exports/rusind/nuclovr.htm (accessed September 22, 2012).

45. International Atomic Energy Agency, "Communication Received from Certain Member States Regarding Guidelines for the Export of Nuclear Material, Equipment or Technology," July 1992, www.iaea.org/Publications/Documents/Infcircs/Others/infcirc254r1p2.pdf.

46. Mark Hibbs, "Nuclear Suppliers Group and the IAEA Additional Protocol," *Nuclear Energy Brief,* Carnegie Endowment for International Peace, August 18, 2010, www.carnegieendowment.org/publications/index.cfm?fa=view&id=41393 (accessed May 11, 2011).

47. Bush, "Speech at the National Defense University on February 10, 2004."

48. Hibbs, "Nuclear Suppliers Group and the IAEA Additional Protocol."

49. Qtd. in Testimony of Fred McGoldrick, Senate Foreign Relations Committee, July 31, 2007 regarding S. 1138, p. 7, http://www.foreign.senate.gov/imo/media/doc/McGoldrickTestimony070731.pdf (accessed March 18, 2011).

50. Reflecting on the failure of the conference, UN Secretary General Kofi Annan opined, the nonproliferation regime faced a "dual crisis of compliance and confidence"; Annan, "Break the Nuclear Deadlock," *International Herald Tribune,* May 30, 2005, www.iht.com/articles/2005/05/29/news/edannan.php (accessed May 20, 2008).

51. Qtd. in David S. Jonas, John Carlson, and Richard S. Goorevich, "The NSG Decision on Sensitive Nuclear Transfers: ABACC and the Additional Protocol," *Arms Control Today,* November 2012, www.armscontrol.org/act/2012_11/The-NSG-Decision-on-Sensitive-Nuclear-Transfers-ABACC-and-the-Additional-Protocol (accessed December 13, 2013).

52. Hibbs, "Nuclear Suppliers Group and the IAEA Additional Protocol."

53. See Jonathan Pearl, "Charting a Smarter Course for a U.S.-Jordan Nuclear Deal," *Bulletin of the Atomic Scientists* (October 25, 2010), www.thebulletin.org/web-edition/op-eds/charting-smarter-course-us-jordan-nuclear-deal (accessed November 19, 2010).

54. Daniel Horner, "Officials Spell Out Nuclear Trade Policy, *Arms Control Today* 42:3 (2012), http://www.armscontrol.org/act/2012_03/Officials_Spell_Out_Nuclear_Trade_Policy (accessed March 23, 2012). Further perspective on these policies was provided in the author's interview with Sharon Squassoni, Washington, DC, October 6, 2010.

55. Richard Stratford, "U.S. Nuclear Cooperation: How and With Whom?" Carnegie International Nuclear Policy Conference, March 29, 2011, http://carnegieendowment.org/files/US_Nuclear_Cooperation-How_and_With_Whom.pdf (accessed March 21, 2012).

56. Qtd. in Daniel Horner, "U.S. Policy on Nuclear Pacts Detailed," *Arms Control Today*, January 2014, https://www.armscontrol.org/act/2014_01–02/US-Policy-on-Nuclear-Pacts-Detailed.

57. Geoffrey L. Herrera, *Technology and International Transformation: The Railroad, the Atom Bomb, and the Politics of Technological Change* (Albany: State University of New York Press, 2006).

58. Interview with senior government official, Washington, DC, February 26, 2014.

59. Ibid.

Chapter 5

1. Madeleine K. Albright and Richard S. Williamson, *The United States and R2P: From Words to Action*, report of the Working Group on the Responsibility to Protect, jointly convened by the United States Holocaust Memorial Museum, United States Institute of Peace, and Brookings Institution (Washington, DC: United States Institute of Peace, 2013), pp. 7–9.

2. Nathaniel Raymond, qtd. in Paul Harris, "George Clooney's Satellite Spies Reveal Secrets of Sudan's Bloody Army" *The Guardian*, March 24, 2012, www.guardian.com.uk/world/2012/mar/24/george-clooney-spies-secrets-sudan.html (accessed June 19, 2013).

3. Alan Bloomfield, "Resisting the Responsibility to Protect: The Advantages Enjoyed by 'Norm Antipreneurs,'" September 2014, p. 2, unpublished manuscript (author's copy).

4. Mark W. Zacher, "The Territorial Integrity Norm: International Boundaries and the Use of Force," *International Organization* 55:2 (2001), p. 216.

5. Hedley Bull, *The Anarchical Society* (New York: Columbia University Press, 1977); George Clark, *Early Modern Europe from about 1450 to about 1720* (London: Oxford University Press, 1972).

6. Louis Henkin, *How Nations Behave: Law and Foreign Policy* (New York: Columbia University Press, 1979).

7. Robert J. Art and Kenneth N. Waltz, "Technology, Strategy, and the Uses of Force," in Robert J. Art and Kenneth N. Waltz, eds., *The Use of Force: International Politics and Foreign Policy*, 2nd ed. (Lanham, MD: University Press of America, 1983), p. 6.

8. For a good perspective on the modern debate about sovereignty and intervention, see Oliver Ramsbotham and Tom Woodhouse, *Humanitarian Intervention in Contemporary Conflict* (Cambridge: Polity Press, 1996).

9. Theodor Meron, "The Martens Clause, Principles of Humanity, and Dictates of Public Conscience," *American Journal of International Law* 94:1 (2000), pp. 78–89.

10. BBC, "Analysis: Defining Genocide," *BBC News*, August 27, 2010, http://www.bbc.co.uk/news/world-11108059 (accessed July 20, 2013).

11. William E. Burrows, *Deep Black: Space Espionage and National Security* (New York: Random House, 1986), p. 32.

12. Jeffrey T. Richelson, *The U.S. Intelligence Community*, 6th ed. (Boulder, CO: Westview, 2011), p. 183; Frank Oliveri, "The U-2 Comes in from the Cold," *Air Force Magazine* (September 1994), pp. 45–50.

13. This is the same Arthur C. Clarke who went on to fame as an author of science fiction novels. See Jonathan Higgins, *Satellite Newsgathering* (Oxford: Focal Press, 1999).

14. See Arthur C. Clarke, "Extra-Terrestrial Relays: Can Rocket Stations Give World-Wide Radio Coverage?" *Wireless World* (1945), pp. 305–308.

15. "Red Moon Over the U.S.," *Time*, October 14, 1957, p. 19.

16. *GRAB*, an electronic intelligence satellite launched by the Navy in June 1960, actually became the first operational U.S. reconnaissance satellite in orbit. National Reconnaissance Office, "Corona Fact Sheet," www.nro.gov/history/csnr/corona/factsheet.html (accessed June 18, 2013).

17. See Ingard Clausen, Edward A. Miller, Robert A. McDonald, and Courtney V. Hastings, eds., *Intelligence Revolution 1960: Retrieving the CORONA Imagery That Helped Win the Cold War* (Washington, DC: Center for the Study of National Reconnaissance, April 2012).

18. Office of the Director, National Reconnaissance Office, "Memorandum for Chairman, United States Intelligence Board. Subject: Study of Requirements for Satellite Reconnaissance Responsive to Warning/Indications Needs," March 12, 1969, http://www.nro.gov/foia/declass/NROStaffRecords/1014.pdf (accessed June 21, 2013).

19. For example: William Potter, ed., *Verification and SALT: The Challenge of Strategic Deception* (Boulder, CO: Westview, 1980); Curtis O. Davis, *Hyperspectral Imaging: Utility for Military, Science, and Commercial Applications* (Washington, DC: Naval Research Laboratory, October 1996).

20. Craig Covault, "Advanced KH-11 Broadens U.S. Recon Capability," *Aviation Week & Space Technology*, January 6, 1997, p. 24.

21. "NRO Presses New Satellite Imagery Architecture," *Aerospace Daily*, May 21, 1998, pp. 175–176.

22. William F. Brinkman, Douglas E. Haggan, and William W. Troutman, "A History of the Invention of the Transistor and Where It Will Lead Us," *IEEE Journal of Solid-State Circuits* 32:12 (1997), http://classes.soe.ucsc.edu/ee171/Winter06/notes/transistor.pdf (accessed July 14, 2013).

23. David Hoffman, "Global Communications Network Was Pivotal in Defeat of Junta," *Washington Post*, August 23, 1991, p. A27.

24. Larry Minear, Colin Scott, and Robert Weiss, *The News Media, Civil Wars and Humanitarian Action* (Boulder, CO: Lynne Rienner 1997).

25. See Thomas G. Weiss, *Military-Civilian Interactions: Intervening in Humanitarian Crises* (Lanham, MD: Rowman & Littlefield, 1999).

26. Qtd. in Nicholas J. Wheeler, *Saving Strangers: Humanitarian Intervention in International Society* (Oxford: Oxford University Press, 2000), p. 147; "Bush: No Obligation to Kurds" *International Herald Tribune*, April 6–7, 1991, p. 1.

27. Martin Shaw, "Global Voices: Civil Societies and the Media in Global Crises," in Timothy Dunne and Nicholas J. Wheeler, eds., *Human Rights in Global Politics* (Cambridge University Press, 1999), p. 229.

28. Wheeler, *Saving Strangers*, p. 149.

29. Daniel Schorr, "Ten Days That Shook the White House," *Columbia Journalism Review*, July/August 1991, pp. 21–23.

30. Qtd. in ibid., p. 21.

31. Robert I. Rotberg and Thomas G. Weiss, eds., *From Massacres to Genocide: The Media, Public Policy, and Humanitarian Crises* (Washington, DC: Brookings Institution, 1996). This new outlook appeared to waver, though, when the international community confronted ethnic violence spilling out of control in Rwanda in 1994.

32. Joshua Muravchik, *Exporting Democracy: Fulfilling America's Destiny* (Washington, DC: American Enterprise Institute Press, 1992).

33. Noel Malcolm, *Bosnia: A Short History* (New York: New York University Press, 1994), pp. 54–55. Research for this section is also derived from collaborative work with Eric Moskowitz; see Jeffrey S. Lantis and Eric Moskowitz, "War in Kosovo: Coercive Diplomacy," in Ralph G. Carter, ed., *Contemporary Cases in U.S. Foreign Policy: From Terrorism to Trade* (Washington, DC: Congressional Quarterly Press, 2002).

34. See Sabrina Petra Ramet, "War in the Balkans," *Foreign Affairs* 71:2 (1992), pp. 174–181.

35. Author's confidential interview, former Bush administration official C, Washington, DC, October 14, 2010.

36. Qtd. in Eytan Gilboa, "Effects of Global Television News on U.S. Policy in International Conflict," in Philip Seib, ed., *Media and Conflict in the Twenty-First Century* (London: Palgrave Macmillan, 2005), pp. 1–32.

37. David D. Pearce, *Wary Partners: Diplomats and the Media* (Washington, DC: CQ Press, 1995), p. 18; Babak Bahador, "Did the Global War on Terror End the CNN Effect?" *Media, War & Conflict* 4:1 (2011), pp. 37–54.

38. Steven Livingston, *Clarifying the CNN Effect: An Examination of Media Effects According to Type of Military Intervention*, Research Paper R-18 (Cambridge, MA: Joan Shorenstein Center, John F. Kennedy School of Government, Harvard University, 1997).

39. Qtd. in interview with PBS; see Frontline, "Interviews: Madeleine Albright," *PBS*, April 18, 1999, http://www.pbs.org/wgbh/pages/frontline/shows/kosovo/interviews/albright.html (accessed July 21, 2013).

40. Michael Hirsh and John Barry, "How We Stumbled into War," *Newsweek*, April 12, 1999, p. 40; Madeleine Albright, *Madam Secretary: A Memoir* (New York: Hyperion, 2003), pp. 378–391.

41. William J. Clinton, "Statement by the President to the Nation," March 24, 1999, http://www2.whitehouse.gov/WH/Newhtml/19990324-2872.html (accessed November 29, 2006).

42. Tom Raum, "Cost of Kosovo Conflict Said to Be $4 Billion," *Washington Post,* June 8, 1999, p. A1.

43. William J. Clinton, "Remarks to Kosovo International Security Force Troops in Skopje, June 22, 2009," *Public Papers of the Presidents of the United States: William J. Clinton, 1999,* Book I, pp. 992–993, https://www.gpo.gov/fdsys/pkg/PPP-1999-book1/html/PPP-1999-book1-doc-pg992.htm (accessed January 13, 2016).

44. Francis M. Deng, "Frontiers of Sovereignty," *Leiden Journal of International Law* 8:2 (2005), pp. 249–286; Francis M. Deng, Sadikiel Kimaro, Terrence Lyons, Donald Rothchild, and I. William Zartman, *Sovereignty as Responsibility: Conflict Management in Africa* (Washington, DC: Brookings Institution Press, 1996).

45. Deng, "Frontiers of Sovereignty"; Deng et al., *Sovereignty as Responsibility.*

46. Weiss, *Military-Civilian Interactions,* p. 24.

47. Cristina G. Badescu and Linnea Bergholm, "The Responsibility to Protect and the Conflict in Darfur: The Big Let-Down," *Security Dialogue* 40:3 (2009), p. 288 (emphasis added).

48. Weiss, *Military-Civilian Interactions,* p. 22.

49. Wheeler, *Saving Strangers;* Jutta Brunnée and Stephen J. Toope, "Norms, Institutions and UN Reform: The Responsibility to Protect," *Behind the Headlines* 63:3 (2006), pp. 1–11.

50. See Badescu and Bergholm, "The Responsibility to Protect and the Conflict in Darfur," pp. 286–291.

51. Letter from John Bolton, Representative of the United States of America to the United Nations, August 30, 2005, http://www.humanrightsvoices.org/site/documents/?d=551 (accessed March 4, 2013).

52. Ban Ki-moon, *Implementing the Responsibility to Protect,* Report from the Secretary-General, United Nations document A/63/677, January 2009; Brunnée and Toope, "Norms, Institutions and UN Reform."

53. United Nations Institute for Training and Research, Operational Satellite Applications Programme, General Information, http://www.unitar.org/unosat/ (accessed January 15, 2016).

54. Human Rights Watch, "Spotting War Crimes from Space," Live chat with Josh Lyons, Satellite Imagery Analyst for HRW's Emergencies Division, on February 5, 2014.

55. Nathaniel A. Raymond, Benjamin I. Davies, Brittany L. Card, Ziad Al Achkar, and Isaac L. Baker, "While We Watched: Assessing the Impact of the Satellite Sentinel Project," *Georgetown University Science & Technology Journal* (Summer/Fall 2013), http://journal.georgetown.edu/2013/07/26/while-we-watched-assessing-t . . . pact-of-the-satellite-sentinel-project-by-nathaniel-a-raymond-et-al (accessed August 11, 2013).

56. Samantha Power, "Dying in Darfur: Can the Ethnic Cleansing in Sudan Be Stopped?" *New Yorker,* August 30, 2004, http://www.newyorker.com/archive/2004/08/30/040830fa_fact1 (accessed February 22, 2012).

57. Glenn Kessler, "Libya, Obama, and the Tragedy in Darfur," *Washington Post*, March 24, 2011, http://www.washingtonpost.com/blogs/fact-checker/post/libya-obama-and-the-tragedy-in-darfur/2011/03/23/ABlu34KB_blog.html (accessed February 23, 2012).

58. Badescu and Bergholm, "The Responsibility to Protect and the Conflict in Darfur."

59. Ban, *Implementing the Responsibility to Protect*.

60. See Robert Latham, ed., *Bombs and Bandwidth: The Emerging Relationship between Information Technology and Security* (New York: New Press, 2003).

61. Raymond, et al., "While We Watched"; Harris, "George Clooney's Satellite Spies Reveal Secrets of Sudan's Bloody Army."

62. Author's interview with Nathaniel Raymond, director of the Harvard Satellite Sentinel Project and the Harvard Signals Program, August 15, 2013.

63. Harris, "George Clooney's Satellite Spies Reveal Secrets of Sudan's Bloody Army."

64. Author's interview with Nathaniel Raymond.

65. Harris, "George Clooney's Satellite Spies Reveal Secrets of Sudan's Bloody Army."

66. Author's interview with Nathaniel Raymond.

67. Akshaya Kumar, qtd. in GooglePlus Hangout, "Using Tech to Fight Atrocities," webinar November 27, 2013, sponsored by the Digital Mass Atrocity Prevention Lab (DMAPLab), with speakers Christopher Tuckwood (Sentinel Project), Akshaya Kumar (Enough Project), Nathaniel Raymond (Signal Program on Human Security and Technology at the Harvard Humanitarian Initiative), and Kyle Matthews (Montreal Institute for Genocide and Human Rights Studies), https://plus.google.com/u/0/events/cuvq5u235lpt7vqb7j2mfis6pgk?authkey=CITI1LOAouamfw.

68. 62 Members of Congress Letter to President Barack Obama, November 21, 2011, cc: The Honorable Hillary Rodham Clinton, Secretary of State, and Princeton N. Lyman, U.S. Special Envoy for Sudan (author's copy).

69. "The Role of the Human Rights Council in Supporting the Practical Implementation of the Responsibility to Protect," Statement by the Delegation of the United States of America, Human Rights Council 20th Session, Geneva, June 19, 2012, http://geneva.usmission.gov/2012/06/19/the-u-s-strong-supporter-of-the-concept-of-responsibility-to-protect-r2p (accessed July 8, 2013).

70. Presidential Study Directive/PSD-10, August 4, 2011, White House Memo (for immediate release); Subject: "Creation of an Interagency Atrocities Prevention Board and Corresponding Interagency Review," http://responsibilitytoprotect.org/index.php/component/content/article/interagency-atrocities-prevention-board (accessed July 8, 2013).

71. White House, Office of the Press Secretary, Presidential Studies Directive on Mass Atrocities, Presidential Study Directive/PSD-10, August 4, 2011, http://www.whitehouse.gov/the-press-office/2011/08/04/presidential-study-directive-mass-atrocities (accessed July 2, 1013).

72. Ibid.

73. Raymond et al., "While We Watched."

74. Ibid.

75. Author's interview with Raymond, August 15, 2013.

76. Author's interview with Joshua Lyons; see also Joshua Lyons, "Documenting Violations of International Humanitarian Law from Space: A Critical Review of Geospatial Analysis of Satellite and Imagery during Armed Conflicts in Gaza (2009), Georgia (2008), and Sri Lanka (2009)," *International Review of the Red Cross* 94:886 (Summer 2012), pp. 739–763.

77. Author's interview with Cameron Hudson, director of the Center for the Prevention of Genocide at the U.S. Holocaust Museum; former chief of staff of U.S. ambassador Princeton Lyman, the U.S. Special Envoy to Sudan; former director of African Affairs at the National Security Council at the White House, 2005–2009; Washington, DC, April 24, 2014.

78. Ibid.

79. Wheeler, *Saving Strangers*.

80. Kofi Annan, "Two Concepts of Sovereignty," *The Economist*, September 18, 1999, p. 49; see also Kofi Annan, *In Larger Freedom: Towards Development, Security, and Human Rights for All*, Report of the Secretary General, A/59/2005 (New York: United Nations, March 21, 2005).

Chapter 6

1. Carl von Clausewitz, *On War*, eds./trans. Michael Howard and Peter Paret (Princeton, NJ: Princeton University Press, 1976), p. 83.

2. Barack Obama, "Remarks by the President at the National Defense University," May 23, 2013, http://www.whitehouse.gov/the-press-office/2013/05/23/remarks-president-national-defense-university (accessed May 24, 2013).

3. Brian Glyn Williams, "A History of the World's First Drone War," *History News Network*, September 25, 2009, http:hnn.us/article/153148; excerpt from his book, *Predators: The CIA's Drone War on Al Qaeda* (Washington, DC: Potomac Books, 2013); Author's interview with Jeremiah Gertler, military aviation specialist at the Congressional Research Service, Washington, DC, February 24, 2014.

4. See Mika Nishimura Hayashi, "The Principle of Civilian Protection and Contemporary Armed Conflict," in Howard W. Hensel, ed., *The Law of Armed Conflict: Constraints on the Contemporary Use of Military Force* (New York: Ashgate Publishers, 2007), pp. 105–129.

5. Louise Doswald-Beck, "The Value of the 1977 Geneva Protocols for the Protection of Civilians," in M. A. Meyer, ed., *Armed Conflict and the New Law: Aspects of the 1977 Geneva Protocols and the 1981 Weapons Convention* (London: British Institute of International and Comparative Law, 1989), pp. 137–172.

6. Qtd. in Adam Roberts and Richard Guelff, eds., *Documents on the Laws of War*, 3rd ed. (Oxford: Oxford University Press, 2000), p. 420.

7. See Franklin L. Ford, *Political Murder: From Tyrannicide to Terrorism* (Cambridge, MA: Harvard University Press, 1985); Ward Thomas, *The Ethics of Destruction* (Ithaca, NY: Cornell University Press, 2001), p. 56.

8. Thomas, Chapter 3 "International Assassination: 'An Infamous and Execrable Practice,'" in *The Ethics of Destruction*, pp. 47–85.

9. Hans Morgenthau, *Politics Among Nations: The Struggle for Power and Peace*, 4th ed. (New York: McGraw-Hill, 1967), p. 225.

10. Hugo Grotius, "De Jure Belli ac Pacis Libri Tres," rev. ed. 1646, reprinted in *The Classics of International Law*, translated by Francis W. Kelsey (Oxford: Clarendon 1925), pp. 649–650.

11. Qtd. in Thomas, *Ethics of Destruction*, p. 58.

12. Qtd. in Stephen F. Knox, *Secret and Sanctioned: Covert Operations and the American Presidency* (New York: Oxford University Press, 1996), p. 171.

13. Yale Law School, Avalon Law Project, "General Orders No.100," http://avalon.law.yale.edu/19th_century/lieber.asp (accessed June 3, 2014).

14. Bert Brandenburg, "Note: The Legality of Assassination as an Aspect of Foreign Policy," *Virginia Journal of International Law* 27:3 (1987); Michael N. Schmitt, "State-Sponsored Assassination in International and Domestic Law," *Yale Journal of International Law* 17 (1992), pp. 609–685.

15. "Plan to Kill Hitler was 'Unsporting,'" *Times of London*, August 5, 1969, p. 5, qtd. in Thomas, *The Ethics of Destruction*, p. 49.

16. "Hunting Hitler," *Sunday Times*, July 26, 1998, pp. 1–2.

17. United States Select Senate Committee to Study Governmental Operations with Respect to Intelligence Activities, *Alleged Assassination Plots Involving Foreign Leaders*, Sen. Rep. No. 94–465 (Washington, DC: Government Printing Office, 1975), p. 259.

18. See Catherine Lotrionte, "Targeting Regime Leaders during Armed Hostilities: An Effective Way to Achieve Regime Change?" in Howard M. Hensel, ed., *The Law of Armed Conflict: Constraints on the Contemporary Use of Military Force* (London: Ashgate, 2005), pp. 21–38.

19. Frank Sauer and Niklas Schörnig, "Killer Drones: The 'Silver Bullet' of Democratic Warfare?" *Security Dialogue* 43:3 (2012), pp. 363–380. On the revolutionary potential of drones, see Michael Sherry, *The Rise of American Airpower: The Creation of Armageddon* (New Haven, CT: Yale University Press, 1989).

20. Jane Mayer, "The Predator War," *New Yorker*, October 26, 2009, p. 38.

21. Andrew Callam, "Drone Wars: Armed Unmanned Aerial Vehicles," *International Affairs Review*, 2010, www.iar-gwu.org/node/144; Thomas P. Ehrhard, "Unmanned Aerial Vehicles in the United States Armed Services: A Comparative Study of Weapon System Innovation," Ph.D. diss. (Johns Hopkins University, 2000); Jeremiah Gertler, *U.S. Unmanned Aerial Systems*, Congressional Research Service Report R42136, January 3, 2012, https://www.fas.org/sgp/crs/natsec/R42136.pdf.

22. Richard Whittle, "The Man Who Invented the Predator," *Air & Space Magazine*, April 2013, http://www.airspacemag.com/flight-today/the-man-who-invented-the-predator-3970502/?all (accessed February 27, 2014).

23. Ibid.

24. Author's interview with Jeremiah Gertler, February 24, 2014.

25. Ibid.

26. Patrick Coffey, "War from Afar: How the Pentagon Fell in Love with Drones," *Salon*, December 8, 2013, http://www.salon.com/2013/12/08/war_from_afar_how_the_pentagon_fell_in_love_with_drones/ (accessed January 22, 2014).

27. P. W. Singer, *Wired for War: The Robotics Revolution and Conflict in the 21st Century* (New York: Penguin, 2009), p. 33.

28. Qtd. in Klaus Brinkbaumer and John Goetz, "Obama's Shadowy Drone War," *Der Spiegel*, October 12, 2010.

29. Frontline, "The Gulf War 1990–1991: An In-Depth Examination of the Persian Gulf Crisis, 1992," http://www.pbs.org/wgbh/pages/frontline/gulf/weapons/drones.html (accessed December 22, 2013).

30. See George Tenet, *At the Center of the Storm: My Years at the CIA* (New York: Harper, 2007).

31. David Axe, "Upgrades to Killer Drone Could Make It Fly for Two Days Straight," *Wired*, April 19, 2012, http://www.wired.com/dangerroom/2012/04/killer-drone-upgrade/ (accessed February 11, 2014).

32. Williams, *Predators*, p. 24.

33. Williams, "A History of the World's First Drone War."

34. Ibid.

35. "A History of Drone Warfare," *New York Times*, May 24, 2013, p. A8.

36. Department of Defense, *FY 2009–2034 Unmanned Systems Integrated Roadmap* (Washington, DC: Department of Defense, 2009), p. 21.

37. Today the Pentagon is believed to have a drone fleet numbering about 20,000 systems; Gertler, *U.S. Unmanned Aerial Systems*.

38. In an interesting twist, Iran claims to be in possession of one following its incursion into Iranian airspace and Iranian shoot-down in December 2011.

39. DARPA, "J-UCAS Program," http://archive.darpa.mil/j-ucas/J-UCAS_Overview.htm (accessed January 17, 2016).

40. BBC, "'Killer Robots' to Be Debated at the UN," *BBC News*, May 9, 2014, http://www.bbc.com/news/technology-27343076 (accessed September 16, 2014).

41. Department of Defense, *FY 2009–2034 Unmanned Systems Integrated Roadmap*, p. xiii.

42. Qtd. in Jane Mayer, "The Manipulator," *New Yorker*, June 7, 2004, p. 61.

43. Yossi Melman, "Why the Plot to Kill Hussein Failed," *Los Angeles Times*, July 21, 1991, pp. M1–M2.

44. Paul Richter, "Congress Ponders Whether the U.S. Should Ease Ban on Assassinations," *Los Angeles Times*, September 18, 1998, http://articles.latimes.com/1998/sep/18/news/mn-24038 (accessed February 11, 2014).

45. "Senators Ask Legality of Assassinating Suspect Terrorist," *Dallas Morning News*, September 4, 1998, p. 13A. See also Jami Melissa Jackson, "The Legality of Assassination of Independent Terrorist Leaders: An Examination of National and

International Implications," *North Carolina Journal of International Law and Commercial Regulation* 24:669 (1999).

46. Qtd. in Nicholas Lemann, "The Next World Order: The Bush Administration May Have a Brand New Doctrine of Power," *New Yorker*, April 1, 2002, www.newyorker.com/fact/content/?020401fa_FACT1 (accessed May 19, 2013).

47. White House, "Statement by President George W. Bush," September 12, 2001, www.whitehouse.gov/news/releases/2001/09/20010912.html (accessed November 22, 2013).

48. Ivo H. Daalder and James M. Lindsay, *America Unbound* (Washington, DC: Brookings Institution Press, 2003), p. 2.

49. George W. Bush, "President Bush Delivers Graduation Speech at West Point," June 1, 2002, www.whitehouse.gov/news/releases/2002/06/print/20020601-3.html (accessed April 22, 2013).

50. White House, *The National Security Strategy of the United States of America*, September 2002, www.whitehouse.gov/nsc/nss.html, p. 15.

51. Steven R. David, "Fatal Choices: Israel's Policy of Targeted Killings," *Mideast Security and Policy Studies* 51:4 (2002), pp. 1–26; and Daniel Byman, "Do Targeted Killings Work?" *Foreign Affairs* 85:2 (March/April 2006), pp. 102–104.

52. Bryan C. Price, "Targeting Top Terrorists: How Leadership Decapitation Contributes to Counterterrorism," *International Security* 36:4 (2012), p. 10.

53. Barton Gellman, "CIA Weighs 'Targeted Killing' Missions," *Washington Post*, October 28, 2001, http://www.washingtonpost.com/ac2/wp-dyn/A63203-2001Oct27.

54. Williams, "A History of the World's First Drone War."

55. Ibid., p. 78.

56. "U.S. Air Strikes Called Very Effective," *CNN.com*, May 18, 2009.

57. Harold H. Koh, "The Obama Administration and International Law," speech to the American Society of International Law, March 25, 2010, http://www.state.gov/s/l/releases/remarks/139119.htm (accessed January 19, 2014).

58. "The Rise—and Decline—of the Drones," *New York Times*, May 21, 2013, p. A1.

59. Anthony Arend, "International Law and the Preemptive Use of Military Force," *Washington Quarterly* 26:2 (2003), pp. 89–103; and Steven Hook and John Spanier, *American Foreign Policy Since World War II*, 16th ed. (Washington, DC: CQ Press, 2004).

60. Jenna Jordan, "When Heads Roll: Assessing the Effectiveness of Leadership Decapitation," *Security Studies* 18:4 (2009), pp. 719–755; Robert A. Pape, "The Strategic Logic of Suicide Terrorism," *American Political Science Review* 97:3 (2003), pp. 1–19.

61. White House, Office of the Press Secretary, "Remarks by the President on Osama bin Laden," May 1, 2011, http://www.whitehouse.gov/blog/2011/05/02/osama-bin-laden-dead (accessed February 26, 2014).

62. Ibid.

63. James Dao and Dalia Sussman, "For Obama, Big Rise in Poll Numbers after Bin Laden Raid," *New York Times*, May 4, 2011, http://www.nytimes.com/2011/05/05/us/politics/05poll.html?_r=0.

64. White House, Office of the Press Secretary, "Press Briefing by Press Secretary Jay Carney," May 4, 2011, http://www.whitehouse.gov/the-press-office/2011/05/04/press-briefing-press-secretary-jay-carney-542011 (accessed March 19, 2014).

65. Daniel Klaidman, "Obama: I Make the Drone Decisions," *Daily Beast*, May 23, 2013, http://www.thedailybeast.com/articles/2013/05/23/obama-i-make-the-drone-decisions.html (accessed March 21, 2014).

66. Ian Cobain, "Obama's Secret Kill List: The Disposition Matrix" *The Guardian*, July 14, 2013, http://www.theguardian.com/world/2013/jul/14/obama-secret-kill-list-disposition-matrix.

67. "John Brennan Delivers Speech on Drone Ethics," Talk of the Nation Report, National Public Radio, May 1, 2012, www.npr.org/2012/05/01/151778804/john-brennan-delivers-speech-on-drone-ethics.

68. Ibid.

69. Ibid.

70. Ibid.

71. New York Times Editorial Board, "The End of Perpetual War," *New York Times*, May 23, 2013, p. A17.

72. White House, Office of the Press Secretary, "Fact Sheet: U.S. Policy Standards and Procedures for the Use of Force in Counterterrorism Operations Outside the United States and Areas of Active Hostilities," May 23, 2013, http://www.whitehouse.gov/the-press-office/2013/05/23/fact-sheet-us-policy-standards-and-procedures-use-force-counterterrorism (accessed February 24, 2014).

73. Ian Hurd, "Breaking and Making New Norms: American Revisionism and Crises of Legitimacy," *International Politics* 44:2 (2007), pp. 194–213, p. 201.

74. Qtd. in Owen Bowcott, "Drone Strikes Threaten 50 Years of International Law, Says UN Rapporteur," *The Guardian*, June 21, 2012, http://www.theguardian.com/world/2012/jun/21/drone-strikes-international-law-un (accessed February 17, 2014).

75. Clifford Bob, "A Framework for Analyzing Conflict over Norms—and Its Application to the Assassination/Targeted Killing Norm," paper prepared for presentation at the Workshop on Anti-Preneurs, International Studies Association Annual Conference, Toronto, March 25, 2014 (author's copy).

76. Qtd. in Michael Isikoff, "Justice Department Memo Reveals Legal Case for Drone Strikes on Americans," *NBC News*, February 4, 2013, http://investigations.nbc-news.com/_news/2013/02/04/16843014-justice-department-memo-reveals-legal-case-for-drone-strikes-on-americans?lite (accessed January 17, 2016).

77. Keith B. Richburg, "Israelis Confirm Assassinations Used as Policy; Key Palestinians Targeted," *Washington Post*, January 8, 2001.

78. https://www.law.upenn.edu/institutes/cerl/conferences/targetedkilling/papers/IsraeliTargetedKillingCase.pdf.

79. Qtd. in Yotam Feldman and Uri Blau, "Consent and Advise," *Haaretz*, January 29, 2009, http://www.haaretz.com/consent-and-advise-1.269127

80. Richburg, "Israelis Confirm Assassinations Used as Policy; Key Palestinians Targeted," p. 1.

81. Spencer Ackerman and Noah Shachtman, "Almost 1 in 3 US Warplanes is a Robot," *Wired*, January 9, 2012, www.wired.com/dangerroom/2012/01/drone-report.

82. Sauer and Schörnig, "Killer Drones."

83. Williams, *Predators*, p. 235.

84. David Hambling, "Air Force Completes Killer Micro-Drone Project," *Wired*, January 5, 2010, www.wired.com/dangerroom/2010/01/killer-mircro-drone/.

85. Qtd. in W. J. Hennigan, "Civilian Use of Tiny Drones May Soon Fly in the US," *Los Angeles Times*, November 27, 2011, p. B4.

Chapter 7

1. President Dwight Eisenhower, June 20, 1958, qtd. in White House, *National Space Policy*, June 28, 2010, http://www.whitehouse.gov/sites/default/files/national_space_policy_6-28-10.pdf (accessed December 20, 2013), p. 1.

2. Michael Krepon and Christopher Clary, *Space Assurance or Space Dominance? The Case Against Weaponizing Space* (Washington, DC: Henry L. Stimson Center, 2003).

3. "Treaty on Principles Governing the Activities of States in the Exploration and Use of Outer Space, Including the Moon and Other Celestial Bodies," United Nations, 1967, http://www.state.gov/t/isn/5181.htm (accessed January 14, 2016).

4. M. J. Peterson, "The Worlds of Global Commons Regimes: The Global Commons: A Regime Analysis by John Vogler," book review, *Mershon International Studies Review* 40:2 (1996), p. 289.

5. Elinor Ostrom, ed., *Governing the Commons: The Evolution of Institutions for Collective Action* (Cambridge: Cambridge University Press, 1990).

6. Michael Byers, "Policing the High Seas: The Proliferation Security Initiative," *American Journal of International Law* 98:3 (2004), pp. 526–545; Daniel Joyner, *International Law and the Proliferation of Weapons of Mass Destruction* (Oxford: Oxford University Press, 2009).

7. Grotius, cited in Jon M. Van Dyke, "International Governance and Stewardship of the High Seas and Its Resources," in Jon M. Van Dyke, Durwood Zaelke, and Grant Hewison, eds., *Freedom for the High Seas in the 21st Century: Ocean Governance and Environmental Harmony* (Washington, DC: Island Press, 1993), p. 14.

8. M. J. Peterson, *Managing the Frozen South: The Creation and Evolution of the Antarctic Treaty System* (Berkeley: University of California Press, 1988).

9. Krepon and Clary, *Space Assurance or Space Dominance?*; Author's interview with Scott Pace, director of the Space Policy Institute at the Elliott School of International Affairs, George Washington University, and former associate administrator for program analysis and evaluation at NASA; Author's interview with Brian Weeden, technical advisor, Secure World Foundation, Washington, DC, February 20, 2014.

10. William E. Burrows, *This New Ocean: The Story of the First Space Age* (New York: Random House, 1998); Author's interview with Scott Pace and Brian Weeden, Washington, DC, February 20, 2014.

11. Peter L. Hays, "Struggling Toward Space Doctrine: U.S. Military Space Plans, Programs, and Perspectives during the Cold War," PhD diss. (Fletcher School of Law and Diplomacy, May 1994); David E. Lupton, *On Space Warfare: A Space Power Doctrine* (Maxwell Air Force Base, AL: Air University Press, June 1988); Paul B. Stares, *The Militarization of Space: U.S. Policy, 1945–1984* (Ithaca, NY: Cornell University Press, 1985).

12. Craig Nelson, *Rocket Men: The Epic Story of the First Men on the Moon* (New York: Penguin, 2009), p. 89.

13. Colin Gray, *American Military Space Policy: Information Systems, Weapon Systems, and Arms Control* (Cambridge, MA: Abt Books, 1982), 77.

14. Nina Tannenwald, "Law Versus Power on the High Frontier: The Case for a Rule-Based Regime for Outer Space," *Yale Journal of International Law* 19:363 (2004), pp. 1–55.

15. "Treaty on Principles Governing the Activities of States in the Exploration and Use of Outer Space, including the Moon and Other Celestial Bodies," 1967. I am grateful to my research assistant, Stephanie Sparrow, for developing the foundations of this discussion.

16. Ibid.

17. Ibid.; see also Fony Osman, *Space History* (London: Michael Joseph Publishers, 1983).

18. Alan J. Levine, *The Missile and Space Race* (Westport, CT: 1994).

19. See Matt Bille and Erika Lishock, *The First Space Race* (College Station: Texas A&M University Press, 2004), p. 15; Central Intelligence Agency, National Intelligence Estimate, 11–5-60, "Soviet Capabilities in Guided Missiles and Space Vehicles," Submitted by the Director of Central Intelligence, Declassified Archive Document no. 333, esp. Annex A, Possible Soviet Space Development Program.

20. Nelson, *Rocket Men*.

21. National Aeronautics and Space Administration, *National Aeronautics and Space Act of 1958, as Amended*, http://history.nasa.gov/spaceact-legishistory.pdf (accessed January 14, 2016).

22. RAND Corporation, *Preliminary Design for an Experimental World-Circling Spaceship* (Santa Monica, CA: Project RAND, 1946; reprinted RAND Corporation 1999), p. 10.

23. See John J. Klein, *Space Warfare: Strategy, Principles, and Policy* (London: Routledge, 2006), p. 24.

24. Bryan R. Early, "Exploring the Final Frontier: An Empirical Analysis of Global Civil Space Proliferation," *International Studies Quarterly* 58:1 (2014), p. 58.

25. See information from the nonprofit Space Launch Report, http://www.spacelaunchreport.com/log2013.html; NASA tracking data from http://www.nasaspaceflight.com/; see also Jonathan's Space Home Page, http://www.planet4589.org/space/ (accessed June 4, 2014).

26. Simon Romero, "Military Now Often Enlists Commercial Technology," *New York Times*, March 10, 2003, p. A19.

27. NSC 5520, 6; the 1958 Purcell Panel, commissioned by President Eisenhower; in NSC 5814; see Matthew J. Mowthorp, "The United States Approach to Military Space during the Cold War," *Air and Space Power Journal* 8 (March 2001); National Aeronautics and Space Council, "US Policy on Outer Space" (January 1960), http://nsarchive.chadwyck.com/collections/content/MS/intro.jsp; John M. Logsdon, moderator, "Legislative Origins of the National Aeronautics and Space Act of 1958: Proceedings of an Oral History Workshop," conducted April 3, 1992, *Monographs in Aerospace History*, Number 8 (NASA Headquarters, Washington DC: Office of Policy and Plans, NASA History Division, July 1998), http://nsarchive.chadwyck.com/collections/content/MS/intro.jsp; NSC-5814, entitled "Preliminary U.S. Policy on Outer Space," August 18, 1958.

28. Stares, *The Militarization of Space*, pp. 261–262.

29. Ashton B. Carter, "Satellites and Anti-Satellites: The Limits of the Possible," *International Security* 10:4 (1986), pp. 46–98.

30. James Clay Moltz, *The Politics of Space Security: Strategic Restraint and the Pursuit of National Interests*, 2nd ed. (Stanford, CA: Stanford Security Studies, 2011).

31. Walter A. McDougall, *The Heavens and the Earth: A Political History of the Space Age* (New York: Basic Books, 1985), p. 127.

32. Joanne Irene Gabrynowicz, "One Half Century and Counting: The Evolution of U.S. National Space Law and Three Long-Term Emerging Issues," *Harvard Law & Policy Review* 4 (2011), pp. 405–406; see also Joanne Irene Gabrynowicz and Sarah M. Langston, *A Chronological Survey of the Development of Article IX of the Outer Space Treaty*, Special Topics in Aerospace Law Series, No. 3: A Supplement to the *Journal of Space Law*, National Center for Remote Sensing, Air, and Space Law, University of Mississippi Law School of Law, 2010, http://www.spacelaw.olemiss.edu/resources/pdfs/article-ix.pdf (accessed March 4, 2013).

33. Qtd. in Walter A. McDougall, *The Heavens and the Earth: A Political History of the SpaceAge* (New York: Basic Books, 1985), p. 108.

34. James S. Lay Jr., "Scientific Satellite Program," Note by the Executive Secretary to the National Security Council (a draft statement in anticipation of NSC meeting May 26 to finalize NSC 5520), May 20, 1955, 3.

35. United States, Department of State, Policy Planning Council, "Planning Implications for National Security of Outer Space in the 1970s," secret report, January 30, 1964, viii, ixiii, available online at the Digital National Security Archive, "U.S. Military Uses of Space, 1945–1991," http://nsarchive.chadwyck.com/collections/content/MS/intro.jsp.

36. "Treaty on Principles Governing the Activities of States in the Exploration and Use of Outer Space, Including the Moon and Other Celestial Bodies."

37. Carter, "Satellites and Anti-Satellites"; Stares, *The Militarization of Space*, pp. 261–262.

38. Sanford Lakoff and Herbert F. York, *A Shield in Space? Technology, Politics, and the Strategic Defense Initiative* (Berkeley: University of California Press, 1989), pp. 87–88.

39. Ibid., pp. 88–92.

40. See Michael Krepon and Julia Thompson, eds., *Anti-Satellite Weapons, Deterrence, and Sino-American Space Relations* (Washington, DC: Stimson Center, September 2013), http://www.stimson.org/images/uploads/Anti-satellite_Weapons.pdf (accessed July 11, 2014).

41. Bruce M. DeBlois, Richard L. Garwin, R. Scott Kemp, and Jeremy C. Marwell, "Space Weapons: Crossing the U.S. Rubicon," *International Security* 19:2 (2004), pp. 50–84.

42. See Rebecca Johnson, "Multilateral Approaches to Preventing the Weaponization of Space," *Disarmament Diplomacy* 56 (April 2001), pp. 8–16; and Philip E. Coyle and John B. Rhinelander, "Drawing the Line: The Path to Controlling Weapons in Space," *Disarmament Diplomacy* 66 (September 2002), pp. 3–7.

43. Jeff Hecht, "U.S. Plans Anti-Satellite Lasers," *New Scientist*, May 3, 2006, p. 83.

44. Sidney D. Drell, Philip J. Farley, and David Holloway, *The Reagan Strategic Defense Initiative: A Technical, Political, and Arms Control Assessment* (Cambridge, MA: Ballinger Publishing, 1985), p. 7.

45. Edward Reiss, *The Strategic Defense Initiative* (Cambridge: Cambridge University Press, 1992), pp. 37–38.

46. "Final Report of the Commission to Assess United States National Security Space Management and Organization," January 11, 2001, p. viii, http://www.defense-link.mil/pubs/space20010111.pdf.

47. George W. Bush, Remarks, December 13, 2001, reprinted in *Arms Control Today*, January/February 2002, http://www.armscontrol.org/act/2002_01–02/docjanfeb02.

48. "Lord: Space Command Focusing on Maintaining Space Superiority," *Inside the Air Force*, January 30, 2004, p. 9; White House, "Fact Sheet: National Space Policy," September 19, 1996, http://history.nasa.gov/appf2.pdf.

49. "Lord: Space Command Focusing on Maintaining Space Superiority."

50. United States Air Force Space Command, *Strategic Master Plan FY 04 and Beyond*, November 5, 2002, p. 5

51. United States Air Force, Counterspace Operations, Air Force Doctrine Document 2–2.1, August 2, 2004, p. 19

52. George W. Bush, *US National Space Policy* (Washington, DC: Office of Science and Technology Policy, August 31, 2006), p. 2.

53. Rex Wingerter, "What Drives the Development of US Missile Defense and Space-Based Weapons? The Role of US Domestic Interest Groups," *Asian Perspective* 35:4 (October 2011), pp. 559–594. https://www.questia.com/library/journal/1P3-2610265141/what-drives-the-development-of-us-missile-defense.

54. Early, "Exploring the Final Frontier"; Deborah Stine, *The Manhattan Project, the Apollo Program, and Federal Energy Technology R&D Programs: A Comparative Analysis*," Congressional Research Service, 2009, http://www.fas. org/sgp/crs/misc/RL34645.pdf (accessed May 1, 2013).

55. Brian Weeden, "The Economics of Space Sustainability," *Space Review*, June 4, 2012, www.thespacereview.com/article/2093/1 (accessed February 20, 2014).

56. Micah Zenko, "Waste of Space," *Foreign Policy*, April 21, 2014, http://www.foreignpolicy.com/articles/2014/04/21/waste_of_space_space_junk_gravity_us_china.

57. Micah Zenko, "Dangerous Space Incidents," Contingency Planning Memorandum 21, April 2014, http://www.cfr.org/space/dangerous-space-incidents/p32790 (accessed June 19, 2014).

58. Interview with Victoria Samson, director of the Secure World Foundation, Washington, DC, February 19, 2014. See also Marc Kaufman and Dafna Linzer, "China Criticized for Anti-Satellite Missile Test: Destruction of an Aging Satellite Illustrates Vulnerability of U.S. Space Assets," *Washington Post*, January 19, 2007, p. 1.

59. Author's interview with Victoria Samson, February 19, 2014.

60. Kaufman and Linzer, "China Criticized for Anti-Satellite Missile Test."

61. Qtd. in Tim Ross and Holly Watt, "WikiLeaks: US vs China in Battle of the Anti-Satellite Space Weapons," *The Telegraph*, February 2, 2011, http://www.telegraph.co.uk/news/worldnews/wikileaks/8299491/WikiLeaks-US-vs-China-in-battle-of-the-anti-satellite-space-weapons.html.

62. Michael Sirak, "Air Force Leadership: Chinese ASAT Test Marked Turning Point; Space No Longer Sanctuary," *Defense Daily*, February 12, 2007.

63. Kaufman and Linzer, "China Criticized for Anti-Satellite Missile Test."

64. P. J. Blount and Joanne Irene Gabrynowicz, eds., *USA-193: Selected Documents*, Special Topics in Aerospace Law Series, No. 1, a supplement to the *Journal of Space Law*, National Center for Remote Sensing, Air, and Space Law, University of Mississippi Law School of Law, http://www.spacelaw.olemiss.edu/resources/pdfs/usa193-selected-documents.pdf (accessed March 4, 2013).

65. Jack Gullum and David Wichner, "How the Satellite Shot Went Down," *Arizona Daily Star*, April 13, 2008, http://www.azstarnet.com/business/234028 (accessed February 22, 2014).

66. "Navy Missile Hits Decaying Satellite over Pacific Ocean," American Forces Press Service, February 20, 2008, http://www.defenselink.mil/news/newsarticle.aspx?id=49024.

67. Jim Garamone, "Transparency of Satellite Shootdown Offers Model," American Foreign Press Service, February 21, 2008, p. 135, in Blount and Gabrynowicz, eds., *USA-193*.

68. Guy Faulconbridge, "U.S. and Russia Track Satellite Crash Debris," *Reuters*, February 12, 2009; Brian Weeden, "Billiards in Space," *Space Review*, February 23, 2009, http://www.thespacereview.com/ article/1314/1.

69. Author's interview with Michael Krepon.

70. White House, *National Space Policy of the United States of America*, June 28, 2010, www.whitehouse.gov/sites/default/files/national_space_policy_6–28–10.pdf, p. 4; White House, "Statement by President on Release of National Space Policy," June 28, 2010, https://www.whitehouse.gov/the-press-office/statement-president-new-national-space-policy.

71. White House, *National Space Policy of the United States of America*, p. 2.

72. Ibid., p. 7.

73. Hillary Rodham Clinton, "Statement to the Press: National Space Policy," Washington, DC, June 28, 2010, www.state.gov/secretary/20092013clinton/rm/2010/06/143728.htm.

74. Wolfgang Rathgeber, Nina-Louisa Remuß, and Kai-Uwe Schrogl, "Space Security and the European Code of Conduct for Outer Space Activities," *Disarmament Forum* 4 (2009), pp. 35–36.

75. Hillary Rodham Clinton, "International Code of Conduct for Outer Space Activities," press statement, Washington DC, January 17, 2012, http://www.state.gov/secretary/20092013clinton/rm/2012/01/180969.htm (accessed January 18, 2016); see also Ajey Lele, "Space Code of Conduct: Inadequate Mechanism," in Ajey Lele, ed., *Decoding the International Code of Conduct for Outer Space Activities* (New Delhi: Institute for Defence Studies and Analyses, Pentagon Security International, 2012), pp. 5–8.

76. Frank A. Rose, "Leading with International Cooperation to Strengthen Stability in Space," Near Space Security Conference, November 3, 2011, www.state.gov/t/avc/rls/176619.htm.

77. Frank A. Rose, "Pursuing Space TCBMs for Long-Term Sustainability and Security," remarks to the International Symposium on Sustainable Space Development and Utilization for Humankind, Shinagawa, Tokyo, Japan, February 28, 2013, www.state.gov/t/avc/rls/2013/205362.htm (accessed March 1, 2014).

78. Remarks by Jeffrey L. Eberhardt, Alternate Representative, Delegation of the United States of America, New York City, October 25, 2013, http://www.state.gov/t/avc/rls/2013/215881.htm.

Chapter 8

1. Thomas Jefferson, Letter from Thomas Jefferson to Samuel Kercheval, July 12, 1816, in *The Writings of Thomas Jefferson: 1816–1826*, vol. 10, pp. 42–43, Paul Leicester Ford, ed. (Washington, DC: Library of Congress, 1899).

2. Barack Obama, "Remarks by the President at the United States Military Academy Commencement Ceremony," May 28, 2014, http://www.whitehouse.gov/the-press-office/2014/05/28/remarks-president-west-point-academy-commencement-ceremony (accessed June 4, 2014).

3. Geoffrey L. Herrera, *Technology and International Transformation: The Railroad, the Atom Bomb, and the Politics of Technological Change* (Albany: State University of New York Press, 2006), p. 2.

4. Renée de Nevers, "Imposing International Norms: Great Powers and Norm Enforcement," *International Studies Review* 9:1 (Spring 2007), pp. 53–80.

5. George W. Bush, *National Strategy for Combating Terrorism*, http//:www.whitehouse.gov/news/releases/2003/02/counter_terrorism/counter_terrorism_strategy.pdf, pp. 23–24.

6. Amitav Acharya, "How Ideas Spread: Whose Norms Matter? Norm Localization and Institutional Change in Asian Regionalism," *International Organization* 58:1 (2004), pp. 239–275.

7. Andrew P. Cortell and James W. Davis, Jr., "Understanding the Domestic Impact of International Norms: A Research Agenda," *International Studies Review* 2:1 (2000), pp. 65–87.

8. Martha Finnemore, "Constructing Norms of Humanitarian Intervention," in Peter J. Katzenstein, ed., *The Culture of National Security: Norms and Identity in World Politics* (New York: Columbia University Press, 1996), pp. 153–185; Martha Finnemore and Kathryn Sikkink, "International Norm Dynamics and Political Change," *International Organization* 52:4 (1998), pp. 887–917; Thomas Risse, Stephen C. Ropp, and Kathryn Sikkink, eds., *The Power of Human Rights: International Norms and Domestic Change* (Cambridge: Cambridge University Press, 1999).

9. Robert Axelrod, "An Evolutionary Approach to Norms," *American Political Science Review* 80:4 (1986), p. 1096.

10. Rodger A. Payne, "Persuasion, Frames, and Norm Construction," *European Journal of International Relations* 7:1 (2001), p. 41.

11. For work in this vein, see Jeffrey S. Lantis, "Nuclear Technology and Norm Stewardship: U.S. Nonproliferation Policies Revisited," *International Studies Perspectives* 16:4 (2015), DOI: 10.1111/insp.12070; Lantis, "Agentic Constructivism and the Proliferation Security Initiative: Modeling Norm Change," *Cooperation and Conflict* (forthcoming 2016); Lantis, "Constructivist Security Studies and Non-proliferation: How Elite Entrepreneurship Can Make or Break International Norms," in Maria Rost Rublee and Avner Cohen, eds., Special issue of *Journal of Global Security Studies* (forthcoming 2016).

12. Wanda J. Orlikowski, "Using Technology and Constituting Structures: A Practice Lens for Studying Technology in Organizations," *Organization Science* 11:4 (2000), pp. 406–428.

13. Herrera, *Technology and International Transformation*, p. 2.

14. For an engaging exposition on this subject, albeit with a different perspective, see Margarita H. Petrova, "Banning Obsolete Weapons or Reshaping Perceptions of Military Utility: Discursive Dynamics in Weapons Prohibitions," Institut Barcelona d'Estudis Internacionals (IBEI) Working Paper Series 31, 2010, www.cidob.org (accessed March 4, 2012).

15. Ann Florini, "The Evolution of International Norms," *International Studies Quarterly* 40:1 (1996), p. 376.

16. For an excellent summary of the literature in this area, see Nicole Deitelhoff and Lisbeth Zimmermann, "Things We Lost in the Fire: How Different Types of Contestation Affect the Validity of International Norms," PRIF Working Paper 18, December 2013.

17. Richard M. Price, *Moral Limit and Possibility in World Politics* (Cambridge: Cambridge University Press, 2008), p. 35.

18. Diana Panke and Ulrich Petersohn, "Why International Norms Disappear Sometimes," *European Journal of International Relations* 18:4 (2012), pp. 719–742.

19. Antje Wiener, *The Invisible Constitution of Politics: Contested Norms and International Encounters* (Cambridge: Cambridge University Press, 2008), p. 33.

20. Ibid, p. 21.

21. Acharya, "How Ideas Spread."

22. Deitelhoff and Zimmermann, "Things We Lost in the Fire."

23. Carmen Wunderlich, "A Rogue Gone Norm Entrepreneurial? Iran within the Nuclear Nonproliferation Regime," in Wolfgang Wagner, Werner Wouter, and Michael Ondercoe, eds., *Deviance in International Relations: "Rogue States" and International Security* (Houndmills, UK: Palgrave Macmillan, 2014), pp. 83–104.

24. Harald Müller and Carmen Wunderlich, eds., *Norm Dynamics in Multilateral Arms Control: Interests, Conflicts, and Justice* (Athens: University of Georgia Press, 2013), p. 20.

25. Maria Rost Rublee, *Nonproliferation Norms: Why States Choose Nuclear Restraint* (Athens: University of Georgia Press, 2010), p. 3.

Bibliography

Abbott, Kenneth W. et al. "The Concept of Legalization." *International Organization* 54:2 (2000): 401–419.

Acharya, Amitav. *Constructing a Security Community in Southeast Asia.* London: Routledge, 2009.

———. "How Ideas Spread: Whose Norms Matter? Norm Localization and Institutional Change in Asian Regionalism." *International Organization* 58:2 (2004): 239–275.

———. *Whose Ideas Matter? Agency and Power in Asian Regionalism.* Ithaca, NY: Cornell University Press, 2009.

"Acheson-Lilienthal Report." Council on Foreign Relations, 2011. Accessed June 4, 2011. http://www.cfr.org/proliferation/acheson-lilienthal-report/p19028.

Ackerman, Spencer, and Noah Shachtman. "Almost 1 in 3 US Warplanes Is a Robot." *Wired*, January 9, 2012. www.wired.com/dangerroom/2012/01/drone-report.

Adamson, Fiona B. "Global Liberalism Versus Political Islam: Competing Ideological Frameworks in International Politics." *International Studies Review* 7:4 (2005): 547–569.

Adler, Emmanuel. "Seizing the Middle Ground: Constructivism in World Politics." *European Journal of International Relations* 3:2 (1997): 319–363.

Albright, David. *Peddling Peril: How the Secret Nuclear Arms Trade Arms America's Enemies.* New York: Free Press, 2010.

Albright, David, and Corey Hinderstein. "Unraveling the AQ Khan and Future Proliferation Networks." *Washington Quarterly* 28:2 (2005): 111–128.

Albright, David, and Kevin O'Neill, eds. *Solving the North Korean Nuclear Puzzle.* Washington, DC: Institute for Science and National Security, 2000.

Albright, Madeleine. *Madam Secretary: A Memoir.* New York: Hyperion, 2003.

Albright, Madeleine K., and Richard S. Williamson. *The United States and R2P: From*

Words to Action. Report of the Working Group on the Responsibility to Protect. Jointly convened by the United States Holocaust Memorial Museum, United States Institute of Peace, and Brookings Institution. Washington, DC: United States Institute of Peace. 2013.

Alston, Philip. "Report of the Special Rapporteur on Extrajudicial, Summary, or Arbitrary Executions." UN General Assembly Report, Human Rights Council, 14th Session, May 28, 2010, A/HRC/14/24/Add.6. http://www2.ohchr.org/english/bodies/hrcouncil/docs/14session/A.HRC.14.24.Add6.pdf.

Amnesty International. "New Satellite Images Reveal Shocking Aftermath of Abuses in Central African Republic." *Amnesty International News*, November 8, 2013. Accessed November 9, 2013. www.amnesty.org/en/news/new-satellite-images-reveal-shocking-aftermath-abuses-central-african-republic-2013-11-08.

Annan, Kofi. "Break the Nuclear Deadlock." *International Herald Tribune*, May 30, 2005. Accessed May 20, 2008. www.iht.com/articles/2005/05/29/news/edannan.php.

———. *In Larger Freedom: Towards Development, Security, and Human Rights for All*. Report of the Secretary General, A/59/2005. New York: United Nations, March 21, 2005.

———. "Two Concepts of Sovereignty." *The Economist*, September 18, 1999.

Arend, Anthony. "International Law and the Preemptive Use of Military Force." *Washington Quarterly* 26:2 (2003): 89–103.

Arnett, Peter. *Live from the Battlefield: From Vietnam to Baghdad: 35 Years in the World's War Zones*. New York: Simon & Schuster, 1994.

Art, Robert J., and Kenneth N. Waltz. "Technology, Strategy, and the Uses of Force." In *The Use of Force: International Politics and Foreign Policy*, 2nd ed., edited by Robert J. Art and Kenneth N. Waltz. Lanham, MD: University Press of America, 1983.

Associated Press. "FBI: Mass. Man Had 'Mission' Against Pentagon." *CBS News*, November 4, 2011. www.cbsnews.com/8301-201_162-57319111/fbi-mass-man-had-mission-against-pentagon.

Atomic Energy Act. U.S. Department of Energy. Accessed June 3, 2011. http://www.etec.energy.gov/regulation/atomic-energy-act.html.

"Atomic Energy Commission Gas Centrifuge Method of Isotope Separation." Note by Secretary W. B. McCool, April 9, 1960. Redacted, US DOE Archives, RG 326 AEC, Secretariat, Box 1427, Folder 3, National Security Archives. Accessed February 18, 2014.

"August 6, 1945: A-Bomb Dropped on Hiroshima." *CNN*. Accessed January 24, 2013. http://www.cnn.com/2003/US/03/10/sprj.80.1945.hiroshima/.

Axe, David. "Upgrades to Killer Drone Could Make It Fly for Two Days Straight." *Wired*, April 19, 2012. http://www.wired.com/dangerroom/2012/04/killer-drone-upgrade/.

Axelrod, Robert. "An Evolutionary Approach to Norms." *American Political Science Review* 80:4 (1986): 1095–1111.

Babington, Charles. "Clinton: Containing Milosevic Is Goal." *Washington Post*, March 25, 1999. Accessed June 11, 2013. http://www.washingtonpost.com/wp-srv/national/daily/march99/clinton25.htm.

Badescu, Cristina G., and Linnea Bergholm. "The Responsibility to Protect and the Conflict in Darfur: The Big Let-Down." *Security Dialogue* 40:3 (2009): 287–309.

Badescu, Cristina G., and Thomas G. Weiss. "Misrepresenting R2P and Advancing Norms: An Alternative Spiral?" *International Studies Perspectives* 11:1 (2010): 354–374.

Bahador, Babak. "Did the Global War on Terror End the CNN Effect?" *Media, War & Conflict* 4:1 (2011): 37–54.

Bailey, Jennifer. "Coalitions and Norm Stability: The Case of Whaling." Paper presented at the Annual Meeting of the International Studies Association, New York, February 17, 2009.

Baldwin, Robert E., and Anne O. Krueger. *The Structure and Evolution of Recent U.S. Trade Policy*. Chicago: University of Chicago Press, 1984.

Balzacq, Thierry. "The Three Faces of Securitization: Political Agency, Audience, and Context." *European Journal of International Relations* 11:2 (2005): 171–201.

Ban Ki-moon. *Implementing the Responsibility to Protect*. Report from the Secretary-General. United Nations document A/63/677. January 2009.

Barnett, Michael N. "Culture, Strategy, and Foreign Policy Change: Israel's Road to Oslo." *European Journal of International Relations* 5:1 (1999): 5–36.

———. "The United Nations and Global Security: The Norm Is Mightier Than the Sword." *Ethics and International Affairs* 9:2 (1995): 37–54.

Barnett, Michael N., and Martha Finnemore. *Rules for the World: International Organizations in Global Politics*. Ithaca, NY: Cornell University Press, 2004.

Barry, Ian Patrick. "The Right of Visit, Search and Seizure of Foreign Flagged Vessels on the High Seas Pursuant to Customary International Law: A Defense of the Proliferation Security Initiative." *Hofstra Law Review* 33:3 (2004): 299–320.

Bass, Gary. *Freedom's Battle: The Origins of Humanitarian Intervention*. New York: Alfred Knopf, 2008.

Baylis, John. "Exchanging Nuclear Secrets: Laying the Foundations of the Anglo-American Nuclear Relationship." *Diplomatic History* 25:1 (2001): 33–62.

BBC. "Analysis: Defining Genocide." *BBC News*, August 27, 2010. http://www.bbc.co.uk/news/world-11108059.

———. "Clinton's Statement on War Crimes Court." *BBC News*, December 31, 2000. Accessed June 11, 2013. http://news.bbc.co.uk/2/hi/1095580.stm.

———. "'Killer Robots' to Be Debated at the UN." *BBC News*, May 9, 2014. Accessed September 16, 2014. http://www.bbc.com/news/technology-27343076.

———. "Libya Protests: Defiant Gaddafi Refuses to Quit." *BBC News*, February 22, 2011. Accessed August 13, 2013. www.bbc.co.uk/news/world-middle-east-12544624.

———. "Syria Crisis: Cameron Loses Commons Vote on Syria Action." *BBC*

News, August 30, 2013. Accessed May 26, 2014. http://www.bbc.com/news/uk-politics-23892783.

Beaton, Leonard. *Must the Bomb Spread?* Baltimore: Penguin, 1966.

Bellamy, Alex. *Responsibility to Protect: The Global Effort to End Mass Atrocities.* Cambridge: Polity Press, 2009.

———. "Responsibility to Protect or Trojan Horse? The Crisis in Darfur and Humanitarian Intervention after Iraq." *Ethics & International Affairs* 19:2 (2005): 31–54.

Benford, Robert. "Dramaturgy and Social Movements: The Social Construction and Communication of Power." *Sociological Inquiry* 62:3 (1992): 36–55.

Beres, Louis Rene. "Assassinating Saddam: A Post-War View from International Law." *Denver Journal of International Law and Policy* 19:3 (1991): 613–623.

Bijker, Wiebe, and John Law, eds. *Shaping Technology/Building Society: Studies in Sociotechnical Change.* Cambridge: MIT Press, 1992.

Bijker, Wiebe E., Thomas P. Hughes, and Trevor Pinch, eds. *The Social Construction of Technological Systems: New Directions in the Sociology and History of Technology.* Cambridge, MA: MIT Press, 2013.

Bille, Matt, and Erika Lishock. *The First Space Race.* College Station: Texas A&M University Press, 2004.

Bird, Kai, and Martin J. Sherwin. *American Prometheus: The Triumph and Tragedy of J. Robert Oppenheimer.* New York: Vintage Books, 2006.

Bleek, Philipp C., and Eric B. Lorber. "Security Guarantees and Allied Nuclear Proliferation." *Journal of Conflict Resolution* 58:3 (2014): 429–454.

Bloomfield, Alan. "Resisting the Responsibility to Protect: The Advantages Enjoyed by 'Norm Antipreneurs.'" September 2014. Unpublished manuscript (author's copy).

Blount, P. J., and Joanne Irene Gabrynowicz, eds. *USA-193: Selected Documents.* Special Topics in Aerospace Law Series, No. 1. A Supplement to the *Journal of Space Law.* National Center for Remote Sensing, Air, and Space Law, University of Mississippi Law School of Law, 2009. http://www.spacelaw.olemiss.edu/resources/pdfs/usa193-selected-documents.pdf.

Bob, Clifford. *The Global Right Wing and the Clash of World Politics.* New York: Cambridge University Press, 2012.

Bob, Clifford, and Sharon Erickson Nepstad. "Kill a Leader, Murder a Movement? Leadership and Assassination in Social Movements." *American Behavioral Scientist* 50:10 (2007): 1370–1394.

Bohr, Niels. *Atomic Physics and Human Knowledge.* New York: John Wiley, 1958.

Bolton, John. "Interview on Meet the Press with Tim Russert." *MSNBC*, February 8, 2004. Accessed April 11, 2013. http://msnbc.msn.com/id/4179618/.

———. "Letter on the Responsibility to Protect." August 30, 2005. Accessed March 4, 2013. http://www.humanrightsvoices.org/site/documents/?d=551.

Boot, Max. "The New American Way of War." *Foreign Affairs* 82:4 (July/August 2003): 41–58.

Boutros-Ghali, Boutros. *Agenda for Peace.* June 17, 1992. Accessed July 21, 2013. http://www.cfr.org/peacekeeping/report-un-secretary-general-agenda-peace/p23439.

Bowcott, Owen. "Drone Strikes Threaten 50 Years of International Law, Says UN Rapporteur." *The Guardian*, June 21, 2012. Accessed February 17, 2014. http://www. theguardian.com/world/2012/jun/21/drone-strikes-international-law-un.

Boyle, Michael J. "The Costs and Consequences of Drone Warfare." *International Affairs* 89:1 (2013): 1–29.

Brandenburg, Bert. "Note: The Legality of Assassination as an Aspect of Foreign Policy." *Virginia Journal of International Law* 27:3 (1987): 609–685.

Braun, Chaim, and Christopher F. Chyba. "Proliferation Rings: New Challenges to the Nuclear Nonproliferation Regime." *International Security* 29:2 (2004): 5–49.

Brennan, John. "CIA Director John Brennan Addresses Senate's Report on CIA Interrogation Program." *ABC News*, December 11, 2014. Accessed December 15, 2014. http://abcnews.go.com/international/transcript-cia-director-john-brennan-senates-report-cia/story?id=27539690.html.

———. "Remarks: The Ethics and Efficacy of the President's Counterterrorism Strategy." April 30, 2012. http://www.wilsoncenter.org/event/the-efficacy-and-ethics-us-counterterrorism-strategy.

Brinkbaumer, Klaus, and John Goetz. "Obama's Shadowy Drone War." *Der Spiegel*, October 12, 2010.

Brinkman, William F., Douglas E. Haggan, and William W. Troutman. "A History of the Invention of the Transistor and Where It Will Lead Us." *IEEE Journal of Solid-State Circuits* 32:12 (1997). Accessed July 14, 2013. http://classes.soe.ucsc. edu/ee171/Winter06/notes/transistor.pdf.

Broad, William J., John Markoff, and David E. Sanger. "Israeli Test on Worm Called Crucial in Iran Nuclear Delay." *New York Times*, January 15, 2011, p. A 1.

Broad, William J., and David E. Sanger. "China Tests Anti-Satellite Weapon, Unnerving U.S." *New York Times*, January 18, 2007. Accessed February 6, 2014. http:// www.nytimes.com/2007/01/18/world/asia/18cnd-china.html?_r=0.

Brooks, Stephen G., and William C. Wohlforth. "Hard Times for Soft Balancing." *International Security* 30:1 (2005): 72–108.

Brooks, Stephen G., and William C. Wohlforth. *World Out of Balance: International Relations and the Challenge of American Primacy*. Princeton, NJ: Princeton University Press, 2008.

Brown, Robert L., and Jeffrey M. Kaplow. "Talking Peace, Making Weapons: IAEA Technical Cooperation and Nuclear Proliferation." *Journal of Conflict Resolution* 58:3 (2014): 402–428.

Brown, Walton L. "Assessing the Impact of American Nonproliferation Policy: 1970–1980." Ph.D. diss. Ann Arbor, MI: University Microfilms, 1982.

———. "Presidential Leadership and U.S. Nonproliferation Policy." *Presidential Studies Quarterly* 24:3 (1994): 563–575.

Brunnée, Jutta, and Stephen J. Toope. "Norms, Institutions and UN Reform: The Responsibility to Protect." *Behind the Headlines* 63:3 (2006): 1–11.

Bukovansky, Mlada. *Legitimacy and Power Politics: The American and French*

Revolutions in International Political Culture. Princeton, NJ: Princeton University Press, 2001.

Bull, Hedley. *The Anarchical Society.* New York: Columbia University Press, 1977.

Bundy, William. *A Tangled Web: The Making of Foreign Policy in the Nixon Presidency.* New York: Hill and Wang, 1998.

Burr, William. "A Scheme of 'Control': The United States and the Origins of the Nuclear Suppliers Group, 1974–1976." *International History Review* 36:2 (2014): 252–276. http://dxdoi.org/10.1080/07075332.2013.864690.

———. "The Secret History of the ABM Treaty." http://www2.gwu.edu/~nsarchiv/NSAEBB/NSAEBB60/index2.html.

Burrows, William E. *Deep Black: Space Espionage and National Security.* New York: Random House, 1986.

———. *This New Ocean: The Story of the First Space Age.* New York: Random House, 1998.

"Bush: No Obligation to Kurds." *International Herald Tribune*, April 6–7, 1991, p. A1.

Bush, George W. *National Strategy for Combating Terrorism.* 2003. http//:www.whitehouse.gov/news/releases/2003/02/counter_terrorism/counter_terrorism_strategy.pdf.

———. "President Announces New Measures to Counter the Threat of WMD, Remarks by President Bush on Weapons of Mass Destruction Proliferation." Fort Lesley J. McNair, National Defense University. February 11, 2004. Accessed February 19, 2013. www.whitehouse.gov/news/releases/2004/02/20040211-4.html.

———. "President Bush Delivers Graduation Speech at West Point." June 1, 2002. Accessed April 22, 2013. www.whitehouse.gov/news/releases/2002/06/print/20020601-3.html.

———. Remarks. December 13, 2001. Reprinted in *Arms Control Today*, January/February 2002. http://www.armscontrol.org/act/2002_01-02/docjanfeb02.

———. "Remarks to Central Intelligence Agency Employees in Langley, Virginia." *Weekly Compilation of Presidential Documents.* Washington, DC, March 26, 2001.

———. "Speech at the National Defense University on February 10, 2004." *New York Times*, February 11, 2004. Accessed January 14, 2012. www.nytimes.com/2004/02/11/politics/10WEB-PTEX.html.

———. *US National Space Policy.* August 31, 2006. Washington, DC: Office of Science and Technology Policy.

Buzan, Barry. *An Introduction to Strategic Studies: Military Technology and International Relations.* London: Macmillan, 1987.

Byers, Michael. "Policing the High Seas: The Proliferation Security Initiative." *American Journal of International Law* 98:3 (2004): 526–545.

Byman, Daniel. "Do Targeted Killings Work?" *Foreign Affairs* 85:2 (March/April 2006): 102–104.

Callam, Andrew. "Drone Wars: Armed Unmanned Aerial Vehicles." *International Affairs Review* 28:3 (2010). www.iar-gwu.org/node/144.

Campbell, Kurt M., Robert J. Einhorn, and Mitchell B. Reiss. *The Nuclear Tipping*

Point: Why States Reconsider Their Nuclear Choices. Washington, DC: Brookings Institution Press, 2004.

Canada Centre for Remote Sensing. "Tutorial: Fundamentals of Remote Sensing Image Interpretation and Analysis." 2008. Accessed June 18, 2013. www.crs.nrcan. gc.ca/resource/tutor/fundam/chapter4/02_e.php.

Cantelon, Philip L., Richard G. Hewlett, and Robert C. Williams, eds. *The American Atom: A Documentary History of Nuclear Policies from the Discovery of Fission to the Present.* Philadelphia: University of Pennsylvania Press, 1991.

Capie, David. "Structures, Shocks and Norm Change: Explaining the Late Rise of Asia's Defence Diplomacy." *Contemporary Southeast Asia* 35:1 (2013): 1–26.

Carter, Ashton B. "America's New Strategic Partner?" *Foreign Affairs* 85:4 (2006): 33–44.

———. "Satellites and Anti-Satellites: The Limits of the Possible." *International Security* 10:4 (Spring 1986): 46–98.

Carter, Jimmy. "Nuclear Non-Proliferation Act of 1978 Statement on Signing H.R. 8638 into Law." March 10, 1978. Accessed March 21, 2011. www.presidency.ucsb. edu/ws/index.php?pid=30475#axzz1HFDCSMwg.

Central Intelligence Agency. "Soviet Capabilities in Guided Missiles and Space Vehicles." National Intelligence Estimate 11–5-60. Submitted by the Director of Central Intelligence, Declassified Archive Document no. 333, Esp. Annex A. Possible Soviet Space Development Program.

Checkel, Jeffrey T. "The Constructivist Turn in International Relations Theory." *World Politics* 50:2 (1998): 332–346.

———. "International Institutions and Socialization in Europe: Introduction and Framework." *International Organization* 59:3 (Fall 2005): 801–826.

———. "Norms, Institutions and National Identity in Contemporary Europe." Arena Working Paper 98/16. Oslo: Advanced Research on the Europeanisation of the Nation-State, University of Oslo, 1998.

———. "Norms, Institutions, and National Identity in Contemporary Europe." *International Studies Quarterly* 43:3 (1999): 83–114.

Checkel, Jeffrey, and Andrew Moravcsik. "A Constructivist Research Program in EU Studies?" *European Union Politics* 2:2 (2001): 219–249.

Cheever, D. "The UN and Disarmament." *International Organization* 19:3 (1965): 436–466.

Chernus, Ira. *Eisenhower's Atoms for Peace.* College Station: Texas A&M University, 2002.

Chestnut, Sheena. "Illicit Activity and Proliferation: North Korean Smuggling Networks." *International Security* 32:1 (2007): 80–111.

Cialdini, Robert, Raymond Reno, and Carl Kallgren. "A Focus Theory of Normative Conduct: Recycling the Concept of Norms to Reduce Littering in Public Places." *Journal of Personality and Social Psychology* 58:6 (1990): 1015–1026.

Clark, George. *Early Modern Europe from about 1450 to about 1720.* London: Oxford University Press, 1972.

Clarke, Arthur C. "Extra-Terrestrial Relays: Can Rocket Stations Give World-Wide Radio Coverage?" *Wireless World* (1945): 305–308.

Clausen, Ingard, Edward A. Miller, Robert A. McDonald, and Courtney V. Hastings, eds. *Intelligence Revolution 1960: Retrieving the CORONA Imagery That Helped Win the Cold War.* Washington, DC: Center for the Study of National Reconnaissance, April 2012.

Clausewitz, Carl von. *On War.* Edited and translated by Michael Howard and Peter Paret. Princeton, NJ: Princeton University Press, 1976.

Clinton, Hillary Rodham. "International Code of Conduct for Outer Space Activities." Press statement. Washington DC, January 17, 2012. Accessed January 18, 2016. http://www.state.gov/secretary/20092013clinton/rm/2012/01/180969.htm.

———. "Situation in Libya." February 22, 2011. Accessed August 13, 2013. www.state.gov/secretary/rm/2011/02/156836.htm.

Clinton, William J. "Remarks to Kosovo International Security Force Troops in Skopje, June 22, 2009." *Public Papers of the Presidents of the United States: William J. Clinton, 1999,* Book I, pp. 992–993. Accessed January 13, 2016. https://www.gpo.gov/fdsys/pkg/PPP-1999-book1/html/PPP-1999-book1-doc-pg992.htm.

———. "Remarks to the People of Rwanda." March 25, 1998. Accessed July 9, 2013. Transcript at http://millercenter.org/president/speeches/detail/4602.

———. "Statement by the President to the Nation." March 24, 1999. Accessed November 29, 2006. http://www2.whitehouse.gov/WH/Newhtml/19990324-2872.html.

Cobain, Ian. "Obama's Secret Kill List: The Disposition Matrix." *The Guardian,* July 14, 2013. http://www.theguardian.com/world/2013/jul/14/obama-secret-kill-list-disposition-matrix.

Coffey, Patrick. "War from Afar: How the Pentagon Fell in Love with Drones." *Salon,* December 8, 2013. http://www.salon.com/2013/12/08/war_from_afar_how_the_pentagon_fell_in_love_with_drones/.

Cohen, Tom. "How Much Say Will Congress Have on Syrian Chemical Weapons Response?" *CNN Politics,* August 30, 2013. www.cnn.com/2013/08/29/politics/obama-congress-syria.

Coll, Steve. *Ghost Wars: The Secret History of the CIA, Afghanistan, and Bin Laden: From the Soviet Invasion of Afghanistan to September 10, 2011.* New York: Penguin, 2004.

Communications Satellite Act of 1962, Pub. L. No. 87–624, 76 Stat. 419 (codified as amended at 47 U.S.C. §§ 701–69 [Supp. II 2008]).

Compton, Arthur Holly. *Atomic Quest.* Oxford: Oxford University Press, 1956.

Cortell, Andrew P., and James W. Davis, Jr. "How Do International Institutions Matter? The Domestic Impact of International Rules and Norms." *International Studies Quarterly* 40:4 (1996): 451–478.

———. "Understanding the Domestic Impact of International Norms: A Research Agenda." *International Studies Review* 2:1 (2000): 65–87.

Covault, Craig. "Advanced KH-11 Broadens U.S. Recon Capability." *Aviation Week & Space Technology,* January 6, 1997.

———. "Secret Inspection Satellites Boost Space Intelligence Ops." *Spaceflight Now*, January 14, 2009. http://www.spaceflightnow.com/news/n0901/14dsp23/.

Coyle, Philip E., and John B. Rhinelander. "Drawing the Line: The Path to Controlling Weapons in Space." *Disarmament Diplomacy* 66 (September 2002): 3–7.

Cruz, Consuelo. "Identity and Persuasion: How Nations Remember Their Pasts and Make Their Futures." *World Politics* 52:2 (2000): 275–312.

Daalder, Ivo H., and James M. Lindsay. *America Unbound*. Washington, DC: Brookings Institution Press, 2003.

Dabney, Virginius. *Mr. Jefferson's University: A History*. Charlottesville: University of Virginia Press, 1981.

Dao, James, and Dalia Sussman. "For Obama, Big Rise in Poll Numbers after Bin Laden Raid." *New York Times*, May 4, 2011, p. A1.

DARPA. "J-UCAS Program." Accessed January 17, 2016. http://archive.darpa.mil/j--ucas/J-UCAS_Overview.htm.

David, Leonard. "Pentagon Report: China's Space Warfare Tactics Aimed at U.S. Supremacy." *Space.com*, August 1, 2003. http://www.space.com/news/china_dod_030801.html.

———. "Weapons in Space: Dawn of a New Era." *Space.com*, June 17, 2005 http://www.space.com/news/050617_space_warfare.html.

David, Steven R. "Fatal Choices: Israel's Policy of Targeted Killings." *Mideast Security and Policy Studies* 51 (September 2002): 1–26.

Davis, Curtis O. *Hyperspectral Imaging: Utility for Military, Science, and Commercial Applications*. Washington, DC: Naval Research Laboratory, October 1996.

Davis, Lynn E., Michael J. McNerney, James Chow, Thomas Hamilton, Sarah Harting, and Daniel Byman. *Armed and Dangerous: UAVs and U.S. Security*. Santa Monica, CA: RAND Corporation. http://www.rand.org/pubs/research_reports/RR449.html.

DeBlois, Bruce M. "The Advent of Space Weapons." *Astropolitics* 1:1 (2003): 29–53.

———. "Space Sanctuary: A Viable National Strategy." *Airpower Journal* 12:4 (Winter 1998): 41–57.

DeBlois, Bruce M., Richard L. Garwin, R. Scott Kemp, and Jeremy C. Marwell. "Space Weapons: Crossing the U.S. Rubicon." *International Security* 29:2 (Fall 2004): 50–84.

Deibert, Ronald J. *Parchment, Printing, and Hypermedia: Communication in World Order Transformation*. New York: Columbia University Press, 1997.

Deitelhoff, Nicole, and Harald Mueller. "Theoretical Paradise—Empirically Lost? Arguing with Habermas." *Review of International Studies* 31:1 (2005): 167–180.

Deitelhoff, Nicole, and Lisbeth Zimmermann. "Things We Lost in the Fire: How Different Types of Contestation Affect the Validity of International Norms." December 2013, PRIF Working Paper 18 (author's copy).

de Nevers, Renée. "Imposing International Norms: Great Powers and Norm Enforcement." *International Studies Review* 9:1 (Spring 2007): 53–80.

Deng, Francis M. "Frontiers of Sovereignty." *Leiden Journal of International Law* 8:2 (2005): 249–286.

Deng, Francis M., Sadikiel Kimaro, Terrence Lyons, Donald Rothchild, and I. William Zartman. *Sovereignty as Responsibility: Conflict Management in Africa*. Washington, DC: Brookings Institution Press, 1996.

Department of Defense. *FY 2009–2034 Unmanned Systems Integrated Roadmap*. Washington, DC: Department of Defense, 2009.

Deudney, Daniel. "Dividing Realism: Structural Realism Versus Security Materialism on Nuclear Security and Proliferation." *Security Studies* 2:3 (1993): 7–36.

———. "Geopolitics as Theory: Historical Security Materialism." *European Journal of International Relations* 6:1 (2000): 77–108.

———. "Nuclear Weapons and the Waning of the Real-State." *Daedalus* 124:2 (1995): 209–231.

D'Olier, Franklin et al. "The United States Strategic Bombing Survey: The Effects of the Atomic Bombings of Hiroshima and Nagasaki." Harry S. Truman Presidential Library, Independence, MO, June 30, 1946. http://www.truman-library.org/whistlestop/study_collections/bomb/large/documents/index.php?documentdate=1946-06-30&documentid=7-1&studycollectionid=&page number=1.

Doswald-Beck, Louise. "The Value of the 1977 Geneva Protocols for the Protection of Civilians." In *Armed Conflict and the New Law: Aspects of the 1977 Geneva Protocols and the 1981 Weapons Convention*, edited by M. A. Meyer, 137–172. London: British Institute of International and Comparative Law, 1989.

Drell, Sidney D., Philip J. Farley, and David Holloway. *The Reagan Strategic Defense Initiative: A Technical, Political, and Arms Control Assessment*. Cambridge, MA: Ballinger Publishing, 1985.

Dulles, John Foster. "Challenge and Response in United States Policy." *Foreign Affairs* 36:1 (1957): 31–33.

———. "The Evolution of Foreign Policy." *U.S. Department of State Bulletin* 30:761 (January 25, 1954): 107–110.

Dyke, Nancy Bearg. *Persian Gulf-Humanitarian Files 1–11*. OA/ID CF01076-015.

"Early Atomic Energy Commission Studies Show Concern over Gas Centrifuge Proliferation Risk." *National Security Archive Electronic Briefing Book* No. 385 (July 23, 2012). www.gwu.edu/-nsarchiv/nukevault/ebb385/.

Early, Bryan R. "Exploring the Final Frontier: An Empirical Analysis of Global Civil Space Proliferation." *International Studies Quarterly* 58:1 (2014): 55–67.

Eberhardt, Jeffrey L. "Statement." Alternate Representative, Delegation of the United States of America New York City. October 25, 2013. Accessed November 4, 2013. http://www.state.gov/t/avc/rls/2013/215881.htm.

Eckstein, Harry. "Case Studies and Theory in Political Science." In *Handbook of Political Science*, edited by Fred Greenstein and Nelson Polsby. Reading, MA: Addison-Wesley, 1975.

Ehrhard, Thomas P. "Unmanned Aerial Vehicles in the United States Armed Services:

A Comparative Study of Weapon System Innovation." Ph.D. diss., Johns Hopkins University, 2000.

Eisenhower, Dwight D. *Mandate for Change, 1953–1956: The White House Years.* New York: Doubleday, 1963.

———. "President of the United States of America, to the 470th Plenary Meeting of the United Nations General Assembly, Tuesday, 8 December 1953, 2:45 pm." http://www.eisenhower.archives.gov/research/online_documents/atoms_for_peace.html.

Entman, Robert M. "Framing: Toward Clarification of a Fractured Paradigm." *Journal of Communication* 43:3 (1993): 51–58.

"Entries from President Truman's Diary." *American Experience Series.* Accessed January 29, 2013. http://www.pbs.org/wgbh/americanexperience/features/primary-resources/truman-diary/.

Etzioni, Amitai. "Social Norms: Internalization, Persuasion, and History." *Law and Society Review* 34:1 (2000): 41–59.

Evangelista, Matthew. *Law, Ethics, and the War on Terror.* Cambridge: Polity Press, 2008.

Evans, Gareth. *The Responsibility to Protect: Ending Mass Atrocity Crimes Once and For All.* Washington, DC: Brookings Institution Press, 2008.

Evans, Gareth, and Mohamed Sahnoun. *The Responsibility to Protect: Report of the International Commission on Intervention and State Sovereignty (ICISS).* Ottawa: International Development Research Centre, 2001.

Evans, Michael. "US Plans to Seize Suspects at Will." *Times of London,* July 11, 2003.

"Excerpted Statements on the Open Debate on Protection of Civilians in Armed Conflict." United Nations Security Council. November 20, 2007. United Nations News Centre. Accessed July 20, 2013. http://www.un.org/apps/news/infocus/sgspeeches/statments_full.asp?statID=153#.UeqexI6zvfg.

"Expounding Bush's Approach to U.S. Nuclear Security: An Interview with John R. Bolton." *Arms Control Today,* March 2002. Accessed June 15, 2016. http://www.armscontrol.org/act/2002_03/boltonmarch02.

Farrell, Theo. "Constructivist Security Studies: Portrait of a Research Program." *International Studies Review* 4:1 (2002): 49–72.

———. *The Norms of War: Cultural Beliefs and Modern Conflict.* Boulder, CO: Lynne Rienner, 2005.

———. "Transnational Norms and Military Development: Constructing Ireland's Professional Army." *European Journal of International Relations* 7:1 (2000): 63–102.

———. "World Culture and Military Power." *Security Studies* 14:3 (2003): 448–488.

Faulconbridge, Guy. "U.S. and Russia Track Satellite Crash Debris." *Reuters,* February 12, 2009.

Federation of American Scientists. "Space Policy Project." *Military Space Programs.* http://www.fas.org/spp/military/program/asat/overview.html.

Feld, Scott. "On the Emergence of Social Norms." *Contemporary Sociology* 31:6 (2002): 638–640.

Feldman, Yotam, and Uri Blau. "Consent and Advise." *Haaretz*, January 29, 2009. http://www.haaretz.com/consent-and-advise-1.269127.

Fetter, Steve, and Frank von Hippel. "Is U.S. Reprocessing Worth the Risk?" *Arms Control Today*, September 2005. Accessed February 1, 2012. http://www.armscontrol.org/act/2005_09/Fetter-VonHippel.

"Final Report of the Commission to Assess United States National Security Space Management and Organization." January 11, 2001. Accessed January 15, 2016. http://www.defenselink.mil/pubs/space20010111.pdf.

Finnemore, Martha. "Constructing Norms of Humanitarian Intervention." In *The Culture of National Security: Norms and Identity in World Politics*, edited by Peter J. Katzenstein, 153–185. New York: Columbia University Press, 1996.

———. *National Interests in International Society*. Ithaca, NY: Cornell University Press, 1996.

———. "Norms, Culture and World Politics: Insights from Sociology's Institutionalism." *International Organization* 50:2 (1998): 325–347.

———. *The Purpose of Intervention: Changing Beliefs about the Use of Force*. Ithaca, NY: Cornell University Press, 2003.

Finnemore, Martha, and Kathryn Sikkink. "International Norm Dynamics and Political Change." *International Organization* 52:4 (1998): 887–917.

———. "Taking Stock: The Constructivist Research Program in International Relations and Comparative Politics." *Annual Review of Political Science* 4:1 (2001): 391–416.

Fischer, David. *History of the International Atomic Energy Agency: The First Forty Years*. Vienna: IAEA Division of Publications, 1997.

Fisher, Adrian S. "Arms Control and Disarmament in International Law." *Virginia Law Review* 50:7 (1964): 1200–1219.

Florini, Ann. "The Evolution of International Norms." *International Studies Quarterly* 40:1 (1996): 363–389.

Ford, Franklin L. *Political Murder: From Tyrannicide to Terrorism*. Cambridge, MA: Harvard University Press, 1985.

"Foreign Affairs 1945–1946: Acheson-Lilienthal Report." *U.S. History.com*. Accessed June 3, 2011. http://www.u-s-history.com/pages/h1839.html.

Friel, Patrick J. "Space-Based Ballistic Missile Defense: An Overview of the Technical Issues." In *Laser Weapons in Space: Policy and Doctrine*, edited by Keith B. Payne, 17–35. Boulder, CO: Westview, 1983.

Frontline. "The Gulf War 1990–1991: An In-Depth Examination of the Persian Gulf Crisis, 1992." *PBS*. Accessed December 22, 2013. http://www.pbs.org/wgbh/pages/frontline/gulf/weapons/drones.html.

———. "Interviews: Ivo Daalder." *PBS*, 2000. Accessed March 14, 2010. http://www.pbs.org/wgbh/pages/frontline/shows/kosovo/interviews/daalder.html.

———. "Interviews: Madeleine Albright." *PBS*. April 18, 1999. Accessed July 21, 2013.

http://www.pbs.org/wgbh/pages/frontline/shows/kosovo/interviews/albright.html.

Fuhrmann, Matthew. "Taking a Walk on the Supply Side: The Determinants of Civilian Nuclear Cooperation." *Journal of Conflict Resolution* 53:2 (2009): 181–208.

Futron's 2012 Space Competitiveness Index (SCI): A Comparative Analysis of How Countries Invest in and Benefit from Space Industry. 5th anniversary ed. Executive Summary. Accessed February 27, 2014. http://www.space.t.u-tokyo.ac.jp/toshiki/FutronSummary.pdf.

Gabrynowicz, Joanne Irene, and Sarah M. Langston. *A Chronological Survey of the Development of Article IX of the Outer Space Treaty.* Special Topics in Aerospace Law Series, No. 3: A Supplement to the *Journal of Space Law.* National Center for Remote Sensing, Air, and Space Law, University of Mississippi Law School of Law, 2010. Accessed March 4, 2013. http://www.spacelaw.olemiss.edu/resources/pdfs/article-ix.pdf.

———. "One Half Century and Counting: The Evolution of U.S. National Space Law and Three Long-Term Emerging Issues." *Harvard Law & Policy Review* 4 (2011): 405–406.

Gamson, William A., and Andre Modigliani. "The Changing Culture of Affirmative Action." In *Research in Political Sociology*, edited by Richard G. Braungart, vol. 3. Greenwich, UK: JAI Press, 1987.

Garamone, Jim. "Transparency of Satellite Shootdown Offers Model." American Foreign Press Service, February 21, 2008, p. 135, in *USA-193: Selected Documents.* Special Topics in Aerospace Law Series No. 1. A Supplement to the *Journal of Space Law*, edited by P. J. Blount and Joanne Irene Gabrynowicz. National Center for Remote Sensing, Air, and Space Law, University of Mississippi Law School of Law, 2009. http://www.spacelaw.olemiss.edu/resources/pdfs/usa193-selected-documents.pdf.

Gartzke, Erik, and Matthew Kroenig. "Nuclear Posture, Nonproliferation Policy, and the Spread of Nuclear Weapons." *Journal of Conflict Resolution* 58:3 (2014): 395–401.

"Gaseous Diffusion Uranium Enrichment." *GlobalSecurity.org*, April 27, 2005. Accessed January 4, 2014.

Gavin, F. J. "Nuclear Nixon: Ironies, Puzzles, and the Triumph of Realpolitik." In *Nixon in the World: American Foreign Relations, 1969–1977*, edited by Fredrik Logevall and Andrew Preston. New York: Oxford University Press, 2008.

Gellman, Barton. "CIA Weighs 'Targeted Killing' Missions." *Washington Post*, October 28, 2001. http://www.washingtonpost.com/ac2/wp-dyn/A63203–2001Oct27.

———. "Slaughter in Racak Changed Kosovo Policy." *Washington Post*, April 18, 1999.

Gellman, Barton, and Dana Priest. "CIA Had Fix on Hussein." *Washington Post*, March 20, 2003, p. A1.

George, Alexander L. "Case Studies and Theory Development: The Method of Structured, Focused Comparison." In *Diplomacy: New Approaches in History, Theory, and Policy*, edited by Paul Gordon Lauren, 43–68. New York: Free Press, 1979.

George, Alexander L., and Andrew Bennett. *Case Studies and Theory Development in the Social Sciences.* Cambridge, MA: MIT Press, 2004.

Gertler, Jeremiah. *U.S. Unmanned Aerial Systems.* Congressional Research Service Report R42136, January 3, 2012. https://www.fas.org/sgp/crs/natsec/R42136.pdf.

Giddens, Anthony. *Central Problems in Social Theory: Action, Structure, and Contradiction in Social Analysis.* Berkeley: University of California Press, 1979.

———. *The Constitution of Society.* Berkeley: University of California Press, 1984.

Gilboa, Eyten. "Effects of Global Television News on U.S. Policy in International Conflict." In *Media and Conflict in the Twenty-First Century,* edited by Philip Seib, 1–32. London: Palgrave Macmillan, 2005.

———. "Global Television News and Foreign Policy: Debating the CNN Effect." *International Studies Perspectives* 6:3 (2005): 325–341.

Gilinsky, Victor, Marvin Miller, and Harmon Hubbard. *A Fresh Examination of the Proliferation Dangers of Light Water Reactors.* Washington, DC: Nonproliferation Policy Education Center, 2004.

Goldgeier, Thomas M., and Phillip E. Tetlock. "Psychology and International Relations Theory." *Annual Review of Political Science* 4:1 (2001): 67–92.

Goldsmith, Jack. "Book Review: Sovereignty, International Relations Theory, and International Law." *Stanford Law Review* 52:4 (2000): 959–960.

Goldsmith, Jack A., and Eric A. Posner. *The Limits of International Law.* Oxford: Oxford University Press, 2005.

Goldstein, Judith, Miles Kahler, Robert O. Keohane, and Anne-Marie Slaughter. "Legalization and World Politics." *International Organization* 54:3 (2000): 385–399.

Goodman, Ryan, and Derek Jinks. "How to Influence States: Socialization and International Human Rights Law." *Duke Law Journal* 54:3 (2004): 621–703.

———. "Incomplete Internalization and Compliance with Human Rights Law." *European Journal of International Law* 19:4 (2008): 725–748.

GooglePlus Hangout. "Using Tech to Fight Atrocities" Webinar. November 27, 2013. Sponsored by the Digital Mass Atrocity Prevention Lab (DMAPLab), with speakers Christopher Tuckwood (Sentinel Project), Akshaya Kumar (Enough Project), Nathaniel Raymond (Signal Program on Human Security and Technology at the Harvard Humanitarian Initiative), and Kyle Matthews (Montreal Institute for Genocide and Human Rights Studies). https://plus.google.com/u/0/events/cuvq 5u235lpt7vqb7j2mfis6pgk?authkey=CITI1LOAouamfw.

Gordon, Michael R., and Mark Landler. "Kerry Cites Clear Evidence of Chemical Weapons Use in Syria." *New York Times,* August 26, 2013, p. A1.

Gottemoeller, Rose. "Letter to the Editor." *New York Times,* March 15, 2012, p. A19.

Gray, Colin. *American Military Space Policy: Information Systems, Weapon Systems, and Arms Control.* Cambridge, MA: Abt Books, 1982.

Grotius, Hugo. "De Jure Belli ac Pacis Libri Tres." In *The Classics of International Law,* translated by Francis W. Kelsey, 649–650. Oxford: Clarendon [1646] 1925.

Gullum, Jack, and David Wichner. "How the Satellite Shot Went Down." *Arizona*

Daily Star, April 13, 2008, p. 1. Accessed February 22, 2014. http://www.azstarnet. com/business/234028.

Hambling, David. "Air Force Completes Killer Micro-Drone Project." *Wired*, January 5, 2010. www.wired.com/dangerroom/2010/01/killer-mircro-drone/.

Hamilton, John Maxwell, and Leonard S. Spector. "The Nonproliferation Predicament: Congress Fights Back." *Society* 20:6 (1983): 38–42.

Harris, John. "Clinton Saw No Alternative to Air Strikes." *Washington Post*, April 1, 1999, p. A1.

Harris, Paul. "George Clooney's Satellite Spies Reveal Secrets of Sudan's Bloody Army." *The Guardian*, March 24, 2012. Accessed June 19, 2013. www.guardian. com.uk/world/2012/mar/24/george-clooney-spies-secrets-sudan.html.

Hayashi, Mika Nishimura. "The Principle of Civilian Protection and Contemporary Armed Conflict." In *The Law of Armed Conflict: Constraints on the Contemporary Use of Military Force*, edited by Howard W. Hensel, 105–129. New York: Ashgate Publishers, 2007.

Hays, Peter L. "Struggling Toward Space Doctrine: U.S. Military Space Plans, Programs, and Perspectives during the Cold War." PhD diss., Fletcher School of Law and Diplomacy, Tuffs University, May 1994.

Hazelton, Jacqueline L. "Drones: What Are They Good For?" *Parameters* 42:4 (Winter–Spring, 2013): 29–33.

Hecht, Jeff. "U.S. Plans Anti-Satellite Lasers." *New Scientist*, May 3, 2006.

Heilbroner, Robert L. "Do Machines Make History?" In *Does Technology Drive History? The Dilemma of Technological Determinism*, edited by Merritt Roe Smith and Leo Marx, 53–65. Cambridge, MA: MIT Press, 1994.

Henkin, Louis. *How Nations Behave: Law and Foreign Policy*. New York: Columbia University Press, 1979.

Hennigan, W. J. "Civilian Use of Tiny Drones May Soon Fly in the US." *Los Angeles Times*, November 27, 2011, p. B4.

Herrera, Geoffrey L. "Technology and International Systems." *Millennium: Journal of International Studies* 32:3 (2003): 559–593.

———. *Technology and International Transformation: The Railroad, the Atom Bomb, and the Politics of Technological Change*. Albany: State University of New York Press, 2006.

Hewlett, Richard G., and Jack M. Holl. *Atoms for Peace and War, 1953–1961*. Berkeley: University of California Press, 1989.

Hibbs, Mark. *The Future of the Nuclear Suppliers Group*. Washington, DC: Carnegie Endowment for International Peace, 2011.

———. "LBJ's Safeguards Legacy." *Arms Control Wonk*, June 25, 2013. carnegieendowment.org/2013/06/25/lbj-s-safeguards-legacy/gc7r.

———. "Nuclear Suppliers Group and the IAEA Additional Protocol." *Nuclear Energy Brief*. Carnegie Endowment for International Peace, August 18, 2010. Accessed May 2011. www.carnegieendowment.org/publications/index.cfm?fa=view&id=41393.

Higgins, Jonathan. *Satellite Newsgathering*. Oxford: Focal Press, 1999.

Hirsch, Theodore. "The IAEA Additional Protocol: What It Is and Why It Matters." *Nonproliferation Review* (Fall/Winter 2004): 140–166.

Hirsh, Michael, and John Barry. "How We Stumbled into War." *Newsweek*, April 12, 1999.

"A History of Drone Warfare." *New York Times*, May 24, 2013, p. A8.

Hitchens, Theresa. "Russian and Chinese Weapons Ban Proposal: A Critique." *Security in Space: The Next Generation*. United Nations Institute For Disarmament Research Conference Report, March 31–April 1, 2008.

———. *Weapons in Space: Silver Bullet or Russian Roulette?* Washington, DC: Center for Defense Information, April 19, 2002.

Hoddeson, Lillian, Paul W. Henriksen, Roger A. Meade, and Catherine Westfall. *Critical Assembly: A Technical History of Los Alamos during the Oppenheimer Years, 1943–1945*. New York: Cambridge University Press, 1993.

Hoffman, David. "Global Communications Network Was Pivotal in Defeat of Junta." *Washington Post*, August 23, 1991, p. A27.

Hoffman, F. G. *Decisive Force: The New American Way of War*. Westport, CT: Praeger, 1996.

Hoffmann, Matthew J. "The Global Regime: Current Status of and *Quo Vadis* for Kyoto." In *A Globally Integrated Climate Policy for Canada*, edited by Steven Bernstein, Jutta Brunnée, David Duff, and Andrew Green, 137–157. Toronto: University of Toronto Press, 2007.

———. "My Norm Is Better Than Your Norm: Contestation and Norm Dynamics." Paper presented at the Annual Meeting of the International Studies Association, Chicago, March 2, 2007.

———. "Norms and Social Constructivism in International Relations." In *The International Studies Encyclopedia*, vol. 9, edited by Robert A. Denemark, 5410–5426. Oxford: Wiley-Blackwell, 2010.

Holt, George C. "The Conference on World Government." *Journal of Higher Education* 17:5 (May 1946): 227–235.

Homeland Security Act of 2002. Public Law 107–296. November 25, 2002. http://www.dhs.gov/xlibrary/assets/hr_5005_enr.pdf.

Homer, Jack A. "ENDC at the General Assembly." Report for the *Bulletin of the Atomic Scientists* (February 1967): 30–33.

Hooghe, Liesbet. *The European Commission and the Integration of Europe: Images of Governance*. Cambridge: Cambridge University Press, 2002.

———. "Several Roads Lead to International Norms, But Few via International Socialization: A Case Study of the European Commission." *International Organization* 59:3 (2005): 861–898.

Hook, Stephen, and John Spanier. *American Foreign Policy Since World War II*. 16th ed. Washington, DC: CQ Press, 2004.

Horner, Daniel. "Officials Spell Out Nuclear Trade Policy." *Arms Control Today* 42:3 (2012). Accessed March 23, 2012. http://www.armscontrol.org/act/2012_03/Officials_Spell_Out_Nuclear_Trade_Policy.

———. "U.S. Policy on Nuclear Pacts Detailed." *Arms Control Today*, January 2014. Accessed January 15, 2016. https://www.armscontrol.org/act/2014_01–02/US-Policy-on-Nuclear-Pacts-Detailed.

Horner, Daniel, and Kelsey Davenport. "Post-2014 Nuclear Security Mulled." *Arms Control Today*, December 2012. Accessed May 14, 2013. www.armscontrol.org/2012_12/Post-2014-Nuclear-Security-Mulled.

Houghton, David Patrick. "Reinvigorating the Study of Foreign Policy Decision Making: Toward a Constructivist Approach." *Foreign Policy Analysis* 3:2 (2007): 24–45.

Hughes, Thomas P. *Networks of Power: Electrification in Western Society, 1880–1930.* Baltimore: Johns Hopkins University Press, 1983.

———. "The Seamless Web: Technology, Science, Etcetera, Etcetera." *Social Studies of Science* 16:2 (1986): 281–292.

Human Rights Watch. "Spotting War Crimes from Space." Live chat with Josh Lyons, Satellite Imagery Analyst for HRW's Emergencies Division. February 5, 2014. http://www.hrw.org/spotting-war-crimes-from-space.

Hurd, Ian. "Breaking and Making Norms: American Revisionism and Crises of Legitimacy." *International Politics* 44:3 (2007): 194–213.

———. "Legitimacy and Authority in International Politics." *International Organization* 53:2 (1999): 379–408.

———. "Legitimacy and Strategic Behavior: The Instrumental Use of Norms in World Politics." Paper presented to the Annual Meeting of the International Studies Association, Chicago, February 28, 2007.

Hymans, Jacques E. C. *Achieving Nuclear Ambitions: Scientists, Politicians, and Proliferation.* Cambridge: Cambridge University Press, 2012.

———. "Proliferation Implications of Civil Nuclear Cooperation: Theory and a Case Study of Tito's Yugoslavia." *Security Studies* 20:1 (2011): 71–98.

———. *The Psychology of Nuclear Proliferation: Identity, Emotions, and Foreign Policy.* Cambridge: Cambridge University Press, 2006.

———. "Veto Players, Nuclear Energy, and Nonproliferation: Domestic Institutional Barriers to a Japanese Bomb." *International Security* 36:2 (Fall 2011): 154–189.

"'The Impulse Toward a Safer World': 40th Anniversary of the Nuclear Nonproliferation Treaty." *The Nuclear Vault.* National Security Archive. July 1, 2008. http://www2.gwu.edu/nsarchiv/nukevault/ebb253/index.htm.

"Informal Communication from Chairman Khrushchev to President Kennedy." September 4, 1962. In *The Kennedy-Khrushchev Letters: Top Secret*, edited by Thomas Fensch, 270. The Woodlands, TX: New Century, 2001.

Ingebritsen, Christine. "Norm Entrepreneurs: Scandinavia's Role in World Politics." *International Studies Perspectives* 37:1 (2002): 11–23.

International Atomic Energy Agency. "Communication Received from Certain Member States Regarding Guidelines for the Export of Nuclear Material, Equipment or Technology." July 1992. www.iaea.org/Publications/Documents/Infcircs/Others/infcirc254r1p2.pdf.

———. *Nuclear Power Reactors in the World.* 2012 edition. Reference Data Series no.

2, IAEA-RDS-2/32. http://pub.iaea.org/MTCD/Publications/PDF/FDS2032_web. pdf.

———. "The Safeguards System of the International Atomic Energy Agency." Organizational document. Accessed January 20, 2013. http://www.iaea.org/OurWork/ SV/Safeguards/documents/safeg_system.pdf.

———. Statute of the International Atomic Energy Agency. Art. III, 5, http://www. iaea.org/About/statute.html (accessed April 11, 2013).

International Institute for Strategic Studies. "Unmanned Aerial Vehicles: Emerging Lessons and Technologies." *The Military Balance 2011*, 20–26. London: IISS, 2012.

Isikoff, Michael. "Justice Department Memo Reveals Legal Case for Drone Strikes on Americans." *NBC News*, February 4, 2013. Accessed January 17, 2016. http://investigations.nbcnews.com/_news/2013/02/04/16843014-justice-department-memo-reveals-legal-case-for-drone-strikes-on-americans?lite.

Jackson, Brian A., David R. Frelinger, Michal J. Lostumbo, and Robert W. Button. *Evaluating Novel Threats to the Homeland*. Santa Monica, CA: RAND Corporation. MG-626-DTRA, 2008. www.rand.org/pub/monographs/MG626.html.

Jackson, Jamie Melissa. "The Legality of Assassination of Independent Terrorist Leaders: An Examination of National and International Implications." *North Carolina Journal of International Law and Commercial Regulation* 24:669 (Spring 1999).

Jefferson, Thomas. Letter from Thomas Jefferson to Samuel Kercheval, July 12, 1816. In *The Writings of Thomas Jefferson: 1816–1826*, vol. 10, edited by Paul Leicester Ford, 42–43. Washington, DC: Library of Congress, 1899.

Jepperson, Ronald. "Institutions, Institutional Effects, and Institutionalism." In *The New Institutionalism in Organizational Analysis*, edited by Paul J. DiMaggio and Walter W. Powell, 143–163. Chicago: University of Chicago Press, 1991.

Jepperson, Ronald, Alexander Wendt, and Peter J. Katzenstein. "Norms, Identity and Culture in National Security." In *The Culture of National Security: Norms and Identity in World Politics*, edited by Peter J. Katzenstein, 33–75. New York: Columbia University Press, 1996.

"John Brennan Delivers Speech on Drone Ethics." *Talk of the Nation Report*, National Public Radio, May 1, 2012. www.npr.org/2012/05/01/151778804/ john-brennan-delivers-speech-on-drone-ethics

Johnson Administration. "Remarks on Signing the Nuclear Nonproliferation Treaty." Transcript from the Miller Center, University of Virginia, July 1, 1968. Accessed May 18, 2013. http://millercenter.org/president/speeches/detail/4037.

———. "U.S. Nuclear and Strategic Delivery System Assistance to France." *National Security Action Memorandum 294*, April 20, 1964. Accessed May 30, 2013. http:// www.lbjlib.utexas.edu/johnson/archives.hom/nsams/nsam294.asp.

Johnson, Lyndon Baines. "Remarks in Seattle on the Control of Nuclear Weapons." *The American Presidency Project at UC Santa Barbara*, September 16, 1964. Accessed May 18, 2013. http://www.presidency.ucsb.edu/ws/?pid=26506.

Johnson, Rebecca. "Multilateral Approaches to Preventing the Weaponization of Space." *Disarmament Diplomacy* 56 (April 2001): 8–16.

Johnston, Alastair Iain. "Thinking about Strategic Culture." *International Security* 19:4 (1995): 32–64.

———. "Treating International Institutions as Social Environments." *International Studies Quarterly* 45:4 (2001): 487–515.

Joint Doctrine for Space Operations. Joint Publication 3–14, Defense Technical Information Center, August 9, 2004. http://www.dtic.mil/doctrine/jel/new_pubs/jp3_14.pdf.

Jonas, David S., John Carlson, and Richard S. Goorevich. "The NSG Decision on Sensitive Nuclear Transfers: ABACC and the Additional Protocol." *Arms Control Today*, November 2012. Accessed May 14, 2013. www.armscontrol.org/act/2012_11/The-NSG-Decision-on-Sensitive-Nuclear-Transfers-ABACC-and-the-Additional-Protocol.

Jordan, Jenna. "When Heads Roll: Assessing the Effectiveness of Leadership Decapitation." *Security Studies* 18:4 (October/November 2009): 719–755.

Joyner, Daniel H. *International Law and the Proliferation of Weapons of Mass Destruction.* Oxford: Oxford University Press, 2009.

———. *Non-Proliferation Export Controls: Origins, Challenges, and Proposals for Strengthening.* London: Ashgate, 2006.

———. "Non-proliferation Law and the United Nations System: Resolution 1540 and the Limits of the Power of the Security Council." *Leiden Journal of International Law* 20:4 (2007): 489–518.

———. "The Nuclear Suppliers Group: History and Functioning." *International Trade Law and Regulation* 11:2 (2005): 84–96.

———. "The Proliferation Security Initiative: Nonproliferation, Counterproliferation and International Law." *Yale Journal of International Law* 507 (2005): 507–548.

Kan, Shirley. *China's Anti-Satellite Weapon Test.* Congressional Research Service Report RS22652, April 23, 2007.

Katz, James Everet. "U.S. Energy Policy: The Impact of the Reagan Administration." *Energy Policy* 23:2 (1984): 136–147.

Katzenstein, Peter J., ed. *The Culture of National Security: Norms and Identity in World Politics.* New York: Columbia University Press, 1996.

Katzenstein, Peter J., Robert O. Keohane, and Stephen Krasner. "International Organization and the Study of World Politics." *International Organization* 52:4 (1998): 645–685.

Kaufman, Marc. "U.S. Finds It's Getting Crowded Out There: Dominance in Space Slips as Other Nations Step Up Efforts." *Washington Post*, July 9, 2008. http://www.washingtonpost.com/wp-dyn/content/article/2008/07/08/AR2008070803185.html.

Kaufman, Marc, and Dafna Linzer. "China Criticized for Anti-Satellite Missile Test: Destruction of an Aging Satellite Illustrates Vulnerability of U.S. Space Assets." *Washington Post*, January 19, 2007, p. 1.

Kay, Sean, and Theresa Hitchens. "Bush Policy Would Start Arms Race in Space." *Cleveland Plain Dealer*, May 25, 2005.

Keck, Margaret, and Kathryn Sikkink. "Transnational Advocacy Networks in International Politics: Introduction." In *Activists Beyond Borders,* edited by Margaret Keck and Kathryn Sikkink, 1–38. Ithaca, NY: Cornell University Press, 1998.

Keeley, James F. *A List of Bilateral Civilian Nuclear Cooperation Agreements. Volume 1: The Treaty List Project.* Calgary, Alberta: University of Calgary, 2009. Accessed March 4, 2011. http://dspace.ucalgary.ca/bitstream/1880/47373/7/Treaty_List_Volume_01.pdf.

Kehoe, R. B. *The Enriching Troika: A History of Urenco to the Year 2000.* Marlow, UK: Urenco Limited, 2002.

Kelly, Cynthia, ed. *The Manhattan Project: The Birth of the Atomic Bomb in the Words of Its Creators, Eyewitnesses, and Historians.* London: Black Dog & Leventhal, 2009.

Kels, Charles G. "Law, Policy, and Drone Warfare: Mixing Legal Doctrines on Targeted Killing Is a Dangerous Recipe for Confusion." *National Law Journal* 35:26 (2013).

Kemp, R. Scott. "Centrifuges: A New Era for Nuclear Proliferation." Report for the Nonproliferation Policy Education Center, June 5, 2012. http://www.npolicy.org/article_file/Centrifuges-_A_new_era_for_nuclear_proliferation.pdf.

———. Quoted in *Countdown to Zero.* Documentary. Magnolia Home Entertainment (2010), min. 68.10.

Kennedy, Greg. "Drones: Legitimacy and Anti-Americanism." *Parameters* 42:4/43:1 (Winter–Spring 2013): 25–41.

Kennedy, John F. "Address to Joint Session of Congress," May 25, 1961. http://www.space.com/11772-president-kennedy-historic-speech-moon-space.html.

———. "News Conference Transcript," March 21, 1963. *The American Presidency Project.* Accessed June 3, 2013. http://www.presidency.ucsb.edu/ws/?pid=9124.

Kennedy, Paul M. *The Rise and Fall of British Naval Mastery.* London: Macmillan, 1983.

Keohane, Robert O., and Elinor Ostrom, eds. *Local Commons and Global Interdependence.* London: Sage Publications, 1995.

Kessler, Glenn. *The Confidante: Condoleezza Rice and the Creation of the Bush Legacy.* New York: St. Martin's Press, 2007.

———. "Libya, Obama, and the Tragedy in Darfur." *Washington Post,* March 24, 2011. Accessed February 23, 2012. http://www.washingtonpost.com/blogs/fact-checker/post/libya-obama-and-the-tragedy-in-darfur/2011/03/23/ABlu34KB_blog.html.

———. "U.S. Decision on Iraq Has Puzzling Past." *Washington Post,* January 12, 2003, p. A1.

Killian, Jr., James R. *Sputnik, Scientists, and Eisenhower: A Memoir of the First Special Assistant to the President for Science and Technology.* Cambridge, MA: MIT Press, 1977.

Kistiakowsky, George. *A Scientist at the White House: The Private Diary of President Eisenhower's Special Assistant for Science and Technology.* Cambridge, MA: Harvard University Press, 1976.

Klaidman, Daniel. "Obama: I Make the Drone Decisions." *Daily Beast,* May 23, 2013.

Accessed March 21, 2014. http://www.thedailybeast.com/articles/2013/05/23/obama-i-make-the-drone-decisions.html.

Klein, John J. *Space Warfare: Strategy, Principles, and Policy.* London: Routledge, 2006.

Kline, Ronald, and Trevor Pinch. "Users as Agents of Technological Change: The Social Construction of the Automobile in the Rural United States." *Technology and Culture* 37:4 (1996): 763–795.

Klotz, Audie. *Norms in International Relations: The Struggle against Apartheid.* Ithaca, NY: Cornell University Press, 1995.

Knowles, Eric S., and Jay A. Linn, eds. *Resistance and Persuasion.* Mahwah, NJ: Lawrence Erlbaum Publishers, 2004.

Knox, Stephen F. *Secret and Sanctioned: Covert Operations and the American Presidency.* New York: Oxford University Press, 1996.

Koh, Harold H. "The Obama Administration and International Law." Speech to the American Society of International Law, March 25, 2010. http://www.state.gov/s/l/releases/remarks/139119.htm.

———. "Why Do Nations Obey International Law?" *Yale Law Journal* 106:8 (1997): 2599–2659.

Kohut, Andrew, and Robert C. Toty. "The People, the Press, and the Use of Force." In *The United States and the Use of Force in the Post-Cold War Era*, edited by Aspen Strategy Group. Queenstown, MD: Aspen Institute 1995.

Kowert, Paul, and Jeffrey Legro. "Norms, Identity, and Their Limits: A Theoretical Reprise." In *The Culture of National Security*, edited by Peter J. Katzenstein, 451–496. New York: Columbia University Press, 1996.

Kratochwil, Friedrich V. *Rules, Norms, and Decisions: On the Conditions of Practical and Legal Reasoning in International Relations and Domestic Affairs.* Cambridge: Cambridge University Press, 1989.

Krepon, Michael, and Christopher Clary. *Space Assurance or Space Dominance? The Case Against Weaponizing Space.* Washington, DC: Henry L. Stimson Center, 2003.

Krepon, Michael, and Julia Thompson, eds. *Anti-Satellite Weapons, Deterrence, and Sino-American Space Relations.* Washington, DC: Stimpson Center, September 2013. Accessed July 11, 2014. http://www.stimson.org/images/uploads/Anti-satellite_Weapons.pdf.

Kroenig, Matthew. "Exporting the Bomb: Why States Provide Sensitive Nuclear Assistance." *American Political Science Review* 103:1 (2009): 113–133.

———. "Force or Friendship? Explaining Great Power Nonproliferation Policy." *Security Studies* 23:2 (2014): 1–32.

———. "Importing the Bomb: Sensitive Nuclear Assistance and Nuclear Proliferation." *Journal of Conflict Resolution* 53:2 (2009): 161–180.

Krook, Mona Lena, and Jacqui True. "Rethinking the Life Cycles of International Norms: The United Nations and the Global Promotion of Gender Equality." *European Journal of International Relations* 18:1 (2010): 103–127.

Krugman, Paul, ed. *Strategic Trade Policy and the New International Economics*. Cambridge, MA: MIT Press, 1986.

Kumar, Akshaya. GooglePlus Hangout, "Using Tech to Fight Atrocities." Webinar November 27, 2013. Sponsored by the Digital Mass Atrocity Prevention Lab (DMAPLab). With Christopher Tuckwood (Sentinel Project), Akshaya Kumar (Enough Project), Nathaniel Raymond (Signal Program on Human Security and Technology at the Harvard Humanitarian Initiative), and Kyle Matthews (Montreal Institute for Genocide and Human Rights Studies). https://plus.google.com/u/0/events/cuvq5u235lpt7vqb7j2mfis6pgk?authkey=CITI1LOAouamfw.

Lakoff, George. *Whose Freedom? The Battle over America's Most Important Idea*. New York: Farrar, Straus, and Girox, 2006.

Lakoff, Sanford, and Herbert F. York. *A Shield in Space? Technology, Politics, and the Strategic Defense Initiative*. Berkeley: University of California Press, 1989.

Lampley, Virginia. Subject Files, Strategic Defense Missiles, OA/ID Number CF01362; Folder ID Number CF01362–075. George H. W. Bush Presidential Library. College Station, TX. Collected April 3, 2014.

Land Remote-Sensing Commercialization Act of 1984, Pub. L. No. 98–365, 98 Stat. 451 (codified at 15 U.S.C. § 4201 [repealed 1992]) (regulating the satellite observation of land masses).

Lantis, Jeffrey S. "Agentic Constructivism and the Proliferation Security Initiative: Modeling Norm Change." *Cooperation and Conflict* (forthcoming 2016).

———. "Constructivist Security Studies and Non-proliferation: How Elite Entrepreneurship Can Make or Break International Norms." Special issue of *Journal of Global Security Studies*, Maria Rost Rublee and Avner Cohen, eds. (forthcoming 2016).

———. "Irrational Exuberance? The 2010 NPT Review, Nuclear Assistance, and Norm Deconstruction." *Nonproliferation Review* 18:2 (July 2011): 389–409.

———. "Nuclear Technology and Norm Stewardship: U.S. Nonproliferation Policies Revisited." *International Studies Perspectives* 16:4 (2015). DOI: 10.1111/insp.12070.

Lantis, Jeffrey S., and Eric Moskowitz. "War in Kosovo: Coercive Diplomacy." In *Contemporary Cases in U.S. Foreign Policy: From Terrorism to Trade*, edited by Ralph G. Carter, 59–87. Washington, DC: Congressional Quarterly Press, 2002.

Latham, Robert, ed. *Bombs and Bandwidth: The Emerging Relationship between Information Technology and Security*. New York: New Press, 2003.

Lawrence, Regina. *The Politics of Force: Media and the Construction of Police Brutality*. Berkeley: University of California Press, 2000.

Lay, James S., Jr. "Scientific Satellite Program." Note by the Executive Secretary to the National Security Council, May 20, 1955. (A draft statement in anticipation of NSC meeting May 26 to finalize NSC 5520.) Both available online at the Digital National Security Archive, George Washington University, Washington, DC.

Lee, Steven P., ed. *Intervention, Terrorism, and Torture: Contemporary Challenges to Just War Theory*. Dordrecht: Springer, 2007.

Legro, Jeffrey W. *Cooperation Under Fire: Anglo-German Restraint during World War II*. Ithaca, NY: Cornell University Press, 1995.

———. *Rethinking the World: Great Power Strategies and International Order*. Ithaca, NY: Cornell University Press, 2005.

Lele, Ajey. "Space Code of Conduct: Inadequate Mechanism." In *Decoding the International Code of Conduct for Outer Space Activities*, edited by Ajey Lele, 5–8. New Delhi: Institute for Defence Studies and Analyses, Pentagon Security International, 2012.

Lemann, Nicholas. "The Next World Order: The Bush Administration May Have a Brand New Doctrine of Power." *New Yorker*, April 1, 2002. Accessed May 19, 2013. www.newyorker.com/fact/content/?020401fa_FACT1.

Lessig, Lawrence. "The Regulation of Social Meeting." *University of Chicago Law Review* 62:3 (1995): 943–1045.

"Letter from Leo Szilard to Mr. Lewis L. Strauss." January 25, 1939. In *The American Atom: A Documentary History of Nuclear Policies from the Discovery of Fission to the Present*, 2nd ed., edited by Philip L. Cantelon, Richard G. Hewlett, and Robert C. Williams, 8–9. Philadelphia: University of Pennsylvania Press, 1991.

Leventhal, Paul. "Cirus Reactor's Role in a U.S.-India Nuclear Agreement." Presentation to Center for Nonproliferation Studies, Washington, DC, December 19, 2005.

Levine, Alan J. *The Missile and Space Race*. Westport, CT: Praeger, 1994.

"Libya Violence Escalates as Qaddafi's Son Vows 'Rivers of Blood.'" *Bloomberg News*, February 21, 2011. Accessed August 13, 2013. www.bloomberg.com/news/2011–02–21/libyan-violence-worsens-as-protesters-claim-control-of-second-largest-city.html.

Lijphart, Arend. "Comparative Politics and the Comparative Method." *American Political Science Review* 65:3 (1971): 682–693.

Livingston, Steven. "Beyond the CNN Effect: The Media-Foreign Policy Dynamic." In *Politics and the Press: The News Media and Their Influences*, edited by Pippa Norris, 291–318. Boulder, CO: Lynne Rienner, 1997.

———. *Clarifying the CNN Effect: An Examination of Media Effects According to Type of Military Intervention*. Research Paper R-18. Cambridge, MA: Joan Shorenstein Center, John F. Kennedy School of Government, Harvard University, 1997.

Livingston, Steven, and W. Lance Bennett. "Gatekeeping, Indexing, and Live-Event News: Is Technology Altering the Construction of News?" *Political Communication* 20:1 (2003): 363–380.

Livingston, Steven, and T. Eachus. "Humanitarian Crises and U.S. Foreign Policy: Somalia and the CNN Effect Reconsidered." *Political Communication* 12:4 (1995): 413–429.

Livingston, Steven, and Douglas A. Van Belle. "The Effects of Satellite Technology on Newsgathering from Remote Locations." *Political Communication* 22:3 (2005): 45–62.

Logsdon, John M., moderator. *Legislative Origins of the National Aeronautics and Space Act of 1958: Proceedings of an Oral History Workshop*. April 3, 1992. Monographs in Aerospace History, Number 8. NASA Headquarters, Washington DC: Office of Policy and Plans, NASA History Division, July 1998.

Lotrionte, Catherine. "Targeting Regime Leaders during Armed Hostilities: An Effective Way to Achieve Regime Change?" In *The Law of Armed Conflict: Constraints on the Contemporary Use of Military Force*, edited by Howard M. Hensel, 21–38. London: Ashgate, 2005.

Lupton, David E. *On Space Warfare: A Space Power Doctrine*. Maxwell Air Force Base, AL: Air University Press, June 1988.

Lynch, Colum, and Karen de Young. "Kerry, Lavrov to Meet on Russian Proposal after Russia Balks at Plan for U.N. Action." *Washington Post*, September 10, 2013. Accessed May 26, 2014. http://www.washingtonpost.com/world/middle_east/france-to-author-security-council-resolution-to-require-syria-to-give-up-chemical-weapons/2013/09/10/0d51a06c-19ff-11e3-a628-7e6dde8f889d_story.html.

Lynch, Marc. *State Interests and Public Spheres: The International Politics of Jordan's Identity*. New York: Columbia University Press, 1999.

Lyons, Joshua. "Documenting Violations of International Humanitarian Law from Space: A Critical Review of Geospatial Analysis of Satellite and Imagery during Armed Conflicts in Gaza (2009), Georgia (2008), and Sri Lanka (2009)." *International Review of the Red Cross* 94:886 (Summer 2012): 739–763.

MacArthur, John R. *Second Front: Censorship and Propaganda in the Gulf War*. Berkeley: University of California Press, 1993.

Mackenzie, Donald. *Inventing Accuracy: An Historical Sociology of Missile Guidance*. Cambridge, MA: MIT Press, 1990.

Mackenzie, Donald, and Judy Wajcman, eds. *The Social Shaping of Technology*. 2nd ed. Philadelphia: Open University Press, 1999.

Malcolm, Noel. *Bosnia: A Short History*. New York: New York University Press, 1994.

Malnes, Raino. "'Leader' and 'Entrepreneur' in International Negotiations: A Conceptual Analysis." *European Journal of International Relations* 1:1 (1995): 87–112.

Man, Zia. "The American Problem: The United States and Noncompliance in the World of Arms Control and Nonproliferation." In *International Law and Organization*, edited by Edward C. Luck and Michael W. Doyle, 247–302. Boulder, CO: Lynne Rienner, 2003.

March, John G., and Johan P. Olsen. "The New Institutionalism: Organizational Factors in Political Life." *American Political Science Review* 78:4 (1984): 734–749.

———. *Rediscovering Institutions: The Organizational Basis of Politics*. New York: Free Press, 1989.

Martin, Lisa L., and Beth A. Simmons. *International Institutions: An International Organization Reader*. Cambridge, MA: MIT Press, 2001.

Matthews, Max W. "Tracking the Emergence of a New International Norm: The Responsibility to Protect and the Crisis in Darfur." *Boston College International and Comparative Law Review* 31:1 (2008): 137–152.

May, Michael M. "Safeguarding Our Space Assets." In *Seeking Stability in Space*, edited by Joseph S. Nye and James A. Schear, 71–85. Lanham, MD: University Press of America, 1987.

Mayer, Jane. "The Manipulator." *New Yorker*, June 7, 2004, p. 61.

———. "The Predator War." *New Yorker*, October 26, 2009, p. 38.

McDonnell, Thomas Michael. "Sow What You Reap? Using Predator and Reaper Drones to Carry Out Assassinations or Targeted Killings of Suspected Islamic Terrorists." *George Washington International Law Review* 44 (2012): 244–315.

McDougall, Walter A. *The Heavens and the Earth: A Political History of the Space Age.* New York: Basic Books, 1985.

McGoldrick, Fred. "Limiting Transfers of Enrichment and Reprocessing Technology: Issues, Constraints, Options." Harvard Kennedy School Belfer Center for Science and International Affairs Project on Managing the Atom, May 2011 (author's copy).

———. *Nuclear Trade Controls: Minding the Gaps.* Report of the CSIS Proliferation Prevention Program. Washington, DC: Center for Strategic and International Studies, January 2013.

———. Testimony of Fred McGoldrick. Senate Foreign Relations Committee, July 31, 2007. Accessed March 18, 2011. http://www.foreign.senate.gov/imo/media/doc/McGoldrickTestimony070731.pdf.

McKeown, Ryder. "Norm Regress: U.S. Revisionism and the Slow Death of the Torture Norm." *International Relations* 23:1 (2009): 5–25.

McKie, Rob. "Sergei Korolev: The Rocket Genius behind Yuri Gagarin." *The Observer*, March 12, 2011. Accessed January 15, 2016. http://www.theguardian.com/science/2011/mar/13/yuri-gagarin-first-space-korolev.

Meitner, Lise, and Otto R. Frisch. "Disintegration of Uranium by Neutrons: A New Type of Nuclear Reaction." Letter to the editor. *Nature* 143 (February 11, 1939): 239–240. Accessed June 26, 2013. http://www.atomicarchive.com/Docs/Begin/Nature_Meitner.shtml.

Melman, Yossi. "Why the Plot to Kill Hussein Failed." *Los Angeles Times*, July 21, 1991, pp. M1–M2.

Meron, Theodor. "The Martens Clause, Principles of Humanity, and Dictates of Public Conscience." *American Journal of International Law* 94:1 (2000): 78–89.

Meyer, Stephen M. *The Dynamics of Nuclear Proliferation.* Chicago: University of Chicago Press, 1984.

Minear, Larry, Colin Scott, and Robert Weiss. *The News Media, Civil Wars and Humanitarian Action.* Boulder, CO: Lynne Rienner, 1997.

"Minutes of National Security Council Meeting." January 29, 1969. In *Foreign Relations of the United States, 1969–1976, Vol. E-2, Documents on Arms Control.* Washington, DC: Department of State, 1998.

Moltz, James Clay. *The Politics of Space Security: Strategic Restraint and the Pursuit of National Interests.* 2nd ed. Stanford, CA: Stanford Security Studies, 2011.

Monk, Ray. *Robert Oppenheimer: A Life Inside the Center.* New York: Doubleday, 2013.

Morgenthau, Hans. *Politics Among Nations: The Struggle for Power and Peace.* 4th ed. New York: McGraw-Hill, 1967.

Mowthorpe, Matthew J. "The United States Approach to Military Space during the Cold War." *Air and Space Power Chronicles* 8 (March 2001).

Müller, Harald. "International Relations as Communicative Action." In *Constructing International Relations: The Next Generation,* edited by K. M. Fierke and K. E. Jorgensen, 160–178. Armonk, NY: ME Sharpe.

Müller, Harald, and Carmen Wunderlich, eds. *Norm Dynamics in Multilateral Arms Control: Interests, Conflicts, and Justice.* Athens: University of Georgia Press, 2013.

Muravchik, Joshua. *Exporting Democracy: Fulfilling America's Destiny.* Washington, DC: American Enterprise Institute Press, 1992.

Nadelmann, Ethan A. "Global Prohibition Regimes: The Evolution of Norms in International Society." *International Organization* 44:4 (1990): 479–526.

National Aeronautics and Space Administration. *National Aeronautics and Space Act of 1958, as Amended.* Accessed January 14, 2016. http://history.nasa.gov/spaceact-legishistory.pdf.

National Aeronautics and Space Council. "US Policy on Outer Space." January 1960. Digital National Security Archive, U.S. Military Uses of Space, 1945–1991. Accessed January 15, 2016. http://nsarchive.chadwyck.com/collections/content/MS/intro.jsp.

National Reconnaissance Office. "Corona Fact Sheet." Accessed June 18, 2013. www.nro.gov/history/csnr/corona/factsheet.html.

National Security Council. "Preliminary U.S. Policy on Outer Space." NSC-5814, August 18, 1958.

———. "US Scientific Satellite Program (NSC 5520)." *Records of the White House Office of the Special Assistant for National Security Affairs,* May 1955. Available online at the Digital National Security Archive, U.S. Military Uses of Space, 1945–1991 Collection. http://nsarchive.chadwyck.com/collections/content/MS/intro.jsp.

National Security Council Undersecretaries Committee. "Memorandum for the President. Subject: U.S. Nuclear Nonproliferation Policy." Record Number 117590, August 25, 1974, secret document of the State Department Policy Planning Staff. Paper copy at National Security Archive, viewed February 21, 2014.

National Security Strategy of the United States of America. September 2002. Accessed April 19, 2013. www.whitehouse.gov/nsc/nss.pdf.

Nelson, Craig. *Rocket Men: The Epic Story of the First Men on the Moon.* New York: Penguin, 2009.

"New Satellite Images Reveal Shocking Aftermath of Abuses in Central African Republic." *Amnesty International News,* November 8, 2013. Accessed November 9, 2013. www.amnesty.org/en/news/new-satellite-images-reveal-shocking-aftermath-abuses-central-african-republic-2013-11-08.

New York Times Editorial Board. "The End of Perpetual War." *New York Times,* May 23, 2013, p. A17.

Niebuhr, Reinhold. *Moral Man and Immoral Society: A Study in Ethics and Politics.* New York: Charles Scribner & Sons, 1932.

Nikitin, Mary Beth. *Proliferation Security Initiative (PSI).* Congressional Research Service Report RL34327, January 8, 2010. Accessed February 4, 2012. www.state. gov/secretary/rm/2005/46951.htm.

"North Korea: U.S., Spanish Special Forces Seize Scud Shipment." *NTI Global Security Newswire*, December 11, 2002. Accessed November 22, 2012. www.nti.org/d_ newswire/issues/thisweek/2002_12_13_misp.html.

"NRO Presses New Satellite Imagery Architecture." *Aerospace Daily*, May 21, 1998, pp. 175–176.

"Nuclear Suppliers Guidelines: Memorandum for Mr. Brent Scowcroft, the White House." December 31, 1975. Record number 117001, Nuclear Nonproliferation 2. Paper copy viewed at National Security Archive, February 21, 2014.

Nuclear Threat Initiative. "Nuclear Non-Proliferation Act of 1978, Partial Text of Public Law 95–242 [H.R. 8638], 92 Stat. 120. approved 10 March 1978." *Nuclear Threat Initiative Research Library.* Accessed March 21, 2011. www.nti.org/db/ china/engdocs/nnpa1978.htm.

———. "Russia: Nuclear Exports to India." Center for Nonproliferation Studies, 2010. Accessed September 2, 2012. www.nti.org/db/nisprofs/russia/exports/ rusind/nuclovr.htm.

Obama, Barack. "Remarks of President Barack Obama." Arms Control Association, Prague, Czech Republic, April 5, 2009. Accessed April 11, 2013. http://www.arms-control.org/node/3626.

———. "Remarks by the President at the National Defense University," May 23, 2013. Accessed May 24, 2013. http://www.whitehouse.gov/the-press-office/2013/05/23/ remarks-president-national-defense-university.

———. "Remarks by the President at the United States Military Academy Commencement Ceremony," May 28, 2014. Accessed June 4, 2014. http://www.whitehouse.gov/the-press-office/2014/05/28/ remarks-president-west-point-academy-commencement-ceremony.

Office of the Assistant Secretary of Defense. "Memorandum on Agreement Concerning Cooperation in the Exploration and Use of Outer Space." National Space Council Document Files, OA/ID Number CF01644-026.

Office of the Director, National Reconnaissance Office. "Memorandum for Chairman, United States Intelligence Board. Subject: Study of Requirements for Satellite Reconnaissance Responsive to Warning/Indications Needs." March 12, 1969. Accessed June 21, 2014. http://www.nro.gov/foia/declass/NROStaffRecords/1014. pdf.

Oliveri, Frank. "The U-2 Comes in from the Cold." *Air Force Magazine* (September 1994): 45–50.

Olsen, J. P. "Garbage Cans, New Institutionalism, and the Study of Politics." *American Political Science Review* 95:1 (2001): 191–198.

O'Neill, Philip D., Jr. "The Development of International Law Governing the Military

Use of Outer Space." In *National Interests and the Military Use of Space*, edited by William J. Durch, 169–199. Cambridge, MA: Ballinger, 1984.

O'Reilly, K. P. "Leaders' Perceptions and Nuclear Proliferation: A Political Psychology Approach to Proliferation." *Political Psychology* 33:6 (2012): 767–789.

Organization for Economic Cooperation and Development. *The Security of Energy Supply and the Contribution of Nuclear Energy*. Paris: OECD Publications, 2010. Accessed May 19, 2013. http://www.oecd-nea.org/pub/security-energy-exec-summary.pdf.

Orlikowski, Wanda J. "Using Technology and Constituting Structures: A Practice Lens for Studying Technology in Organizations." *Organization Science* 11:4 (2000): 404–428.

Osman, Fony. *Space History*. London: Michael Joseph Publishers, 1983.

Ostrom, Elinor, ed. *Governing the Commons: The Evolution of Institutions for Collective Action*. Cambridge: Cambridge University Press, 1990.

Panke, Diana, and Ulrich Petersohn. "Why International Norms Disappear Sometimes." *European Journal of International Relations* 18:4 (2012): 719–742.

Pape, Robert A. "The Strategic Logic of Suicide Terrorism." *American Political Science Review* 97:3 (August 2003): 1–19.

Park, Andrew T. "Incremental Steps for Achieving Space Security: The Need for a New Way of Thinking to Enhance the Legal Regime for Space." *Houston Journal of International Law* 28:3 (2006): 872–910.

Payne, Rodger A. "Persuasion, Frames and Norm Construction." *European Journal of International Relations* 7:1 (2001): 37–61.

Pearce, David D. *Wary Partners: Diplomats and the Media*. Washington, DC: CQ Press, 1995.

Pearl, Jonathan. "Charting a Smarter Course for a U.S.-Jordan Nuclear Deal." *Bulletin of the Atomic Scientists*, October 25, 2010. Accessed November 19, 2010. www.thebulletin.org/web-edition/op-eds/charting-smarter-course-us-jordan-nuclear-deal.

Peña, Charles V., and Edward L. Hudgins. "Should the United States 'Weaponize' Space? Military and Commercial Implications." *Policy Analysis* 427 (March 18, 2001): 5–10. Washington DC: Cato Institute.

Perry, Timothy C. "Blurring the Ocean Zones: The Effect of the Proliferation Security Initiative on the Customary International Law of the Sea." *Ocean Development & International Law* 37:1 (2006): 33–53.

Peterson, M. J. *Managing the Frozen South: The Creation and Evolution of the Antarctic Treaty System*. Berkeley: University of California Press, 1988.

———. "Whalers, Caetologists, Environmentalists, and the International Management of Whaling." *International Organization* 46:1 (1992): 147–186.

———. "The Worlds of Global Commons Regimes: The Global Commons: A Regime Analysis by John Vogler." Review by M. J. Peterson, *Mershon International Studies Review* 40:2 (October 1996): 289–291.

Peterson, Stephen R. *Space Control and the Role of Anti-Satellite Weapons*. Research

Report AU-ARI-90–7. Maxwell Air Force Base, AL: Air University Press, 1991. http://www.fas.org/spp/military/petersen.pdf.

Petrova, Margarita H. "Banning Obsolete Weapons or Reshaping Perceptions of Military Utility: Discursive Dynamics in Weapons Prohibitions." Institut Barcelona d'Estudis Internacionals (IBEI). Working Paper Series 31, 2010. Accessed March 4, 2012. www.cidob.org.

Pilat, Joseph F., and Warren H. Donnelly. "The Nuclear Export Policy of the Reagan Administration." *Energy Policy* 11:2 (June 1983): 168–171.

Pinch, Trevor J., and Wiebe E. Bijker. "The Social Construction of Facts and Artefacts: Or How the Sociology of Science and the Sociology of Technology Might Benefit Each Other." *Social Studies of Science* 14:3 (1984): 399–441.

"Plan to Kill Hitler was 'Unsporting.'" *Times of London*, August 5, 1969.

Polenberg, Richard, ed. *In the Matter of J. Robert Oppenheimer: The Security Clearance Hearing*. Ithaca, NY: Cornell University Press, 2002.

Posen, Barry R. "Command of the Commons: The Military Foundations of U.S. Hegemony." *International Security* 28:1 (Summer 2003): 5–46.

Potter, William, ed. *Verification and SALT: The Challenge of Strategic Deception*. Boulder, CO: Westview, 1980.

Power, Samantha. "Dying in Darfur: Can the Ethnic Cleansing in Sudan Be Stopped?" *New Yorker*, August 30, 2004. Accessed February 22, 2012. http://www.newyorker. com/archive/2004/08/30/040830fa_fact1.

Presidential Study Directive/PSD-10. August 4, 2011. White House Memo (for immediate release); Subject: Creation of an Interagency Atrocities Prevention Board and Corresponding Interagency Review. Accessed July, 8, 2013. http://responsibilitytoprotect.org/index.php/component/content/article/ interagency-atrocities-prevention-board.

Price, Byran C. "Targeting Top Terrorists: How Leadership Decapitation Contributes to Counterterrorism." *International Security* 36:4 (2012): 9–46.

Price, Richard M. *Moral Limit and Possibility in World Politics*. Cambridge: Cambridge University Press, 2008.

———. "Reversing the Gun Sights: Transnational Civil Society Targets and Land Mines." *International Organization* 52:3 (1998): 613–644.

Price, Richard, and Christian Reus-Smit. "Dangerous Liaisons? Critical International Relations Theory and Constructivism." *European Journal of International Relations* 4:1 (1998): 259–294.

Protocol Additional to the Geneva Conventions of 12 August 1949, and Relating to the Protection of Victims of International Armed Conflicts (Protocol I) arts. 51(2), 51(1), June 8, 1977, 1125 U.N.T.S. 3.

Protocol to the Convention for the Suppression of Unlawful Acts Against the Safety of Maritime Navigation. Completed Rome Treaty Document, March 10, 1988. Accessed June 11, 2013. http://www.un.org/en/sc/ctc/docs/conventions/Conv8. pdf.

Public Papers of the Presidents of the United States, Ronald Reagan, 1987. Washington, DC: U.S. Government Printing Office, 1989.

Pursell, Carroll W., Jr. *The Machine in America: A Social History of Technology.* Revised ed. Baltimore: Johns Hopkins University Press, 2007.

———. *Readings in Technology and American Life.* New York: Oxford University Press, 1969.

———. *Technology in Postwar America: A History.* New York: Columbia University Press, 2007.

Ramsbotham, Oliver, and Tom Woodhouse. *Humanitarian Intervention in Contemporary Conflict: A Reconceptualization.* Cambridge, MA: Polity Press, 1996.

Ramet, Sabrina Petra. "War in the Balkans." *Foreign Affairs* 71:2 (1992): 174–181.

RAND Corporation. *Preliminary Design for an Experimental World-Circling Spaceship.* Santa Monica, CA: Project RAND, [1946] 1999.

Rathgeber, Wolfgang, Nina-Louisa Remuß, and Kai-Uwe Schrogl. "Space Security and the European Code of Conduct for Outer Space activities." *UNIDIR Disarmament Forum* 4 (2009): 35–36.

Raum, Tom. "Cost of Kosovo Conflict Said to Be $4 Billion." *Washington Post,* June 8, 1999, p. A1.

Raymond, Gregory A. "Problems and Prospects in the Study of International Norms." *Mershon International Studies Review* 41:1 (1997): 205–245.

Raymond, Nathaniel A., Benjamin I. Davies, Brittany L. Card, Ziad Al Achkar, and Isaac L. Baker. "While We Watched: Assessing the Impact of the Satellite Sentinel Project." *Georgetown University Science & Technology Journal* (Summer/Fall 2013). Accessed August 11, 2013. http://journal.georgetown.edu/2013/07/26/while-we-watched-assessing-t . . . pact-of-the-satellite-sentinel-project-by-nathaniel-a-raymond-et-al.

Reagan, Ronald. "Address to the Nation on the Defense Budget." White House, March 23, 1983.

———. "Statement on United States Nuclear Nonproliferation Policy." July 16, 1981. Reprinted in *The Public Papers of Ronald Reagan,* University of Texas Library. Accessed April 14, 2012. http://www.reagan.utexas.edu/archives/speeches/1981/71681a.htm.

"Red Moon Over the U.S." *Time,* October 14, 1957.

Reed, Thomas C., and Danny B. Stillman. *The Nuclear Express: A Political History of the Bomb and Its Proliferation.* Minneapolis: Zenith, 2009.

Reiss, Edward. *The Strategic Defense Initiative.* Cambridge: Cambridge University Press, 1992.

Reiss, Mitchell. *Without the Bomb: The Politics of Nuclear Proliferation.* New York: Columbia University Press, 1988.

"Remarks by the President and Secretary of Defense Donald Rumsfeld Swearing-In Ceremony." Oval Office, Office of the Press Secretary, January 26, 2001. http://georgewbush-whitehouse.archives.gov/news/releases/20010126-6.html.

Reus-Smit, Christian, ed. *The Politics of International Law*. Cambridge: Cambridge University Press, 2004.

Rhodes, Richard. *The Making of the Atomic Bomb*. Revised ed. New York: Simon and Schuster, 2012.

———, ed. *Visions of Technology*. London: Touchstone, 1999.

Richburg, Keith B. "Israelis Confirm Assassinations Used as Policy; Key Palestinians Targeted." *Washington Post*, January 8, 2001.

Richelson, Jeffrey T. *The U.S. Intelligence Community*. 6th ed. Boulder, CO: Westview, 2011.

Richter, Paul. "Congress Ponders Whether the US Should Ease Ban on Assassinations." *Los Angeles Times*, September 18, 1998, p. A8.

Risse, Thomas. "'Let's Argue!': Communicative Action in World Politics." *International Organization* 54:1 (2000): 1–39.

Risse, Thomas, Stephen C. Ropp, and Kathryn Sikkink, eds. *The Power of Human Rights: International Norms and Domestic Change*. Cambridge: Cambridge University Press, 1999.

Risse-Kappen, Thomas. "Ideas Do Not Float Freely: Transnational Coalitions, Domestic Structures, and the End of the Cold War." *International Organization* 48:2 (1994): 185–214.

Roberts, Adam, and Richard Guelff, eds. *Documents on the Laws of War*. 3rd ed. Oxford: Oxford University Press, 2000.

"The Role of the Human Rights Council in Supporting the Practical Implementation of the Responsibility to Protect." Statement by the Delegation of the United States of America, Human Rights Council 20th Session, Geneva. June 19, 2012. Accessed July 8, 2013. http://geneva.usmission.gov/2012/06/19/the-u-s-strong-supporter-of-the-concept-of-responsibility-to-protect-r2p.

Romero, Simon. "Military Now Often Enlists Commercial Technology." *New York Times*, March 10, 2003, p. A19.

Rose, Frank A. "Leading With International Cooperation to Strengthen Stability in Space." Near Space Security Conference, London, November 3, 2011. www.state.gov/t/avc/rls/176619.htm.

———. "Pursuing Space TCBMs for Long-Term Sustainability and Security." Remarks to the International Symposium on Sustainable Space Development and Utilization for Humankind. Shinagawa, Tokyo, Japan, February 28, 2013. Accessed March 1, 2014. www.state.gov/t/avc/rls/2013/205362.htm.

———. "Rebalancing Toward Asia with Space Cooperation." Speech to the National Space Symposium, Colorado Springs, CO, April 11, 2013. Accessed March 1, 2014. www.state.gov/t/avc/rls/2013/207434.htm.

Rosenberg, Zach. "The Coming Revolution in Orbit." *Foreign Policy*, March/April 2014. Accessed January 4, 2015. http://foreignpolicy.com/2014/03/12/the-coming-revolution-in-orbit/.

Rosert, Elvira. "Norms Matter—But Not Only in the Way They Are Supposed To:

Exploring Unintended Effects of International Norms." Paper prepared for the International Studies Association Convention 2011, Montreal, March 16–19, 2011.

Rosert, Elvira, Una Becker-Jakob, Giorgio Franceschini, and Annette Schaper. "Arms Control Norms and Technology." In *Norm Dynamics in Multilateral Arms Control: Interests, Conflicts, and Justice*, edited by Harald Müller and Carmen Wunderlich, 109–140. Athens: University of Georgia Press, 2013.

Rosert, Elvira, and Sonja Schirmbeck. "Zur Erosion internationaler Normen. Folterverbot und nukleares Tabu in der Diskussion." *Zeitschrift für Internationale Beziehungen* 14:2 (2007): 253–288.

Ross, Tim, and Holly Watt. "WikiLeaks: US vs China in Battle of the Anti-Satellite Space Weapons." *The Telegraph*, February 2, 2011. http://www.telegraph.co.uk/news/worldnews/wikileaks/8299491/WikiLeaks-US-vs-China-in-battle-of-the-anti-satellite-space-weapons.html.

Rotberg, Robert I., ed. *Mass Atrocity Crimes: Preventing Future Outrages*. Washington, DC: Brookings Institution Press, 2010.

Rotberg, Robert I., and Thomas G. Weiss, eds. *From Massacres to Genocide: The Media, Public Policy, and Humanitarian Crises*. Washington, DC: Brookings Institution Press, 1996.

Rublee, Maria Rost. *Nonproliferation Norms: Why States Choose Nuclear Restraint*. Athens: University of Georgia Press, 2010.

———. "Taking Stock of the Nuclear Nonproliferation Regime: Using Social Psychology to Understand Regime Effectiveness." *International Studies Review* 10 (2008): 420–450.

Ruggie, John Gerard. "Continuity and Transformation in the World Polity: Toward a Neorealist Synthesis." *World Politics* 35:2 (1983): 261–285.

———. "What Makes the World Hang Together? Neo-Utilitarianism and the Social Constructivist Challenge." *International Organization* 52:1 (1998): 855–885.

Sandholtz, Wayne. "Humanitarian Intervention: Global Enforcement of Human Rights." In *Globalization and Human Rights*, edited by Alison Brysk, 201–225. Berkeley: University of California Press, 2002.

———. *Prohibiting Plunder: How Norms Change*. Oxford: Oxford University Press, 2007.

Sandholtz, Wayne, and Kendall Stiles. *International Norms and Cycles of Change*. Oxford: Oxford University Press, 2008.

Sanger, David E. *Confront and Conceal: Obama's Secret Wars and Surprising Use of American Power*. New York: Broadway Books, 2013.

———. *The Inheritance*. New York: Crown, 2009.

Sanger, David E., and Thom Shanker. "Threats and Responses: War Matériel; Reluctant U.S. Gives Assent for Missiles to Go to Yemen." *New York Times*, December 12, 2002, p. A1.

Sassen, Saskia. "Towards a Sociology of Information Technology." *Current Sociology* 50:3 (2002): 365–388.

Satellite Sentinel Program. Harvard Humanitarian Initiative Report. Prepared by the

Human Rights Documentation Team for the Satellite Sentinel Project. Charlie Clements, Executive Director of the Carr Center for Human Rights Policy. Cambridge, MA: John F. Kennedy School of Government, Harvard University, 2011.

Sauer, Frank, and Niklas Schörnig. "Killer Drones: The 'Silver Bullet' of Democratic Warfare?" *Security Dialogue* 43:3 (2012): 363–380.

Sauer, Tom. "The Nuclear Non-proliferation Regime in Crisis." *Peace Review* 18:3 (2006): 333–340.

Schindler, Dietrich, and Jiri Toman, eds. *The Laws of Armed Conflicts: A Collection of Conventions, Resolutions, and Other Documents.* 3rd ed. Dordrecht: Martinus Nijhoff, 1988.

Schlosser, Eric. *Command and Control: Nuclear Weapons, the Damascus Accident, and the Illusion of Safety.* New York: Penguin, 2013.

Schmitt, Eric. "The World: The Bombs Are Smart, People Are Smarter." *New York Times,* July 4, 1999, p. D6.

Schmitt, Michael N. "Preemptive Strategies in International Law." *Michigan Journal of International Law* 24:1 (2003): 513–518.

———. "State-Sponsored Assassination in International and Domestic Law." *Yale Journal of International Law* 17:2 (1992): 609–686.

Schorr, Daniel. "Ten Days That Shook the White House." *Columbia Journalism Review* 30:2 (July/August 1991): 21–23.

Schumpeter, Joseph. *The Theory of Economic Development.* Cambridge, MA: Harvard University Press, 1934.

Scott, W. Richard. "Unpacking Institutional Arguments." In *The New Institutionalism in Organizational Analysis,* edited by Walter W. Powell and Paul J. DiMaggio, 164–182. Chicago: University of Chicago Press, 1991.

"Secret: Discussion Paper on U.S. Non-Proliferation Policy." Department of State Briefing Memorandum to Secretary Kissinger from Winston Lord, July 11, 1974. Declassified record number 115198: Nuclear Nonproliferation 2. July 11, 1974. Paper copy at National Security Archive, viewed February 21, 2014.

"Secretary of Defense Donald Rumsfeld Interview on Fox News Sunday." *Fox News.* News transcript, Feb. 11, 2001.

Seib, Philip. *The Global Journalist: News and Conscience in a World of Conflict.* Lanham, MD: Rowman & Littlefield, 2002.

Semmel, Andrew. "UN Security Council Resolution 1540: The U.S. Perspective." Remarks at Conference on Global Nonproliferation and Counterterrorism, Chatham House, London, October 12, 2004. Accessed June 10, 2013. http://2001-2009.state.gov/t/isn/rls/rm/37145.htm.

"Senators Ask Legality of Assassinating Suspected Terrorist." *Dallas Morning News,* September 4, 1998, p. 13A.

Shaker, Mohamed I. *The Nuclear Non-Proliferation Treaty: Origin and Implementation, 1959–1979.* London: Oceana Publications, 1980.

Shannon, Vaughn P. "Norms Are What States Make of Them: The Political Psychology of Norm Violation." *International Studies Quarterly* 41:1 (2000): 293–316.

Shapiro, Michael. *Reading the Postmodern Polity: Political Theory as Textual Practice.* Minneapolis: University of Minnesota Press, 1992.

Sharkey, Jaqueline E. "When Pictures Drive Foreign Policy." *American Journalism Review* 15:1 (1993): 14–19.

Shaw, Martin. *Civil Society and Media in Global Crises: Representing Distant Violence.* London: St. Martin's Press, 1996.

———. "Global Voices: Civil Societies and the Media in Global Crises." In *Human Rights in Global Politics*, edited by Timothy Dunne and Nicholas J. Wheeler, 214–232. Cambridge: Cambridge University Press, 1999.

Sheehan, Michael. *The International Politics of Space.* London: Routledge, 2007.

Sherry, Michael. *The Rise of American Airpower: The Creation of Armageddon.* New Haven, CT: Yale University Press, 1989.

Sherwin, Martin J. *A World Destroyed: The Atomic Bomb and the Grand Alliance.* New York: Knopf, 1975.

Sikkink, Kathryn. "Beyond the Justice Cascade: How Agentic Constructivism Could Help Explain Change in International Politics." Revised paper from Millennium Annual Conference, London, October 22, 2011. Accessed January 4, 2013. http://www.princeton.edu/politics/about/file-repository/public/Agentic-Constructivism-paper-sent-to-the-Princeton-IR-Colloquium.pdf.

———. "Transnational Politics, International Relations Theory, and Human Rights." *PS: Political Science and Politics* 31:3 (1998): 516–523.

Simpson, Gerry. *Great Powers and Outlaw States: Unequal Sovereigns in the International Order.* Cambridge: Cambridge University Press, 2004.

Singer, P. W. *Wired for War: The Robotics Revolution and Conflict in the 21st Century.* New York: Penguin, 2009.

Sirak, Michael. "Air Force Leadership: Chinese ASAT Test Marked Turning Point; Space No Longer Sanctuary." *Defense Daily*, February 12, 2007.

Slaughter Burley, Anne-Marie. "International Law and International Relations Theory: A Dual Agenda." *American Journal of International Law* 205:2 (1993): 205–239.

Smith, Gerard, and Helena Cobban. "A Blind Eye to Nuclear Proliferation." *Foreign Affairs* 68:3 (1989): 53–70.

Smith, Merritt Roe, and Leo Marx, eds. *Does Technology Drive History? The Dilemma of Technological Determinism.* Cambridge, MA: MIT Press, 1994.

Smyth, Henry DeWolf. *Atomic Energy for Military Purposes: The Official Report on the Development of the Atomic Bomb under the Auspices of the United States Government, 1940–1945.* Princeton, NJ: Princeton Univ. Press, 1945.

Sofaer, Abraham D. "Terrorism, the Law, and the National Defense." *Military Law Review* 89 (1989): 89–123.

Sokolski, Henry D. *Best of Intentions: America's Campaign against Strategic Weapons Proliferation.* Westport, CT: Praeger, 2001.

Spacy, William L. II. *Does the United States Need Space-Based Weapons?* Maxwell Air Force Base, Alabama: Air University Press, 1999.

Squassoni, Sharon. "Looking Back: The 1978 Nuclear Nonproliferation Act." *Arms Control Today*, December 2008. Accessed March 31, 2011. www.armscontrol.org/act/2008_12/lookingback_NPT.

———. "Nuclear Cooperation and Nonproliferation: Reconciling Commerce and Security." Prepared statement before the House Foreign Affairs Committee, Washington, DC, September 24, 2010. (author's copy).

———. *Proliferation Security Initiative*. CRS Report for Congress RS21881. September 24, 2006.

Stares, Paul B. "Anti-Satellite Arms Control in a Broader Security Perspective." In *Seeking Stability in Space: Anti-Satellite Weapons and the Evolving Space Regime*, edited by Joseph S. Nye Jr. and James A. Schear, 109–124. Washington, DC: Aspen Strategy Group, 1987.

———. *The Militarization of Space: U.S. Policy, 1945–1984*. Ithaca, NY: Cornell University Press, 1985.

———. "Rules of the Road for Space Operations." In *Technology and the Limitation of International Conflict*, edited by Barry Blechman, 99–116. Washington, DC: Johns Hopkins Foreign Policy Institute, 1989.

———. *Space and National Security*. Washington, DC: Brookings Institution Press, 1987.

Stine, Deborah. *The Manhattan Project, the Apollo Program, and Federal Energy Technology R&D Programs: A Comparative Analysis*. Congressional Research Service Report RL34645, June 30, 2009. Accessed May 1, 2013. http://www.fas. org/sgp/crs/misc/RL34645.pdf.

Stratford, Richard. U.S. Department of State. "U.S. Nuclear Cooperation: How and With Whom?" Carnegie International Nuclear Policy Conference, Washington, DC, March 29, 2011. Accessed March 21, 2012. http://carnegieendowment.org/files/US_Nuclear_Cooperation-How_and_With_Whom.pdf.

Streeck, Wolfgang, and Kathleen Thelen, eds. *Beyond Continuity: Institutional Change in Advanced Political Economies*. Oxford: Oxford University Press, 2005.

Strulak, Tadeusz. "The Nuclear Suppliers Group." *Nonproliferation Review* 1:1 (1993): 2–10.

Suchman, Mark C. "Managing Legitimacy: Strategic and Institutional Approaches." *Academy of Management Review* 20:4 (1995): 571–610.

"Summary of the Atomic Energy Act." United States Environmental Protection Agency, March 2, 2001. Accessed June 3, 2011. http://www.epa.gov/regulations/laws/aea.html.

Sunstein, Cass. "Social Norms and Social Roles." *Columbia Law Review* 96:4 (1996): 903–968.

Sweet, Alec Stone. "Judicialization and the Construction of Governance." *Comparative Political Studies* 32:2 (1999): 147–184.

Sweet, Alec Stone, and Wayne Sandholtz. "Integration, Supranational Governance, and the Institutionalization of the Europe Polity." In *European Integration and*

Supranational Governance, edited by Wayne Sandholtz and Alex Stone Sweet, 297–317. Oxford: Oxford University Press, 1998.

Tannenwald, Nina. "Law Versus Power on the High Frontier: The Case for a Rule-Based Regime for Outer Space." *Yale Journal of International Law* 19:363 (Summer 2004): 1–55.

———. *The Nuclear Taboo: The United States and the Non-Use of Nuclear Weapons since 1945.* Cambridge: Cambridge University Press, 2007.

Tarrow, Sidney. *Power in Movements: Social Movements, Collective Action and Politics.* New York: Cambridge University Press, 1994.

Taylor, Adam. "Did Boko Haram Attack Leave 150 Dead—or 2000? Satellite Imagery Sheds New Light." *Washington Post*, January 14, 2015. Accessed January 17, 2015. www.washingtonpost.com/blogs/worldviews/wp/2015/01/14/did-bokoharam-attack-leave-150-dead-or-2000-satellite-imagery-sheds-new-light.

Tellis, Ashley J. *India as a New Global Power: An Action Agenda for the United States.* Washington, DC: Carnegie Endowment for Peace, July 2005. Accessed March 8, 2012. www.carnegieendowment.org/files/CEIP_India_strategy_2006.FINAL.pdf.

———. "Punching the US Military's 'Soft Ribs': China's Antisatellite Weapon Test in Strategic Perspective." Carnegie Endowment for International Peace, Policy Brief 51, June 2007.

Tenet, George. *At the Center of the Storm: My Years at the CIA.* New York: Harper, 2007.

Terrill, Andrew W. "Drones over Yemen: Weighing Military Benefits and Political Costs." *Parameters* 42:4/43:1 (Winter-Spring 2013): 17–23.

Thelen, Kathleen. "How Institutions Evolve: Insights from Comparative Historical Analysis." In *Comparative Historical Analysis in the Social Sciences*, edited by James Mahoney and Dietrich Rueschemeyer, 208–240. Cambridge: Cambridge University Press, 2003.

Thomas, Kenneth R. *Selected Theories of Constitutional Interpretation.* Congressional Research Service Report 7-5700, February 15, 2011. Accessed November 15, 2012. http://www.fas.org/sgp/crs/misc/R41637.pdf.

Thomas, Ward. *The Ethics of Destruction.* Ithaca, NY: Cornell University Press, 2001.

"Treaty on the Non-Proliferation of Nuclear Weapons." United Nations, 1970. Accessed February 2, 2012. http://www.un.org/en/conf/npt/2005/npttreaty.html.

"Treaty on Principles Governing the Activities of States in the Exploration and Use of Outer Space, Including the Moon and Other Celestial Bodies." United Nations, 1967. Accessed January 14, 2016. http://www.state.gov/t/isn/5181.htm.

Truman, Harry. Statement by the President of the United States. White House Press Release, August 6, 1945. Harry S. Truman Library. Accessed May 4, 2013. http://www.trumanlibrary.org/whistlestop/study_collections/bomb/large/documents/index.php?pagenumber=1&documentdate=1945–08 06&documentid=59&studycollectionid=abomb.

United Nations. "Convention on the High Seas." Adopted at Geneva, Switzerland, on 29 April 1958. Accessed June 14, 2013. http://untreaty.un.org/ilc/texts/instruments/english/conventions/8_1_1958_high_seas.pdf.

———. "Declaration of Legal Principles Governing the Activities of States in the Exploration and Use of Outer Space." 1963.

———. *A More Secure World: Our Shared Responsibility*. Report of the High Level Panel on Threats, Challenges, and Change, 2004. Accessed March 4, 2012. www.un.org/secureworld/report2.pdf.

———. Security Council Resolution 688. April 5, 1991. http://www.fas.org/news/un/iraq/sres/sres0688.htm (accessed July 10, 2013).

———. Summary Record of the U.N. Committee on the Peaceful Uses of Outer Space (1966). UNDoc. A/AC.105/C.2/SR.66, at 6 (statement of the Permanent Representative of the Soviet Union).

———. "United Nations Convention on the Law of the Sea [UNCLOS])," 1982. 1833 U.N.T.S. 397. Articles X and 38.

———. "United Nations Convention on the Law of the Sea." Hearing before the Committee on Environment and Public Works, United States Senate, 108th Cong., 2nd Sess. March 23, 2004. Washington DC: U.S. Government Printing Office, 2005.

United Nations Division for Ocean Affairs and the Law of the Sea. *Oceans: The Source of Life*. New York: United Nations, 2002.

United Nations General Assembly. Resolution 1962, UN Doc. A/RES/1962, December 24, 1963, 3 I.L.M. 157.

———. Resolution 60/288, United Nations Global Counter-Terrorism Strategy. A/RES/60/288. New York: United Nations, September 20, 2006.

United Nations Inter-Agency Programme for Iraq, Kuwait and the Iraq/Turkey and Iraq/Iran Border Areas: Updated and Consolidated Appeal for Urgent Humanitarian Action. Nancy Bearg Dyke Files, Persian Gulf-Humanitarian [2], OA/ID CF01076-013. May 15, 1991.

United Nations Institute for Disarmament Research. Agenda—Information & Communication Technologies and International Security—24–25 April 2008. Accessed October 12, 2011. http://www.unidir.org/pdf/activites/pdf-act371.pdf.

United Nations Institute for Training and Research (UNITAR). "Operational Satellite Applications Programme, General Information." Accessed January 15, 2106. http://www.unitar.org/unosat/.

United States Air Force. *Counterspace Operations*. Air Force Doctrine Document 2-2.1. August 2, 2004.

United States Air Force Space Command. *Strategic Master Plan FY 04 and Beyond*. November 5, 2002.

United States Arms Control and Disarmament Agency and U.S. Department of State Policy Planning Staff. Analytic Staff meeting on non-proliferation strategy, July 31, 1974. Record number 117436: Nuclear Nonproliferation 2. Paper copy housed at National Security Archive—a secret document that was declassified in 2010.

United States Congress. "Treaty on Outer Space: Hearings before the Senate

Committee on Foreign Relations." Statement of Arthur J. Goldberg, US Ambassador to the UN. 90th Cong. (1967).

United States Congress Office of Technology Assessment. *Anti-Satellite Weapons, Countermeasures, Arms Control* (1985), reprinted in Congressional Office of Technology Assessment, *Strategic Defenses: Ballistic Missile Technologies, Anti-Satellite Weapons, and Arms Control*. Princeton, NJ: Princeton University Press, 1986.

United States Delegation to the 2010 Nuclear Non-Proliferation Treaty Review Conference. "Treaty on the Non-Proliferation of Nuclear Weapons." U.S. State Department, April 8, 2010. Accessed May 18, 2011. http://www.state.gov/documents/organization/141503.pdf.

United States Department of State. Cable 142418 to U.S. Mission of the United Nations. "NPT and Resumed GA [General Assembly]," April 5, 1968.

———. Conversation between President Nixon and Assistant for National Security Affairs Kissinger. June 13, 1972, 11:43 am–1:18 pm. Electronic publication, Document 58. *Foreign Relations of the United States, 1969–1976, Vol. E-2, Documents on Arms Control and Nonproliferation, 1969–1972*. Washington, DC: U.S. Government Printing Office, 2007.

———. *Documents on Disarmament, 1960*. Pub. No. 7172, July 1961. Washington, DC, U.S. Government Printing Office, 1961.

———. Draft Position Paper, "Non-Proliferation of Nuclear Weapons." August 14, 1968. *Foreign Relations of the United States, 1964–1968, Vol. XI, Arms Control and Disarmament*, Document 44. Washington, DC: U.S. Government Printing Office, 1997.

———. "Memorandum from the Director of the Arms Control and Disarmament Agency (Foster) to President Johnson." April 6, 1967. *Foreign Relations of the United States, 1964–1968, Vol. XI, Arms Control and Disarmament*, Document 193. http://history.state.gov/historicaldocuments/frus1964-68v11/d193.

———. *National Strategy for Combating Terrorism*. Washington, DC: 2003. Accessed July 14, 2004. http://www.state.gov/documents/organization/60172.pdf.

———. *Nuclear Weapons and Rogue States: Challenge and Response*. Washington DC: Bureau of Nonproliferation, 2003. Accessed June 4, 2013. www.state.gov/t/us/rm/26786pf.htm.

———. Report by the Committee on Nuclear Proliferation, January 21, 1965. *Foreign Relations of the United States, 1964–1968, Vol. XI, Arms Control and Disarmament*, Document 64. Washington, DC: U.S. Government Printing Office, 1997.

United States Department of State, Policy Planning Council. "The Further Spread of Nuclear Weapons: Problems for the West." February 14, 1966. Secret. National Archives, Record Group 59, Records of the Department of State (RG 59). Records of the Policy Planning Council, 1965–1968, Subject: Country and Area Files. Box 384, Atomic Energy-Armaments 2 of 4.

———. "Planning Implications for National Security of Outer Space in the 1970s." Secret report, January 30, 1964. Available online at the Digital National Security Archive, "U.S. Military Uses of Space, 1945–1991," http://nsarchive.chadwyck.com/collections/content/MS/intro.jsp.

United States Select Senate Committee to Study Governmental Operations with Respect to Intelligence Activities. *Alleged Assassination Plots Involving Foreign Leaders.* Washington, DC: U.S. Government Printing Office, 1975.

United States Senate. Committee on Foreign Relations, Nuclear Proliferation: Learning from the Iraq Experience. Hearing before the Committee on Foreign Relations. 102 Cong. 1st Sess. October 17, 1991.

United States Space Command. *Vision for 2020* (February 1997); *Long Range Plan: Implementing US SPACECOM Vision for 2020* (March 1998).

"U.S. Cautious over Plan for Kurds' Haven." *The Independent,* April 10, 1991, p. 1.

U.S. Government Accountability Office. *Nonproliferation: Agencies Could Improve Information Sharing and End-Use Monitoring on Unmanned Aerial Vehicle Exports.* US GAO Report 12–536. July 2012. http://dronewarsuk.files.wordpress.com/2012/09/us-gao-_-noproliferation-of-uavs.pdf.

"U.S. Military Uses of Space, 1945–1991." NSC-5814: "Preliminary U.S. Policy on Outer Space." August 18, 1958. Accessed January 15, 2016. http://nsarchive.chadwyck.com/collections/content/MS/intro.jsp.

Verdier, Daniel. "Multilateralism, Bilateralism, and Exclusion in the Nuclear Proliferation Regime." *International Organization* 62:2 (2008): 439–476.

Von Hippel, Frank N. *Managing Spent Fuel in the United States: The Illogic of Reprocessing.* Research Report No. 3. International Panel on Fissile Materials. January 2007. Accessed February 19, 2012. http://www.npolicy.org/article_file/Managing_Spent_Fuel_in_the_United_States-The_Illogic_of_Reprocessing.pdf.

———. "Why Reprocessing Persists in Some Countries and Not in Others: The Costs and Benefits of Reprocessing." Paper for the Non-proliferation Education Center, April 9, 2009 (author's copy).

Wallop, Malcolm. On SDI, July 31, 1992, in Presidential Archive, John A. Gordon Files, SDI, September 1992, OA/ID CF01653-027.

Walzer, Michael. *Just and Unjust Wars: A Moral Argument with Historical Illustrations.* New York: Basic Books, 2006.

Warhol, Andy. *The Philosophy of Andy Warhol.* Accessed May 27, 2011. http://www.quotationspage.com/quote/25824.html.

Weber, Steven, and Sidney Drell. "Attempts to Regulate Military Activities in Space." In *U.S.-Soviet Security Cooperation,* edited by Alexander L. George, Philip J. Farley, and Alexander Dallin, 373–431. New York: Oxford University Press, 1988.

Weeden, Brian. "Billiards in Space." *Space Review,* February 23, 2009. Accessed February 20, 2014. http://www.thespacereview.com/ article/1314/1.

———. "The Economics of Space Sustainability." *Space Review,* June 4, 2012. Accessed February 20, 2014. www.thespacereview.com/article/2093/1.

———. "Through a Glass, Darkly: Chinese, American, and Russian Anti-Satellite Testing in Space." *Space Review,* March 17, 2014.

Weeden, Brian, and K. Shortt. "Development of a Sun-Synchronous Zoning Architecture to Minimize Conjunctions." Paper presented at AIAA Space Ops, Heidelberg, Germany, May 2008.

Weigley, Russell F. *The American Way of War: A History of United States Military Strategy and Policy*. New York: Macmillan, 1973.

Weiss, Leonard. "U.S.-India Nuclear Cooperation: Better Later Than Sooner." *Nonproliferation Review* 14:3 (2007): 430–457.

Weiss, Thomas G. *Humanitarian Intervention: Ideas in Action*. Cambridge: Polity Press, 2007.

———. *Military-Civilian Interactions: Humanitarian Crises and the Responsibility to Protect*. Lanham, MD: Rowman & Littlefield, 2005.

———. *Military-Civilian Interactions: Intervening in Humanitarian Crises*. Lanham, MD: Rowman & Littlefield, 1999.

———. "On R2P, America Takes the Lead." *Current History* 111:748 (2012).

Wells, A. A. "Control of and Cooperation in Gas Centrifuge Research and Development Technology." Memorandum to Philip J. Farley, United States Atomic Energy Commission, February 19, 1960, pp. 44–48. Accessed February 8, 2014. www.documentcloud.org/documents/399992-doc-3-wells-report.html.

Wells, H. G. *The World Set Free: A Story of Mankind*. New York: E.P. Dutton, 1914.

Wendt, Alexander. "Anarchy Is What States Make of It: The Social Construction of Power Politics." *International Organization* 46:2 (1992): 391–425.

———. "Collective Identity Formation and the International State System." *American Political Science Review* 88:2 (1994): 384–396.

———. "Constructing International Politics." *International Security* 20:1 (1995): 71–81.

Western, Jon. "Sources of Humanitarian Intervention: Beliefs, Information, and Advocacy in the U.S. Decisions on Somalia and Bosnia." *International Security* 26:4 (2002): 112–142.

Wheeler, Nicholas J. *Saving Strangers: Humanitarian Intervention in International Society*. Oxford: Oxford University Press, 2000.

Wheelon, Albert D. "Technology and Intelligence." *Technology in Society* 26:2 (2004): 245–255.

"Where Are We; Where Are They—Dr. Oppenheimer Speaks." *Newsweek*, November 11, 1957, p. 75.

White House. *The National Security Strategy of the United States of America*. September 2002. www.whitehouse.gov/nsc/nss.html.

———. *National Space Policy of the United States of America*. June 28, 2010. http://www.whitehouse.gov/sites/default/files/national_space_policy_6-28-10.pdf.

———. *National Strategy to Combat Weapons of Mass Destruction*. Washington, DC: U.S. Government Printing Office, December 2002. Accessed October 28, 2005. www.whitehouse.gov/news/releases/2002/12/WMDStrategy.pdf.

———. "President's Statement on Proliferation Security Initiative." June 23, 2006. Accessed February 26, 2013. www.whitehouse.gov/news/releases/2006/06/20060623.html.

———. Press release on Hiroshima, August 6, 1945. *Foreign Relations of the United*

States, Potsdam. Vol. 2, pp. 1380–1381. Washington, DC: U.S. Government Printing Office, 1960.

———. "Remarks to the People of Rwanda." Kigali, Rwanda, March 25, 1998. Accessed July 9, 2013. http://millercenter.org/president/speeches/detail/4602.

———. "Statement by the President." September 11, 2001. http://georgewbush-whitehouse.archives.gov/news/releases/2001/09/20010911-16.html.

———. "Statement by President on Release of the National Space Policy of the United States of America." June 28, 2010. https://www.whitehouse.gov/the-press-office/statement-president-new-national-space-policy.

———. Transcript of President Obama's Speech on Counterterrorism Policy. May 23, 2013. Accessed November 22, 2013. www.whitehouse.gov.

White House, National Science and Technology Council. "Fact Sheet: National Space Policy." September 19, 1996. http://history.nasa.gov/appf2.pdf.

White House, Office of the Press Secretary. "Address by the President on the State of the Union." January 29, 1991. Housed in William Tobey files, GPALS [Global Protection Against Limited Strikes] 3, OA/ID CF01419-020.

———. "Fact Sheet: U.S. Policy Standards and Procedures for the Use of Force in Counterterrorism Operations Outside the United States and Areas of Active Hostilities." May 23, 2013. http://www.whitehouse.gov/the-press-office/2013/05/23/fact-sheet-us-policy-standards-and-procedures-use-force-counterterrorism.

———. *National Space Policy.* US National Space Policy Document, November 16, 1989. Housed in the George HW Bush Archives, OA/ID Number CF00770. Folder ID Number CF00770–024.

———. Presidential Studies Directive on Mass Atrocities, PSD-10. August 4, 2011. Accessed January 10, 2016. http://www.whitehouse.gov/the-press-office/2011/08/04/presidential-study-directive-mass-atrocities.

———. "Press Briefing by Press Secretary Jay Carney." May 4, 2011. http://www.whitehouse.gov/the-press-office/2011/05/04/press-briefing-press-secretary-jay-carney-542011.

——— "Remarks by the President on Osama bin Laden." May 1, 2011. http://www.whitehouse.gov/blog/2011/05/02/osama-bin-laden-dead.

———. "Remarks by the President at the United States Military Academy Commencement Ceremony." May 28, 2014. http://www.whitehouse.gov/the-press-office/2014/05/28/remarks-president-west-point-academy-commencement-ceremony.

———. "Statement by the President on Syria." August 31, 2013. Accessed September 5, 2013. www.whitehouse.gov/the-pres-office/2013/08/31/statement-president-syria.

Whittle, Richard. "The Man Who Invented the Predator." *Air & Space Magazine,* April 2013. Accessed February 27, 2014. http://www.airspacemag.com/flight-today/the-man-who-invented-the-predator-3970502/?all.

Wiener, Antje. "Contested Compliance: Interventions on the Normative Structure of World Politics." *European Journal of International Relations* 10:2 (2004): 189–234.

———. "The Dual Quality of Norms and Governance beyond the State: Sociological and Normative Approaches to 'Interaction.'" *Critical Review of International Social and Political Philosophy* 10:1 (2007): 47–69.

———. *The Invisible Constitution of Politics: Contested Norms and International Encounters.* Cambridge: Cambridge University Press, 2008.

———. *A Theory of Contestation.* Berlin: Springer Verlag, 2014.

Wiener, Antje, and Uwe Puetter. "The Quality of Norms Is What Actors Make of It: Critical Constructivist Research on Norms." *Journal of International Law and International Relations* 5:1 (2009): 1–16.

Williams, Brian Glyn. "A History of the World's First Drone War." *History News Network.* Accessed June 27, 2104. http:hnn.us/article/153148

———. *Predators: The CIA's Drone War on Al Qaeda.* Washington, DC: Potomac Books, 2013.

Williams, Robert Chadwell, and Philip L. Cantelon, eds. *The American Atom: A Documentary History of Nuclear Policies from the Discovery of Fission to the Present, 1939–1984.* Philadelphia: University of Pennsylvania Press, 1984.

Wingerter, Rex. "What Drives the Development of US Missile Defense and Space-Based Weapons? The Role of US Domestic Interest Groups." *Asian Perspective* 35:4 (2011): 559–594. https://www.questia.com/library/journal/1P3-2610265141/what-drives-the-development-of-us-missile-defense.

Wood, Heather Jacques, Taylor Nuttall, and Kendall Stiles. "Humanitarian Intervention." In *International Norms and Cycles of Change,* edited by Wayne Sandholtz and Kendall Stiles, 263–288. New York: Oxford University Press, 2008.

Wunderlich, Carmen. "The Good, the Bad, and the Bias: Towards a Reconceptualization of Norm Entrepreneurship." Paper prepared for the 54th Annual Convention of the International Studies Association, San Francisco, April 3–6, 2013.

———. "A Rogue Gone Norm Entrepreneurial? Iran within the Nuclear Nonproliferation Regime." In *Deviance in International Relations: "Rogue States" and International Security,* edited by Wolfgang Wagner, Werner Wouter, and Michael Ondercoe, 83–104. Houndmills, UK: Palgrave Macmillan.

———. "Theoretical Approaches in Norm Dynamics." In *Norm Dynamics in Multilateral Arms Control: Interests, Conflicts, and Justice,* edited by Harald Müller and Carmen Wunderlich, 20–47. Athens: University of Georgia Press, 2013.

Zacher, Mark W. "The Territorial Integrity Norm: International Boundaries and the Use of Force." *International Organization* 55:2 (2001): 215–250.

Zenko, Micah. "Dangerous Space Incidents." Contingency Planning Memorandum 21, April 2014. Accessed June 19, 2014. http://www.cfr.org/space/dangerous-space-incidents/p32790.

———. "Waste of Space." *Foreign Policy,* April 21, 2014. Accessed June 19, 2014. http://www.foreignpolicy.com/articles/2014/04/21/waste_of_space_space_junk_gravity_us_china.

Ziegler, David W. *Safe Heavens: Military Strategy and Space Sanctuary Thought.* Maxwell Air Force Base, AL: Air University Press, 1998.

Zoellner, Tom. *Uranium: War, Energy, and the Rock That Shaped the World.* New York: Viking 2009.

Index